Foul Balls

ALISON GORDON

General
— PAPERBACKS —
Toronto, Canada

General Paperbacks edition published 1986

ISBN 0-7736-7117-X

Cover Design by Brant Cowie/Artplus

Cover photograph: Toronto Blue Jays Baseball Club

Printed and bound in Canada

Contents

For Ruth Gordon, my first editor

This book could not have been written without a lot of help over the years: from the Blue Jay front office, most notably Howie Starkman, with aid and comfort from Paul Beeston and George Holm; from the players, T. J. and Big John, Willie and Lloyd, Ernie and Buck, Collie, Diamond and most of the rest; from Jan Walter and Charis Wahl; from Avie Bennett; from the *Star* sports department, especially Paul Warnick, Wayne Parrish and Gay Leno; and most particularly from my husband, Paul Bennett. Thanks.

Foreword

Baseball players, like children, are at their most appealing when they are asleep. Walking up the aisle of the DC10 high over middle America, on the red-eye from the coast during the last road trip of 1983, I looked at the Toronto Blue Jays, snoozing in their first-class seats. Their heads lolled to the side, as if the weight of their cassette-deck headsets, playing gospel music here, country over there, Latin American *salsa* two rows back, was too much for their necks to bear. There were weary smudges under their eyes, and they looked peaceful and innocent, a Cub pack on the way back from a field trip, not overpaid athletes with egos as big as all outdoors.

I stopped to chat with a couple of the players still awake, standing by the galley, cadging free drinks from the flight attendant. It was she who asked the usual question: "Why are you travelling with the team?"

"I'm a sportswriter," I replied.

"Oh," she said, with a dimpled smile, "I thought you were a mother."

I knew it was time to quit.

That particular road trip had started almost five years previously, in the spring of 1979, when *The Toronto Star* hired me as a baseball writer, but the journey had begun almost two decades before that. I spent my early childhood in and around New York City, my maternal grandfather's granddaughter and my brother's kid sister, with confused baseball allegiances. My grandfather, Isaac Anderson, was a drily witty and courtly gentleman, as I remember him, a man who always had a twinkle in his eye. He lived with us and rooted for the Brooklyn Dodgers, as they still were, and later for the Boston Red Sox. My brother Charley, two years older and ever-so-much wiser than I, followed the Yankees and, like kid sisters do, I tagged along.

In the sixth grade, I took my portable radio to school and was allowed to listen to it during class and give my schoolmates inning-by-inning updates of the 1953 Yankee-Dodger World Series. It was the fifth consecutive championship for the Yankees. Billy Martin was the star.

As it turned out, we followed the team from halfway around the world in the mid-fifties, when my father's job with the United Nations found us living in Tokyo, Cairo, and Rome. We came back in time for the 1958 World Series, and my love affair with the Yankees began again in earnest.

As broadening as travel may be, it was of no use in preparing a skinny sixteen-year-old for the social complexities of being a teen-ager in Irvington, New York, in that era, and I was a bit of an outcast, the kind of kid who had compositions read out in English class and had to ask relatives to take me to the prom.

Baseball became my refuge, beginning with that extraordinary World Series in 1958 when the Yankees came back from being down 3-1 to the Milwaukee Braves to win it. Ryne Duren became my new hero. Casey Stengel was my personal saint.

Our next-door neighbour had season tickets at Yankee Stadium and he sometimes gave me one. I had to take the commuter local to New York and the subway to the Bronx, but the excitement of being in the ballpark made the long trip worthwhile, and I felt surrounded by friends.

My last ballgame of that era was in 1960, the year I graduated from high school and came to university in Canada. It would be seventeen years before I saw another game.

Appropriately, it was also in Yankee Stadium. The year the Blue Jays were born I played hookey from work one April Monday and flew to New York to see them play. I brought down a couple of Blue Jay T-shirts and went to the game with Sean Kelly, an expatriate humourist and Yankee hater, and an equally zany friend of his.

Walking up the ramp into the afternoon sunshine and looking up at the gleaming white pediments of the renovated playground was as close as I've come to an epiphany, and the sight of the

8

green diamond brought a lump to my throat. It was a homecoming of sorts, and the game, which the Blue Jays won, was a welcome back to a joy I had forgotten.

We sat a dozen rows behind the Blue Jay dugout in the almost empty stadium, cheering mightily for the newly hatched Jays. The Yankees made four errors, Reggie Jackson struck out, and the underdogs played like champs. Fans around us, civilized people who cherish weekday afternoon games, praised us generously on the quality of our team. After the Jays went ahead in the sixth inning the crusty usher patrolling our section, one of those colourful characters that give the joint its special tone, wandered over to fix us with a mock glare. "Don't say a *woid*," he growled, pointing a stern finger in our direction.

I remember well the bemused look on the players' faces as they trotted back to the dugout between innings and looked at the three loonies cheering them on. Finally, one of them, Jim Mason, I think, tipped his cap. We cheered some more.

And somewhere in the middle of that blissful afternoon I realized how very much I had missed the game.

I came back from New York a fan again, a Blue-Jay fan this time, following the team with a lot of anguish and some small moments of joy for the first two seasons. I was working at the time at CBC radio, a producer on the current-affairs program *As It Happens*, but had begun to do some freelance writing on the side. In the summer of 1978, I quit that job to write full-time and lucked into some baseball features for the now defunct *City Magazine*.

In January of 1979, *The Toronto Star* approached me about sharing the baseball beat with Neil MacCarl, a veteran of more than thirty years in the business. Perhaps naively, I jumped at the chance without really thinking through the consequences. Had I known then what I now know about the nature of the sport and about the men who play it, manage it, and report on it, I might not have been so quick to sign on, so I thank my ignorance.

Had timidity won out, or good sense prevailed, I would have missed meeting a raft of fascinating people. Some were real heroes, fine men who deserved the admiration they got. Others were phonies, as despicable in private as they were noble in public. I met players, managers and scouts, broadcasters, reporters and fans – the people, more than the numbers, that make baseball a joy for me.

The strangest thing for me, looking back, was how unlikely it was that I would enjoy myself with these people. Intellectually, temperamentally, and politically I couldn't have been further away from these people I came to love. A socialist, feminist, hedonist with roots in the sixties, a woman who had marched against the bomb, done drugs, and never, ever even wanted to date the head jock at school, had nothing in common with these children of Ozzie and Harriet, locked in a fifties timewarp. The only ballplayer I could relate to was Bill Lee of the Montreal Expos, and the only time I ever met him we were so locked into baseball rules I couldn't even give him a sign of recognition. It says a lot about baseball as a common denominator that I cherish the time I spent in their world.

I certainly dodged foul balls, literal and figurative. The baseball diamond can be a dangerous place to roam during batting practice, and I quickly learned to dodge balls hit or thrown (some of the latter by players whose idea of a good joke was to brush back reporters with throws that, oops, accidentally got away).

One ball I've saved was hit during batting practice in the spring of 1980. I was standing by the Blue Jay clubhouse in right field in Dunedin, Florida, talking to Blue Jay broadcaster Tom Cheek, when a foul ball hit by one of the Pittsburgh Pirates came our way.

Although the players all shouted "heads up," neither of us could see it. It was obvious by the reaction of others that it was headed straight for us, so I ducked, knees bent and hands over my head to protect myself.

Then I found the ball. On the fly, it landed in the pocket formed by my skirt and my thighs, just above my knees, and stuck, as if in baseball's best glove. I never saw a better catch, on or off the field, and I kept the ball to commemorate the event.

Cheek signed it for me, with the explanation that the feat had rendered him speechless, an event almost as rare as the catch itself.

I had laughter and good times on the beat and others that brought me to tears, but it was seldom dull. How could it be, with a game every day? The road was often bumpy, but it was an unforgettable trip. I'm glad I took it but almost as glad, finally, that I turned in my ticket and got off.

Chapter

1

Opening Day

The ghosts all come out on opening day, lurking happily in the outfield corners, floating through the dugouts, raising small eddies of red-clay dust around second base, settling into the bleachers with the flesh-and-blood paying customers.

They are the ghosts of baseball and gather wherever the game is played, not just in historic venues like Comiskey Park and Yankee Stadium. They even come to modern horrors like Exhibition Stadium on the shores of Lake Ontario. They don't even have to go through customs.

Some of the ghosts are dressed in baggy flannel uniforms with their stirrup straps barely showing an inch of white over their polished black shoetops. Others wear dark jackets, high collars and ties, and straw boaters on their heads. The women have fox-furs draped across their shoulders and hats with a jaunty tilt. They sit incongruously among their rude modern counterparts who use language once reserved for the locker rooms under the stands, but in all their hearts is the same joy.

Baseball is as eternal as green grass and blue sky, and has been passed down through the generations, both on the diamond and in the stands. There are Ty Cobb and Babe Ruth, shagging flies in the outfield. Jackie Robinson, Honus Wagner, and Lou Gehrig take infield practice with Willie Upshaw, Alfredo Griffin, and Damaso Garcia. Cy Young leans against the bullpen fence while Dave Stieb warms up before the game. And every fan in the stands carries a memory of a father or a grandfather who took him to his first game, and the line goes back for more than a century.

Despite the changes in the game: despite skin-tight uniforms in shocking colours and night games and the designated hitter, despite silly seven-foot-tall furry animals cavorting on the dugout roofs and plastic playing fields, the game is still the same as the day it was decided to put the bases that magical ninety feet apart and the mound sixty feet, six inches from home plate.

I once stood outside Fenway Park in Boston, a place where the ghosts never go away, and watched a vigorous man of middle years helping, with infinite care, a frail and elderly gentleman through the milling crowds to the entry gate. Through the tears that came unexpectedly to my eyes I saw the old man strong and important forty years before, holding the hand of a confused and excited five-year-old, showing him the way.

Baseball's best moments don't always happen on the field.

The dugout is a special place, at once utilitarian and almost sacred, a place of physical and spiritual renewal where players can hide from accusing eyes and spend a few moments with men who are surely their friends while outside the spectators howl and opposing players glare their game-time hatred.

It is a cosy cave, whether it is set down from the playing field by steep steps like the ones in Detroit and Baltimore or a field-level modern adaptation like the one in Toronto, a dug-in.

Before a game, before batting practice has even begun, there's the feeling of a private club here. Players hang from the dugout roof, stretching, or lounge on the narrow benches, chewing tobacco and spitting it on the floor, already stained and disgusting from generations of juice, splintered and pitted from generations of sharp spikes.

The dugout isn't pretty, but it's home. Here is where the tales are told, over and over again. Usually the stories are old ones, with even rookies digging back into their early minor league days for conversation, when they talk at all. Usually, following unwritten rules, rookies listen to coaches and veterans talking about players and ballparks only they know.

"You remember Fred Smumphl?" one coach asks.

"Yeah, I played with him in Rochester," another answers. "Now he could hit. He could *flat* hit."

Nods all around. A player leans on his bat and spits.

"Not only that, he could throw," he chimes in. "He could *flat* throw. I remember one time in winter ball I saw him throw out Jose Alapwunnra – remember him? – and Fred must have been forty at the time."

"Yup." Pause, spit. "Jose could run, too."

"I played against him in Mexico." Agreement from down the bench. "He could *flat* run."

Like the oral tradition of any group, the stories are comforting, a reminder of the sanctity of the game. A reminder that in this world a man is measured by a simple yardstick. Education doesn't matter; nor does family background. In fact, high breeding and college degrees are suspect. What matters are hands and wrists and legs and heart, and the guys in the dugout know all about those.

They are workmen surrounded by their tools before their shift begins. Their bats are in the rack at the end of the dugout, compartmentalized by uniform number so that each player can find his own quickly and choose from several: the batting practice bat, taped on the barrel; the gamer, with several good hits left in it; and the backups. Each has the player's number written in felt pen on the butt of the handle either by the bat boy or the player himself, depending on his superstition. Some players have secret signs or hexes for luck, a particular style of numeral that has worked in the past, elaborate as the graffiti on a New York subway car.

The helmets are on top of the rack, numbered on the back, some battered, some brand new. Players take them from team to team when they are traded, painting their new team colours on top of the old.

Big, square canvas bags with zippered tops hold balls, ready for batting practice and infield drills. These are used balls, scuffed and grass-stained: new balls are used only in games and for pitching workouts. There are towels folded and laid on the ledge behind the benches.

The water fountain holds a place of honour in most dugouts, inevitably bearing the scars of countless kicks and bat attacks by players who have failed at the plate. Somehow the water cooler is always to blame; but it keeps bubbling cheerfully, supplying cold, if somewhat brackish, water for thirsty throats.

The players are in charge of their own gloves, and these lie on the steps and benches. Players have practice gloves, too, either new ones they are working into shape to use in a game or, for some infielders, smaller models for practice to improve their fielding. Like the batter who swings a weight in the on-deck circle so that his bat will feel light and free at the plate, the fielder uses the small glove so that his bigger gamer will catch more balls.

Many players and most coaches arrive early on game days, leaving the hotel at 2:00 for a 7:30 game on the road, because the unstructured rituals are as important to them as the formal warmups to come. They play cards in the clubhouse, gossip in the dugout, or sun themselves in the empty stands.

The team bus arrives with the stragglers shortly after 5:00, and by 5:30 almost everybody is on the field. It's the home team's turn for batting practice first, so the visitors stretch and warm up, often chatting with a friend from the opposing team while doing it, or stand behind the batting cage and heckle.

This is the private time, the time when the diamond belongs to them. Soon the gates will open and they will be on show, but for now the only people in the park are the ones who belong there: players, the press, ground crew, vendors and ushers getting their final briefing in the stands. An umpire is always on duty, standing by the dugout in street clothes, supposedly enforcing the rule against fraternization between opposing team members. There is a sweet calm.

In the bullpen, the pitchers work out with their coach, especially the starters who aren't scheduled to pitch for a couple of days. Dave Stieb or Jim Clancy goes out with Al Widmar to work on a new pitch or perfect an old one. The tutelage will last as long as their careers.

While the home team takes batting practice, the visitors warm up, playing catch, slow toss at first at relatively close range, then harder and harder, farther and farther. Some play pepper, a simple fielding game that can get very intense. A player with a bat taps the ball toward a line of three or four fielders, one after the other. The fielder catches the ball and tosses it back to the batter to hit. A fielder who misses must move to the bottom of the line and if the batter misses, the first fielder gets to bat, usually over vociferous protest.

It's almost worth the price of the ticket to come out early and watch the Milwaukee Brewers play their variation on pepper, called flip. It is a viciously played game in which the ball is flipped from glove to glove among jostling players who do their best to make the next guy miss it. A game does not go by without several players sent sprawling by body checks more at home in a hockey rink. Most major league teams have banned flip for fear of injuries, but it is as much a part of the Brewers' macho image as Pete Vuckovich's scowl.

Lloyd Moseby is always a joy to watch in pregame play. He may be a hero now to Little League dreamers, but he has lively fantasies of his own and before the working day begins, he is Walter Mitty in spikes. Playing catch, usually with Willie Upshaw, Moseby becomes a pitcher, throwing sliders, curveballs, and changeups, commenting on each as it hits Upshaw's glove. He's like every twelve-year-old who has ever done a play-by-play of his fielding games against the front steps.

"A hard slider – strike three!" he shouts, raising his arms over his head in triumph. "Moseby notches his twentieth save! How about that?"

In batting practice, Moseby hits one into the leftfield stands, an opposite-field home run, and dances out of the cage screaming, "I don't believe it! The Blue Jays win the pennant! The Blue Jays win the pennant!"

Not content with chasing fly balls in his normal centrefield turf, Moseby asks the coaches to hit ground balls to him at third base. He makes great diving stops and rifles the ball to first, laughing when he misses. He then comes into the dugout to confide, quite seriously, that he could be the greatest third baseman ever to play the game. There is always that kind of joy in the best of the players, though few of them have Moseby's exuberance.

These moments before the game are as much a part of the pleasure of baseball as the game itself and typify the special nature of the sport as well as anything else. Let football players spend their pregame period throwing up and getting mean. Baseball players spend theirs getting loose. The relaxed intensity necessary to play the game well is the reason for the tradition of zaniness that has built up in baseball.

The fans who come out early, who are there when the gates

open an hour and a half before game time, share in this. They can watch big, ugly Cliff Johnson pick up tiny Garth Iorg (in baseball, anyone under 5'11" is referred to as a "little man") and race him around in a fireman's carry. They can hear the insults being shouted from dugout to dugout, cheerful jibes about the players' ability, looks, drinking capacity, or, these days, salary. The players mimic each other mercilessly. One player jumps out of his dugout with a bat and replays the way another bailed out on an inside pitch the night before, and members of both teams point at the embarrassed culprit and laugh uproariously.

As game time approaches, everyone gets a bit more serious. The starting pitcher retreats to the clubhouse where, like a matador, he dons his psychological suit of lights. Some pitchers refuse to go on the field before a start, but even the most even-keeled need a short quiet period alone. The other players settle into familiar routines, the same drills they have done from the lowest minors right on up before every game, day or night, with no exception, even during the World Series. These are the drills that help the players switch off their minds and fine-tune their reflexes for the game ahead.

Batting practice is taken in groups of four or five, the starters separately from the extra men. Each player first bunts twice, once down the first-base line, once toward third. They begin with six or seven swings, depending on the time available, taking turns, and work down until they are popping in and out of the cage, taking one swing each while the next group watches the clock and complains they are taking too much time. (Baseball players all have selective arithmetical amnesia. When they're in the cage, they can't figure out how many swings make five. When they're outside waiting, their math improves.)

The batting coach usually leans against the back of the cage watching. Occasionally he comments between swings or takes a player aside between turns with some advice.

The rest of the players are busy in the field, shagging flies in the outfield (although pitchers' shagging looks suspiciously like standing around with arms folded talking to the next guy) or fielding infield ground balls, hit by coaches standing beside the batting cage on either side.

After both teams have had batting practice and the protective screens and cages have been rolled away, it's time for the final

16

drills: outfielders catch fly balls and base hits and practise throwing to third and home; then the infielders practise fielding and throwing to different bases and to home; the pitchers stand in foul territory, first playing pepper, then relaying balls from the outfield back to the coaches; the catchers practise fielding bunts.

As the drills end, the players leave the field one by one, fielding one last ground ball as each leaves until only the catcher remains. One final popup and he's free to go and the ground crew race out with their rakes and barrows full of lime to fluff up the infield one last time.

The umpires stroll onto the field at last, with their hulking authority, and wait for the lineup cards to be delivered to them at the plate by a representative of each team. Then they all solemnly discuss the ground rules they have gone over dozens of times before.

The rituals whet the fans' appetites, and they greet the home team with great cheers when they run on the field and doff their caps for the anthems. Whenever the Blue Jays or Expos play, both American and Canadian anthems are played. Larry Millson of the *Globe and Mail* once estimated that if each anthem averages a minute and a half, players for Canadian teams spend a full eight hours listening to anthems in the course of a 162-game season – a working day's worth of phony patriotism.

A dream game is always played in the sunshine, memory omitting the lights or the cold of reality. It is watched from the boxes down the first-base line in Fenway Park in Boston or Royals Stadium in Kansas City, with a hot dog from Detroit in one hand and a beer from Milwaukee in another, surrounded by Baltimore fans waiting for the operatic vendor from Al Lang Field in St. Petersburg to pass by, singing "East Side, West Side" in a ringing baritone. Dreams are like that, you remember the best.

The game proceeds at just the right pace: the one detractors call boring. It is gentle and relaxed, full of spaces for reflection or conversation, quiet moments in which to relish a play just made or a confrontation about to occur. What's the rush? The longer the game, the more there is to enjoy.

It's hard to understand people who hate baseball, but easy to pity them. Never to have felt the surge of joy watching a ball sail over the fence or a fielder making a running, leaping catch is to have missed a great pleasure indeed. For that matter, to have missed the anger and despair when the ball sailing over the fence beats your favourite team in an important game is equally sad, because the caring feels so good. To find baseball boring is to have missed drama and nuance, the laughter and the tears that come from joy or sorrow. It's a shame.

The unfortunate thing about baseball for the novice fan is that the more you know about it the more attractive it becomes, and there aren't enough teachers to go around.

It's not hard to find the excitement in a high-scoring game the home team wins, but the pleasure of a pitchers' duel is more elusive. To find the joy in a low-scoring game, you have to understand that the central confrontation of the game is being won by the pitcher, this time, but the battle is rejoined with each pitch.

That's what is at the core of the sport. Standing on a hill precisely ten inches high is a man who uses every bit of muscle and talent and brain he has to throw a ball harder or with more spin of one kind or another than anyone in the stands ever could. He has a lone enemy and eight accomplices on the field with him. His catcher is crouched behind the plate doing some (or, occasionally, all) of his thinking for him, suggesting which pitches to throw. Seven other men, four in the infield and three in the outfield, are ready to make the pitcher look good. His enemy stands next to the plate with a stick in his hand, all by himself. It's as simple as that. The guy with the stick is trying to hit the ball thrown by the man on the hill, preferably out of range of the gloved accomplices.

The complications come in when we peek inside each man's head, the real battleground of baseball. The pitcher and catcher remember what they have learned from the scouts and from their own experience with the hitter. Does he have trouble with curveballs? Will he go for the slider low and outside? Does he swing at the first pitch or watch it? In short, is there an easy way to get this guy out? The fielders are remembering, too. Does the hitter pull the ball? Should the outfielders shade him to left or right? What's the pitcher going to throw?

The hitter, for his part, is reviewing what he knows about the pitcher and catcher, while trying to watch the fielders in case they open a hole he can hit through. All of the cerebration goes on in the time it takes the pitcher to get the sign from the catcher, wind up, and throw the ball, to the accompaniment of a hellacious hullabaloo from the paying customers in the stands.

Add a base runner or two and the equation becomes even more complex. The pitcher and catcher are worrying that the runner will try to steal and are trying to prevent it. The catcher will often call for a fastball with men on base to give himself a fighting chance.

That will please the hitter, because fastballs are easier to hit, but he has to worry about the base runner, too. He gets signs from the third-base coach to tell him whether he should swing or not, hit behind the runner into rightfield, or simply swing away. And, oh yes, he has to hit a round ball with a round bat, reckoned by some to be the most difficult endeavour in all of sport.

The experienced fans understand all of this, and even have some thinking of their own to do. Anyone can see the hitter's batting average on the scoreboard and guess at his chances, but the ardent fans know more. They might remember the last time the two players squared off, when the pitcher gave up a home run, or know that the hitter is in a three-game slump. They might even know that the pitcher's wife just had a baby and he's tired.

The numbers define the game, but so do human factors. These athletes, unencumbered (with the exception of catchers) by the padding, helmets, and masks of hockey and football, have faces, and their isolation on the field gives them no place to hide. This is one reason that newspapers and magazines profile these players more than they do those in football or hockey, and why readers are eager to learn more about them.

Their personalities also show clearly in the way they play. No one watching Pete Rose in action can have any doubt about the type of man he is. Compare the way Eddie Murray arrogantly approaches the plate with the excuse-me diffidence of Todd Cruz and see if you can figure out which is the slugger. This body language even shows what kind of a day a player is having. The difference between a relief pitcher struggling for control and the same one in command of his game is like watching two different men.

Sometimes the confrontation is classic, usually when it is the team's best pitcher against the other team's best hitter when the game is on the line. There's intimidation on both sides. The batter digs his spikes into the dirt and glares, saying with his eyes, "Throw the damn ball."

The pitcher responds. He throws it right at the batter's throat. "Out of my way, mother. Get back where you belong."

The batter picks himself up out of the dirt and laughs. The fans howl for the pitcher's head. The show goes on.

In Yankee Stadium on October 10, 1980, the confrontation was between George Brett, the Royal third baseman who had hit .390 in the regular season, and Goose Gossage, the Yankee reliever who had a 2.27 earned run average and twenty saves. The league's best reliever was up against the league's best hitter in the third game of the league championship series, but it was even more than that. It was also the fourth time the two teams had met in the playoffs, and the Yankees had won the three previous times. The Royals had never made it to the World Series but they had a 2-0 lead in games this time. They were hungry.

The score was 2-1 Yankees in the seventh inning and there were two men on when Brett came to bat, speedy Willie Wilson and U.L. Washington. Brett hadn't had a hit in seven at bats.

There were 56,000 fans in the stands, and every one of them was screaming: "GOOOOoose, GOOOOooose" echoed off the pillared facades of the historic park. They were banshees, drowning out the few voices shouting in the visiting dugout: "It's going to happen! It's going to happen!"

It was a moment so exciting, so purely dramatic, that years later it still gives me chills. In memory the two are frozen for an instant before Gossage threw his first pitch. Then whap, it was over in the blink of an eye – the delivery, the swing, and then the ball flying harder and faster than physics should allow into the third deck of the rightfield grandstand. There was no doubt about it. Brett was the Royals and Gossage the Yankees, and the series was won and lost on that single pitch.

In April of 1982 I remembered that night again after another confrontation almost as classic, though not as crucial. Reggie Jackson was making his first trip back to New York in an Angel uniform after going to California as a free agent when the Yankees didn't try to sign him. Jackson was bitter, as were the New York fans who had adored him through five years and three World Series. They felt, Jackson and his fans, that Yankee owner George Steinbrenner had let them all down.

The day before Jackson's return, Steinbrenner tried to upstage the event by firing manager Bob Lemon for the second time in five years and rehiring the man Lemon had replaced the season before, Gene Michael.

Jackson had been slumping, with a .173 batting average so far that season, and his nine hits had all been singles. He was at the ballpark early, taking extra batting practice and holding a press conference. ("Hi, guys, I'm Reggie," he began.)

When the lineups were announced, 35,000 fans gave Jackson a standing ovation. They cheered his first at bat, a weak popup. His second time up, he singled, and the fans chanted "Reg-gie, Reg-gie!" as they had so many times before.

Finally, when he hit the first pitch Ron Guidry threw his third time at bat off the facing of the third tier in rightfield, they stood and chanted "Steinbrenner sucks," over and over. It was as if they had rehearsed it for weeks, so clearly were the unlovely words enunciated by men and women, boys and girls, young and old, in perfect unison. And even the Yankees couldn't quite hold back their smiles as they stood on the field and listened.

On the way downtown after the game I encountered a gleeful cabbie, a middle-aged man who had lived in New York and hated the Yankees all his life. His radio was tuned to the Yankee network.

"Reggie stuck it in Steinbrenner's ear, didn't he?" the cabbie gloated. "I was on the Brooklyn Bridge when he hit it."

As the ride continued through the less appetizing parts of Harlem the man talked about other great moments in baseball history, including Brett's home run two seasons previously. "That was a great one, too," he chortled. "I was gassing up the cab over in the Bronx when he hit it."

It finally dawned on me that this very dedicated fan saw very few games. He was too busy trying to support a family to take nights or afternoons off, but he listened to every game on his radio and fixed them in his own peculiar geography.

The Giants were the cabbie's team before they went west, and his all-time hero was Willie Mays. "When he retired, they gave him a day," he said, evoking the majesty of the occasion. "I'll never forget it. When he made his speech I just pulled the cab over to the side of 85th Street and cried. It was like he was my father."

21

Baseball has more than moments like those two home runs, those sweet moments of revenge. What makes baseball special is almost daily surprise. Watching tiny Alfredo Griffin hit a home run is as delightful as watching elephantine Cliff Johnson steal a base because each is so unexpected that fans laugh and clap each other on the back. Did you *see* that? Players in the dugout hide their smiles behind their hands, and Griffin crosses the plate or Johnson dusts his uniform off at second trying to look cool, as if it happened every day.

If it wasn't for surprise only a handful of the twenty-six teams in the major leagues could survive. The others wouldn't draw flies to watch them lose, overmatched, game after game. But baseball is the underdog's sport, and on any given day virtually anything can happen, and that's what keeps fans showing up to see even the least successful teams. Because any team can win any game; because a Gold Glove can make an error and a bum can make a great play; because the worst team in baseball can score twenty runs some days baseball is still alive. A trip to the ballpark is full of anticipation: what's going to happen today?

In the early Blue Jay years, all fans could hope for was astounding surprises. They got their share, but the underdog battle I remember best was fought out of town, in Yankee Stadium. It was a game few others will recall so vividly. Tommy John and Billy Martin might, even though it had no real bearing on a championship. Phil Huffman will never forget it.

The Blue Jays started a four-game series in New York on June 19, 1979. Now these were truly dreadful players having a terrible year, and it was a mid-week series, but there were 36,000 crazed fans on hand that Tuesday night. Not for the Blue Jays, no, but to welcome back Billy Martin as manager.

At the beginning of the week, Steinbrenner, perhaps realizing that advance ticket sales were pathetic for the series, perhaps wanting to guarantee Martin a few quick wins, had announced that Bad Billy would replace Bob Lemon, the man who had replaced him the season before. The move was cynically motivated, but the fans lined up around the block to be there.

To further ensure success, Martin moved John (10-2 at the time) up a game in the starting rotation to pitch the first night against the hapless Jays. All they had to face the ace was Huffman, a fuzzy-cheeked rookie with a 3-7 record who would turn twenty-one the next day. Huffman, although he tried to hide it with a moustache that refused to grow, had the fair freckled face, mischievous grin, and baby blue eyes of a Norman Rockwell painting.

Banners hung from every tier of the stadium to welcome Martin back, and when he came jogging out of the dugout with the lineup card before the game the din was frightening, especially to Huffman, out in the bullpen warming up. "When they all started yelling for Billy, I got the chills," he recalled afterwards. "I got the butterflies real bad. I was so pumped up I couldn't even hear the names of the batters when they were announced."

It was probably just as well. If he had realized who he was facing he probably wouldn't have got them out, but he lasted six innings, holding the Yankees to three runs while the Blue Jays had every blooper they hit drop in. They ended up winning the game 5-4. David slew Goliath, and the cynics lost their shirts.

The heroes of that night were men who will never be called to Cooperstown. Not one of them lasted in the majors past the end of the next season. Huffman lost eighteen games that year and was sent to the minors, never to return. Tom Buskey, the journeyman reliever who saved the game, now works for the state employment office in Pennsylvania and coaches a junior college team. J.J. Cannon, who made the catch of the game to rob Graig Nettles of a home run, now coaches in the low Blue Jay minors.

It's nice to think that those men, Cannon and Buskey and Huffman, have that game to remember, and you know they remember it still. That was the night when they were truly big league. The Cinderella night when they beat the Yankees, broke all those New York hearts, and felt like they could play forever. Their lives have turned back into pumpkins and field mice, but they still carry the glass slipper around in their minds.

I remember Cannon's catch in particular. He was a late-inning defensive replacement for the genial, lead-footed Otto Velez in rightfield, and when Nettles hit the ball, Cannon was the only one in the park who didn't believe it was gone and that the Yankees had won the game. He raced back into the rightfield corner, timing his leap to the flight of the ball, as he later explained it, and snatched it off the padding at the top of the fence, ten feet high.

It was a perfect moment, a perfect catch, and he hangs up there frozen in my memory for all time, the cheering fans frozen behind him at the very moment they realize they've been robbed, their jaws slackening out of the smiles of triumph.

I remember Huffman, too. There are more reporters in Yankee Stadium than anywhere else in the league, especially on a night like this one, vultures coming out to circle Martin again. They all wanted to talk to the kid pitcher who had spoiled Billy's fun. Huffman was all calm bravado and offhand – nothing to it, just another day in a big-league pitcher's life, ho hum – convincing unless you had suffered with him through the seven losses and seen the doubt and despair in his eyes. He was a kid in over his head, and he knew it, but he was enjoying the bluff. I waited until the New Yorkers had left before I talked to him.

"What about the first pitch in the third inning?" I asked, about a ball thrown so wildly it sailed over the catcher's head and hit the screen, totally out of control.

Huffman looked around to make sure we were alone and then began to giggle. He laughed and laughed and didn't stop until he had used all the happiness up. Then he went out with the big guys and had a birthday celebration he will never forget.

These moments are the soul of baseball: the ball perfectly hit, perfectly caught, or perfectly thrown; the strikeout that ends a game, the pitcher's hand punching the air, the catcher running toward the mound. We can unwrap the moments later, when it's quiet, and enjoy them all over again. Each fan has a private collection, and his moments are more precious than another fan's whole game.

I certainly cherish Huffman's game more than another one played almost two years later, even though the second game already has its own niche in the Hall of Fame, and in Len Barker's heart. It was a pretty boring night in Cleveland on Friday night, May 15, 1981. Two lacklustre teams, in contention for nothing more interesting than last place, were meeting because the schedule told them to, and nobody much cared. Paid attendance was announced as 7,290 but some of those who had paid for tickets obviously had stayed at home. Those who showed up looked like no more than a handful in the huge park. The Blue Jays and Indians drew big crowds only on bat day.

It was a chilly evening and neither team was doing anything very exciting. The Indians scored a couple of unearned runs in the first inning, but Luis Leal kept it close with a good pitching job. Barker, for his part, hadn't allowed a Blue Jay to reach base by hit, walk, or error; but this caused little excitement in the press box.

Partial no-hitters are more common than one might think. Baseball writers see them all the time. The first couple of times it's exciting, but after that it's just an excuse to set up a pool. After three no-hit innings, a dollar will buy you one of ten numbered slips of paper. The number you get, from one to nine, indicates what position you hold in the batting order, and the zero gives you the no-hitter to cheer for. The guy who pulled that slip that night groaned.

Even five perfect innings aren't really unusual. Players say they don't start noticing until after the sixth, after the second time through the batting order. That's why Barker's perfect innings that night, one after another, didn't cause much of a stir at first.

This wasn't Nolan Ryan out there, for Pete's sake. This was Len Barker and the Indians, and someone was bound to get on base sooner or later. Even the Blue Jays, no matter how they were slumping (they had been shut out in two previous games), would get on base with a hit, a walk, or an error before the game was over.

In the press box we simply waited for the play that would open the game up and noticed admiringly that the game, however dull, was moving along nicely. There was a chance to get our stories in before deadline.

Only as the game began winding down did the excitement begin. As the seventh inning passed, then the eighth, a strange, superstitious silence filled the stadium. The clapping and cheering were slightly subdued, the balance seemed so precarious. All eyes were on Barker as he left the mound after an inning, and then came back for the next. This large, rather ordinary pitcher became a different man.

In the press box we had been making jokes about the legitimacy of such a feat against the Blue Jays and whether it should carry an asterisk in the record books, but we stopped kibitzing and began to watch each pitch carefully, trying to fix it in our minds. This wasn't just another boring game – this was history!

We called our editors, spoiling their hopes for an easy night:

"Uh, I know you don't want to hear this on deadline, but we might have a perfect game here."

During the top of the ninth inning, with the Indians up to bat, Terry Pluto, the beat writer from the *Cleveland Plain Dealer*, rushed breathlessly into the press box. It was every writer's nightmare come true. Len Barker was pitching a perfect game, and Pluto had taken the day off.

He watched with the rest of us as Barker walked to the mound in the bottom of the ninth, picked up the ball, and immediately bobbled and dropped it. His nerves were showing. The scoreboard in centrefield flashed the answer to the night's trivia question: "The Toronto Blue Jays and Seattle Mariners." The question had asked which two teams had never been involved in a no-hitter in the major leagues. It looked mightily like the jinx was on, but Barker, calmer than anybody in the place, faced his last three men and got them.

Ernie Whitt, the last batter, hit a fly ball into centrefield. Rick Manning ran in and caught it, then kept on running with it clutched in his hand, fought through the mob on the mound, and gave it to Barker. Whitt dragged his bat back to the Blue Jay dugout, where the rest of the team just stood and watched, completely stunned. They stayed on the field for a long time, waiting with the rest of the crowd for Barker to come back out on the field and acknowledge the cheers.

Whitt insisted to me later, even off the record, that he had been trying as hard as he ever did to get a hit in that last at-bat. He wanted to ensure that Barker had earned it. He said that when he had come in to pinch-hit he had even considered pulling a Babe Ruth, pointing into centrefield to show where he was going to hit it out. All in all, it wasn't the way he wanted to get into the history books.

There had not been a perfect game pitched since 1968, when Catfish Hunter did it to the Minnesota Twins for the Oakland A's. One after another, Barker had set down twenty-seven Blue Jays. No hits, no walks, no errors. Two foul outs, five fly ball outs, nine groundouts, eleven strikeouts. It was perfect, and it was, for the most part, a yawn. Funny.

When it was over, Barker's hands were shaking with after-the-fact jitters as he passed champagne around to his teammates.

(Every ballclub must have a secret supply of bubbly hidden away for such occasions.) He said he felt like he was "in an airplane 45,000 feet off the ground."

Someone mentioned Addie Joss, the last Indian to pitch a perfect game (in 1908, against the White Sox), but Barker had never heard of him. "But whoever he was," he said, "I'm sure he pitched a hell of a game!"

It was almost an anticlimax, but the sense of history was strong. We were there. We saw it happen. And don't you know that in years to come the people who claim to have been there that night could fill the stadium to the rafters.

There was something especially nice about seeing it pitched in that cavernous old barn of a ballpark, a fitting place for history to be made. I watched half a thousand games from the press box in my five years on the beat, but never even came close again.

I could identify with Pluto the next season when Jim Clancy took a perfect game into the ninth inning against the Twins while I was taking a few days off to get married. I was listening to the game on the radio at home, trying to decide whether to rush down to the stadium to see the end of it. Clancy was one of my favourite players, and I hated the thought of him throwing it without me. The first batter in the inning took the quandary away with a bloop single, and Clancy became just another pitcher who almost made it.

Perfect games are rare. The special combination of skill and luck necessary has rolled around in the major leagues only eight times this century. Luckily for us all, a game doesn't need to be perfect to be splendid.

Chapter

2

The Players

Shoulders broad and sculptured, arms with muscles and sinews as well defined as a thoroughbred's, hips slim, legs strong – the body is designed to hit and run and throw. In repose, it would not look out of place in the Louvre.

A few lockers down, fat fleshes low on the waist, the beer can is held in a hammy hand. The feet are flat, the legs are short, and the buttocks hang over the stool. You could find the like on any tavern softball team.

Elsewhere in the clubhouse are little skinny guys who look like they couldn't pick up a bat, let alone swing it, and guys who are simply average, fit but not muscular. Each athlete has a body defined by its function and by its owner's dedication to perfection.

The outfielders and middle infielders are in the best shape because they are the ones for whom speed and flexibility are most important in the field. There is no extra bulk on a base stealer, but the sluggers carry more than their share. They need the weight to put into their swings. In the American League, these are usually designated hitters like Greg Luzinski, who has the physique of a sumo wrestler, but there are those who play first base and leftfield out of necessity, and their teams suffer for it defensively. You can tell a catcher by the extra beef in his thighs and by the bruises on his body. It is physically the toughest position to play in the game, and the catcher wears the evidence all over him.

When scoffers talk about the lack of athleticism among baseball players, they are usually talking about pitchers. It is on the mound that the belly of LaMarr Hoyt of the White Sox or Dodger Fernando Valenzuela invites derision: "You call these guys *athletes?*" Kent Tekulve of the Pirates could pose for the "before" picture in the old Charles Atlas ads. Tiny Tippy Martinez of the Orioles is the butt of the big players' jokes. But each has the body he needs, and all four pitchers are aces on their teams.

There is room for physical difference in baseball, as there is for the whole range of temperament, from the silence of Steve Carlton to the quipping of Dan Quisenberry, from surly Eddie Murray to sweet Frank White, from high-flying Lloyd Moseby to matter-of-fact Barry Bonnell, just doing his job. Jim Clancy answers "yup" and "nope"; Jim Gott talks in chapters.

And the question asked me more than any by fans I meet is inevitably, "What are ballplayers *really* like?"

Ballplayers are like accountants or tightrope walkers, veterinarians or computer programmers, streetcar drivers or university professors: some good, some bad, some smart, some dumb, some dedicated, some lazy, and an awful lot in between.

There are, to be sure, traits most share. Ballplayers tend to be inordinately self-absorbed. During the season, their teammates come second, followed distantly by wives, families, and fans. The "real world," outside baseball, concerns them not at all. Oh, they can whip up some interest in the Kentucky Derby or the NBA finals, but don't ask them about the situation in Lebanon. ("Beirut?" goes the joke, "I thought Hank Aaron was a better pure hitter.")

It's not even their fault, really. A star athlete has been special since he was very small. A player who makes it to the big leagues is a good bet to have been the best player on his little league team, his high school team, his college team, and every step along the way in the minor leagues.

Tell a boy, then a man, that he is special often enough and he's going to believe it. Then give him privilege, special treatment academically, deals on cars and stereos, free equipment, restaurant meals on the house, and sex on demand, and he's going to come to expect it as his due. There are fans everywhere who would give anything to befriend a real live major league ballplayer, to rub up against a star, and some of those fans have a lot to give.

In every town in the major leagues, there is a deal to be had, and no matter how much money these guys make, they hate to buy retail. In Texas, the players know where to get boots cheap. In Milwaukee, it's stereo equipment, the monster tape decks of five years ago now mercifully replaced by discreet Walkmans. Leather jackets here, jewellery there. Women. In some cases, drugs.

Nothing is ever demanded in return except the player's presence, an autograph, an evening spent, tickets to a game. No wonder they're spoiled. No wonder they never want to grow up.

The other side of the coin is that their Peter Pan world is very insecure. For men not encouraged to define themselves by anything but their talents, failure can be emotionally devastating. And by the very nature of baseball, they fail every day, and when it happens, they know it. If the fans don't boo, they at least groan. There's no place to hide on a baseball diamond after an error that leads to a run or a strikeout with the bases loaded.

Players realize that catcalls are part of the job description, but it doesn't mean they have to enjoy them. Many players have told me the same fantasy. They would like to go and watch one of their fans at his office and subject him to the treatment they get every day of the season. "Boo, boo, you dialled a wrong number, how can you be so stupid?" the fantasy heckling inevitably goes. "Boo, you're five minutes late back from lunch. Oh, no! Is that a spelling mistake? You're horseshit. Boo, boo, boooooooooo!"

That players are paid very good money for their work does not make it easier for most of them. It is part of the fairy-tale reality of baseball that a player is "worth" $500,000 a year for playing a game, and they are certainly not going to question it. All it does is make them more likely to panic at the thought of losing the job.

The insecurity is the root of the anger, the moodiness, and their distrust of the press, whom they see as vultures waiting to pounce on their every mistake. The fishbowl of celebrity is difficult for them, especially when they are young. Nowhere in all the years of training, in all the hours spent by coaches along the line refining their physical tools, has anyone given any formal attention to their emotional development, and they are seldom mature enough to handle the attention with grace. They either believe their good notices too much or take the bad ones too seriously.

The lucky player finds a mentor, a sensitive parent, a good coach, a veteran player, an agent who cares about more than his percentage, or a strong wife who challenges him to put his life and work into perspective. The unlucky one finds nothing but sychophants who have their own reasons to keep him immature. He is offered irresistible doses of flattery wrapped around offers of drugs or can't-miss investments for his unaccustomed wealth.

When the inevitable crash comes the players find that the friends and the money are gone. Successful players have seen it happen to friends, and some have come close to the edge themselves. What often happens to the young phenoms who get stalled inexplicably in the low minor leagues isn't a matter of finding too many players who can hit their sliders or too many pitchers who throw curveballs. Often it is simply because straight out of high school or college, even the good times and bright lights of a minor league burg like Kinston, North Carolina, or Knoxville, Tennessee, can be pretty seductive. The players are just kids, some away from home for the first time, making good money for playing a game, and a lot of them go a bit wild.

Most of the players who make it through the low-level pitfalls to major league careers have found their own way to cope with the stresses of celebrity, the pressure of performing, and the fear of failure. For many of them, the mechanism is religion. I always figured that God had better things to do than watch ball games, but there seem to be plenty of ballplayers who think otherwise. These guys thank the Lord for home runs.

Former Oriole manager Earl Weaver came up with the definitive word on the God Squad, in an often-quoted exchange with born-again outfielder Pat Kelly.

"Aren't you happy I walk with the Lord, Earl?" Kelly asked.

"I'd rather you walked with the bases loaded," the Pearl replied.

It is easy to be cynical about the believers, perhaps a bit too easy. There are certainly some hypocrites among them, those who go straight from Saturday night adultery to Sunday morning baseball chapel, but that's not unique to athletes. There are also those who use Jesus as a cop-out for their own mistakes, but most of the religious athletes I knew were sincere.

They haven't chosen the easiest route to take in the "man's-man" world of sport. There is a sissy taint to Bible reading and a distrust of the motives of religious players.

Barry Bonnell experienced this kind of prejudice when he first joined the Atlanta Braves. "I had just come up and Dale Murphy had converted to Mormon while we were on a road trip in the minor leagues," Bonnell recalled, some years later, the memory still smarting. "Everybody knew that I'd been involved in it.

"The Braves were going somewhere on the bus and it was really full for some reason, but no one sat next to me. They stood in the aisles instead. I hated that."

Bonnell was also the victim of an attitude all too prevalent in baseball, that those who walk with the Lord lack the fire in the belly that drives great players.

I was told by players and coaches more than once that Bonnell didn't hustle because he was too much at peace with his maker. Jesse Barfield slumped badly in the last half of 1982, and I was told that it had more to do with his being born again than with the effects of an ankle injury.

This attitude is something they must each struggle with, since winning baseball isn't necessarily good Christian behaviour. Jim Gott told me that when he converted to Mormonism he had trouble figuring out how to live his faith and stay aggressive on the ball diamond. He finally resolved it by leaving charity outside of the white lines.

I think that religion finally has very little to do with how a player behaves on the field. It has a lot to do with how he behaves off the field, though, and the athletes with strong faith certainly bring healthier bodies to the ballpark each day than the carousers.

More importantly, crutch or not, religion has straightened out some athletes who needed help. Two I knew well, Gott and Barfield, were pretty messed up before the conversions, living self-centred and destructive lives that almost ruined their careers. It happened in the minor leagues. After a fast start when every day holds triumph and every night a chance to celebrate it, each fell into difficulty.

Gott admits that he drank and used drugs, that he had a tough time with authority and came close to losing everything. He was wild on and off the mound and after his second pro season his father kicked him out of the house and told him to straighten himself out. Gott went to stay with his older brother, who was on a golf scholarship at Brigham Young University. In the straitlaced but idyllic atmosphere of Happy Valley, as the Mormon campus is called by the students, Gott calmed down. He also met Clenice, the devout and tough-minded woman he later married. She quickly straightened him out and is still the strongest force in his life.

The Gotts told me a story that showed their relationship in the early days. Gott had been working out with weights and was showing off his muscles for his wife. Clenice barely glanced at him. "When your character is that well developed it will be worth a look," she said. Within two years, he was a clean-living major league pitcher.

This is not to say there is anything sanctimonious about either of the Gotts. The two of them tell the story with affection and laughter, and approach life with glee. When Gott arrived in Toronto in 1982, his rookie year, he had the irresistible eagerness of a St. Bernard puppy, always cheerful, always talking, always asking questions. After every win, Gott was the first to bound out of the dugout to shake the pitcher's hand.

Gott's particular charm came from his refusal to bow to clubhouse pressure, subtle as it might have been, to stay cool, to play the ballplayer role. He didn't understand why his teammates spent so much time sniping at each other and didn't like playing their psychological games. He not only tolerated reporters, which was just marginally cool, he actually sought them out. And the things he talked to them about were uncommon. The latest performance of the National Ballet? C'mon. Gott is a rare one, and not just because he listens to Itzhak Perlman tapes on his headphones. In the world of supercool, his warmth is as welcome as sunshine.

May he never change, and may he become a good enough pitcher to stay around and set an example for lots of rookies to come. The game needs more like him.

Barfield's conversion was not as dramatic a change in his life. He simply went back to the habits of his childhood, turning to prayer when his career was going badly. He was rewarded by almost immediate advancement to Toronto. When he backslid, he slumped at the plate. When he promised himself again to Jesus, his career straightened out. He got the message. He also married a woman who was born again, with teammate Roy Lee Jackson as his best man. A gentle, affectionate, and humorous young man, Barfield doesn't see his faith as a panacea. He stops short of crediting the Lord with the home runs he hits. He simply understands that he is in better control of his life when he shares out the responsibility.

We had a conversation one day that I found unsettling at first, but remember now warmly. He called me early one afternoon in Kansas City and asked if he could come and talk to me. I agreed, hoping that he wanted to talk about demanding a trade or to complain about the manager off-the-record, but was pretty sure I wouldn't be so lucky.

When Barfield arrived, he sat down and unzipped the case in which he carried his Bible and I knew I was in for it. He began, in his words, to "share" scripture with me, continuing a discussion we had begun in spring training. He went at it for an hour, until we had to catch the team bus.

My first reaction was a combination of hilarious disbelief – I was afraid I was going to be seized by a giggling fit – and anger at the imposition. There was certainly something absurd about the situation. Here I was, a reasonably intelligent and well-educated forty-year-old woman being lectured by a born-again ballplayer young enough to be my son. As he read, though, I changed my mind. I was moved by Barfield's sincerity and generosity. It was really a very loving gesture, showing more concern for me than most players ever had. Because it was not made in a form with which I was comfortable did not make it any less thoughtful.

One thing Barfield said that afternoon has stayed with me because of the loneliness he unwittingly expressed. "I was reading the Bible on the plane on the way here," he said. "I looked around me at the other people on the plane and as I looked at each one I realized he was Hell-bound. There were only three of us who weren't Hell-bound."

On the other side of the spiritual coin is the superstition that is everywhere in baseball. Otherwise reasonable men, who work in a world in which luck, of both sorts, is everywhere, tend to do what they can to court it. Games are won and lost on the hop of a ground ball, and careers are made and broken on series of circumstances in no one's control, so anything that can give a player an edge is grabbed quickly.

Some superstitions are universal. Just watch players, coaches, and managers go on and off the field. If you find one who dares to step on the white lines on the way past, he's likely doing it out of some sort of reverse superstition, like people who make a point of walking under ladders.

Many superstitions have to do with clothing. Some players invariably put on one leg of their trousers first. Others line their shoes up in their locker a special way. If they are in a winning or hitting streak, they will often wear the same T-shirt day after day. Some refuse to shave until the luck turns sour.

Dave Collins started the 1983 season badly. He could barely hit his weight, and he's not very heavy. He cracked jokes about it – the best was his remark that he didn't mind hitting .220 during day games because people seeing it on the scoreboard might think it was the time – but he was obviously troubled by the slump and tried all sorts of voodoo to change his luck.

In the second half of the season he began to hit. In celebration, he decided not to cut his hair until he stopped hitting, and by the last day of the season he had curls almost to his shoulders. I asked him when he was going to cut it.

"Tomorrow," he said. "I can't stand long hair. It's driving me crazy." But not crazy enough to fiddle with luck.

Wade Boggs, the American League batting champion in 1983, is famous for always eating chicken before a game, and those sorts of pregame rituals are not even considered strange.

Others place importance on tokens. I gave Willie Upshaw a lucky penny one day when he was in a slump and he went on to get three hits in the game. After that he came and asked me for another whenever he began to have trouble at the plate. I consider myself personally responsible for his half of the team most valuable player award in 1983.

Even managers weren't immune. Earl Weaver was the worst I ever met. I was in the Oriole manager's office after one game in Toronto to see it in action. His team had just swept three from the Jays and the little manager had every right to put his feet on the desk, have a beer, and dispense genius. Instead, he was in a raging flap.

"Who's got my Kansas City Royals' pen?" he asked. "I can't find my pen."

"Your lineup pen? Your four-game-streak pen?" The panic edged into the reporters' voices, too. This was a crisis indeed! They put down their pads and began to look around the room.

Weaver put great stock in rituals around the preparation and presentation of his lineup cards. On a winning streak he would make sure he used the same pen to write the lineup until the team lost a game, at which point he would switch.

Now he was desperate. On a four-game streak, he'd lost his pen and the team was due to leave for Boston in an hour. The Oriole reporters, on deadlines like the rest of us, immediately put their interviews on hold to look for the talismanic ballpoint. One actually dug through the contents of the wastebasket, but they never found the pen, and there was a palpable pall in the room for the rest of the interview. The next day, the Orioles lost to the Red Sox. Make of it what you will.

Weaver was also superstitious about the delivery of the cards to the umpires before the game. While most managers take their own lineups to home plate for the ceremonial meeting with the opposing manager and the umpires just before the game, Weaver took turns with his coaches. When the Orioles won the game, the same coach would take the lineup each game until the team lost. Weaver could tell you how long each coach's best streak had lasted.

Frank Robinson was very lucky, but the coach I remember best was Jimmy Frey, now the Cubs' manager. Frey was in charge of the lineup card for one game late in the 1979 season after the Orioles had lost several in a row, and Weaver was dubious about Frey's ability to come through. The Orioles won the game, though, and I stopped at Frey's locker after the game to ask him the secret of his success. "I'm in the contract stretch," he said.

The ego is a powerful force in baseball, and there are those players who cope by being completely self-centred. They were, in many cases, the biggest stars, and the ones I could most easily do without. They are a joy to watch play the game, but a pain in the neck to deal with. These are the ones who talk about themselves in the third person. To hear Pete Rose complain about "a player of my stature" being benched or listen to Reggie Jackson for more than five minutes always made me want to be elsewhere.

Undeniably a star with an extraordinary sense of the moment, Jackson was one of the most fascinating, but unpleasant, characters I encountered in baseball. It's only a fluke I feel that way.

There were some reporters I respect whom he liked and who assured me that Jackson was a sensitive and intelligent man, unfairly at the mercy of the sharks that surrounded him. It could be. I wouldn't know because he thought I had a fin on my back, too. He was a bit like Billy Martin in that way. If you encountered either one on a good day you came away thinking he was a prince. On a bad day they were jerks. I never hit a good day with either one.

Had I not been a print reporter it would have been a different matter. Jackson loved television interviewers once the camera was turned on because this was an image he could control. He was wonderful in front of the cameras, self-effacing and God-fearing, all "Hi, Mom" and five-dollar words. Out of their range, he was completely unpredictable.

Being a reporter from the boonies didn't help either. What importance could a reporter from Toronto have in the world of baseball, for heaven's sake? I wasn't Peter Gammons of the *Boston Globe* or Tom Boswell of the *Washington Post*, so why bother? I didn't cover the Yankees or the Angels when he played for those teams. I wasn't in the inner circle.

On the fringe, I watched as he manipulated my colleagues, who practically tugged their forelocks in deference. He sighed at what he considered dumb questions while winking at the reporters who covered him daily, exempting them from his scorn. They ate it up. Then he would turn and snarl at the offender, asking him exactly what he meant by his question. He reduced the meek to jelly and enjoyed it. It made me ashamed of my profession to be reduced to acting a role in Jackson's drama of the moment. The man was only a ballplayer, after all, whatever inflated importance he placed on it, and not that great a ballplayer either, day in and day out.

That these men are perceived to be more important than doctors or scientists or firemen or teachers, on the evidence of what they are paid, struck me often, but the disproportion never seemed greater than when I dealt with Jackson. Here was a supreme egotist with one skill, the ability to hit a baseball out of any park in the major leagues when the game was on the line, and for that he was deified by the fans. He was by no means a well-rounded athlete. There are dozens in the game better than he. He couldn't run or catch or throw particularly well. He exemplified none of the greater virtues of sport, team play and sportsmanship, but he was a greater hero than those who did. What I'm not sure of is whether that's Jackson's fault, or baseball's.

And yet there was another side to him. He was kind to young players, dispensing bits of himself to star-struck rookies and making them feel at home on his turf. Once, in 1979, in Toronto, he was walked by Phil Huffman. He yelled at the young pitcher all the way to first base, accusing him of not having the guts to throw him a pitch he could hit. Huffman, cocky himself, yelled right back. A week later, in New York, in the last game Huffman would pitch in the major leagues, in his eighteenth loss of the season, Huffman struck Jackson out. When the game was over and Huffman was packing up his stuff, the clubhouse attendant walked up to him at his locker and handed him a baseball. It was inscribed "To Phil – I admire your toughness. Reggie Jackson."

I admired the gesture, which meant a lot to Huffman, but I also saw it as an extraordinarily condescending thing to do to a player who was, after all, a fellow major leaguer, not a beseeching twelve-year-old fan. But I'm sure that baseball now holds place of pride among Huffman's souvenirs.

I can find some sympathy in my heart for the likes of Jackson or Rose, constantly in the public eye. They are booed as heartily on the road as they are cheered at home, loved and hated with equal ferocity. They are forced to suffer legions of fools, some with press passes, who want to get close to their celebrity. A slump is examined as if with a microscope; behaviour off the field is as public as that on it. The demands on the superstars are great, indeed.

But, hey, that's what they signed on for. It comes with the territory, and the admirable players are the ones who understand their responsibility to the press and to the fans they represent. Mike Schmidt, one of the greatest players in today's game, showed me his character after the 1983 World Series. The Phillies had lost, in part because this extraordinary hitter had picked the wrong time of the year to have a slump. In the five games, in twenty at bats, he had managed nothing more than a single, striking out six times. As the press rushed into the losing clubhouse when the series ended, most of the players were cooling off in private, but Schmidt stood at his locker, waiting for us with a rueful joke: "Me first, huh?"

Rickey Henderson was another star with a sense of responsibility. An Oakland boy grown up to be an All-Star hero, he never forgot his roots. On the day the A's returned to Oakland after Henderson had broken Lou Brock's stolen-base record, there were hundreds of fans waiting outside the stadium for him after the game. He soon appeared, casually elegant in the expensive sports clothes favoured by ballplayers. A bat boy was with him, carrying two bases: the 118th, which tied the record, and the 119th, which broke it.

When Henderson spotted the crowd, he gave the kid with the bases his keys and a few other things he was carrying and asked him to deliver the goods to his car, while he set about the business at hand. As long as there were people there who wanted his autograph, Henderson signed, chatted, waved at friends, simply gave of himself to the fans who cared so much. I watched for twenty minutes before the Blue Jay team bus pulled out for the hotel. When we left, he was still signing.

Men like these have the wit to understand that without the fans and the press, they wouldn't be making good money to play a game for a living, but it's more than greedy pragmatism that motivates them. They simply behave like human beings dealing with other human beings.

I think the difference between Henderson and someone like Jackson is that Henderson remembers where he came from. He remembers when he was the kid screwing up his courage to ask a big star for an autograph and when a shy tyke wordlessly holds out paper and pen he treats the kid like he wished that big leaguer from his childhood had treated him. The guys with the monster egos have forgotten.

The rookies have had no time to forget. You see them in hotel lobbies and on the field before every game, signing anything they are offered because they are one step closer to that little kid and his dreams. They just hope that they don't hear, "Who was that, Daddy?" as they move on.

I always like the rookies because they wear their hearts on their sleeves. Their hopes and dreams are hung out for everybody to see. They soon enough learn to hide the hunger behind big league bravado, but when they stroll, ever so casually, into a major league dugout for the first time and look out over the field, you can see the stars in their eyes.

There is a magic in a rookie doing well that we all feel, even sitting in the stands. In our hearts we want the kids to win, and we admire the animal exuberance of their raw talent. Cal Ripken, Jr., was a joy in his first season with the Orioles, his dad standing in the third-base coaching box with pride in his eyes. John Stupor for the Cardinals in 1982 and Mike Boddicker for the Orioles in 1983 – boys being sent to do a man's job in the World Series and winning – made us shake our heads in admiration.

Covering a team as bad as the Blue Jays were for the first few years gave me a chance to see a lot of baseball debuts. Most of the rookies rushed to the big leagues have gone back to the minors or have left baseball, but some of them have stuck. Lloyd Moseby was called up in late May of 1980, and he hit the ground running. The Yankees were in Toronto, and Moseby, twenty-one at the time, got five hits, including two doubles and a home run, in his first two games.

"I thought maybe I had just had first-day luck," Moseby said after the second game. "Today, going against Tommy John was a big thrill. Tommy John! I thought to myself, 'Be realistic, this is a Cy Young pitcher, one of the greats.' But I did all right."

The home-run ball, retrieved by an usher, was waiting for him in an envelope. For most it would have been a thrill, but Moseby hid it well. "A baseball? Only a baseball?" he joked. "I see hundreds of them every day. I hoped it was going to be money!"

The team went from Toronto to New York, where UPI columnist Milt Richman called him "the next Dave Parker," and Moseby went into a slump that lasted two years.

Dave Stieb pitched his first major league game in Baltimore in June of 1979. He had no such rookie luck. Stieb had risen through the minor leagues with amazing speed. He was drafted out of college the year before, spent a season in the Florida State (Class A) League, alternating between pitching and playing the outfield, and began the 1979 season in the same place. After winning five games there, he was jumped to the Triple A Syracuse Chiefs for another five wins before he made the great leap to the big leagues.

He was twenty-two when he made his debut. He approached it with a combination of cockiness and awe. The confidence was foolish, but understandable. He had never known failure. But still, this was the big time in Memorial Stadium, and the Orioles had won eighteen of their last twenty games. He sat in the corner of the dugout during batting practice, hardly believing that he was there. The other players greeted him casually on their way to the bat rack. Most of the Blue Jays knew him only by name anyway; his baseball peers were still in the low minors. Regulars are usually wary around a rookie when he's first called up, anyway, waiting to see if the kid will stick.

It was lonely on the mound. He did pretty well, for a debut against a team as hot as the Orioles, even striking out five, but back-to-back home runs by Doug DeCinces and Lee May with two out in the sixth did him in.

After the game, he sat slumped at his locker, sad and vulnerable, refusing to content himself with having impressed both teams with his pitching. "I don't mind the runs I gave up early," he finally admitted, "but no one had ever hit a home run off me before." At that moment, he was still only a kid, albeit an extraordinarily talented one. Not many pitchers get to the major leagues without giving up a home run. Stieb went on to become one of the best pitchers in the league, but that night, that loss, his shyness and chagrin were touching.

Now, when I watch a ball sail over the outfield fence as he glares around him, I remember the first one and bet that somewhere inside him he does, too.

"Now I know that everything is better in the big leagues," he said then with a grimace. "The travel is better, the ballparks, the uniforms, everything is better. Even the hitters are better."

To my mind, the players who cope best in baseball are neither those blessed with belief in a deity nor those who believe divinity lies with themselves, but those who know how to laugh. A good sense of humour is as valuable in sport as it is in what we occasionally refer to as "the real world," and the players who can laugh at themselves and at others survive well. The best baseball humour, I found, is self-deprecating.

The jokers I remember were often the guys who played behind baseball's front line, those who served their time on the bench. Pinch hitters, defensive replacements, relief pitchers, and utility men fill up the roster, and the dugout, just in case something goes wrong with a starter. It's not the easiest burden for an ego to bear, but it creates a whole different breed of ballplayer. There's a lot of time when you're sitting on the bench, and some use it wisely. They become baseball experts, the kind who go on to become great coaches and managers. Others become expert at heckling and playing pranks. They won't last as long in the sport, but they have a lot more fun on the ride.

The Montreal Expos had a group several years ago that called itself the Bus Squad, the "Busted, Underpaid Superstars." The Blue Jays' equivalent aggregation called themselves the Turds, which stood for nothing at all.

In my first year covering the Jays, Tim Johnson, an aging utility infielder, was the leader of the pack, which also included pitchers Dave Lemanczyk and Dave Freisleben and catcher Rick Cerone, a regular who qualified for Turdship on the basis of sheer rowdiness. Balor Moore, nicknamed Yahoo, was another. These guys were the reprobates, the ones who were sometimes known to stay out late and show up for day games with a hangover, but they were my champions, my knights in tarnished armour. I think they were delighted to be on the same side that the conservative elements in baseball abhorred.

They also liked me because I reported the unhappiness of the players with their manager, Roy Hartsfield, whom they couldn't stand. When Hartsfield announced his plans to stop speaking to me after one particularly critical article, and suggested his players do the same, the Turds were the first to come and tell me about it.

On the last day of the 1979 season, the morning after a night before that had featured the annual team blowout paid for with fines levied by Lemanczyk's kangaroo court, they honoured me. Getting on the bus on the way to the game, Johnson and Freisleben giggled and pointed at me. Freisleben was carrying a large paper bag, which he hid as he scurried past my seat. I suspect he was still drunk. After the game was over, a game in which Hartsfield took his final revenge by playing every one of the Turds, even those who could barely run onto the field, Johnson accosted me in the clubhouse and made his presentation. It was two big bottles of good scotch, "to get you through the World Series," and an assurance that I, too, was a Turd. I was honoured.

Johnson was an incorrigible agitator and his favourite target was Rico Carty, the veteran slugger whom Johnson thought took himself a bit too seriously. Beside Johnson's locker was his "Wall of Shame," composed of photographs clipped out of newspapers with rude captions. Carty made the wall one day, with a vengeance.

It had been Poster Day at Exhibition Stadium, and Carty was that season's pinup. The pose was a standard baseball one. Carty knelt on one knee, resting a hand on his bat, flashing the famous smile. Johnson put it up on the wall with the legend, "Here's Rico, running out a ground ball."

Johnson was one of my favourite ballplayers from the first day on the job, as was John Mayberry, but through the years, others also were helpful and considerate to me. More often than not, the ones I liked and respected most were black players, and it galled me to see the way they were treated.

Is baseball racist? Of course it is, institutionally. It's obvious when you count the few blacks at the positions traditionally felt to demand intelligence: pitching and catching. They are in the outfield where all they have to do is run and catch and throw, or at first where all they have to do is catch and hit. This is not a coincidence.

Neither is it a coincidence that most managers and coaches are white. Frank Robinson was the first black manager in the major leagues when he was hired by the Cleveland Indians in 1975, twenty-eight years after Jackie Robinson first broke the colour barrier as a player. Frank Robinson was fired halfway through the 1977 season and didn't get another managing job until he was hired by the San Francisco Giants in 1981. Yet he is an excellent baseball man in a sport that recycles managers with experience, and a lot of managing jobs came and went before Robinson got another chance.

Of course baseball is racist when it is acceptable to comment on how many blacks are on a team. Knowledgable baseball people, who should know better, believed that the Pittsburgh Pirates in the late seventies had a problem because there were too many blacks on the team. I showed their 1981 media guide (which had a black cover with the team name and logo embossed in gold) to one general manager.

"Oh, a team picture," he joked.

A minor, but very galling example of racism came in the television coverage of the 1979 World Series. The cameras commonly panned to the wives of players, but when they came to Colette

Singleton, a white woman married to a black man, they cut away from this "offending" shot without delay. The Red Sox have very few black faces in their lineup (or among the fans in the stands) because it is assumed that the people of Boston would stop supporting the team if they had too many blacks. And older scouts and team personnel often still refer to blacks as "boys," the way they did forty years ago, and are surprised if anyone takes offense.

Latin American players are also discriminated against. Because English is their second tongue, one they are still learning when they come to the big leagues, they are thought stupid and quaint.

All of these things are very subtle and seldom present when you get down to where the interaction is most direct: among the players. The clubhouse is completely egalitarian, and the camaraderie within it is strong. The experiences and goals teammates share outweigh any differences in racial or national origin, and the intensity of their friendships and their loyalty to one another are obvious. Considering the redneck backgrounds of a lot of the white players, that in itself is heartening.

In all their varying guises, I found the athletes I spent five years following fascinating. They were men unlike any I had ever known well. As a feminist, I had qualms before stepping inside their world but found, to my relief, that for every player who was a flat-out pig, there were a dozen decent human beings. I can't say that I made any lifelong friendships in five years on the beat. I doubt if I'll ever see even those I came to consider my friends again, and I'm sure I'm not missed around the clubhouse, but I had encounters I'll never forget. These young men changed my view of sport and of humanity. I hope that I changed theirs a bit.

Chapter

3

The Bosses

There are few jobs as thankless and insecure as managing a dugout full of the walking egos baseball breeds, and few jobs as misunderstood. When a reliever comes in and gives up the losing run, whose fault is it? The manager who brought him in. When a starter stays in and gives up the losing run, whose fault is it? The manager who left him in. When a team full of big-money superstars falls to the league's cellar, who gets fired? The same guy.

When things are going badly for his team, the manager is booed by the fans when he walks on the field, second-guessed by the writers in the paper the next day, and undermined by sulking players who don't think they are getting the respect they deserve.

Why do otherwise sane men take such a job? It reminds me of the old story about the man whose job it is to give enemas to the elephants at the circus. When he is asked why he doesn't quit, he replies, "What? And leave show business?"

Managers manage because they can't think of anything else they like better than baseball, no matter how much crap is involved. The process excites the good ones, the challenge of balancing strengths and weaknesses and of outsmarting the other managers. There are those who claim that American League managers do nothing but push buttons, that taking the bat out of the pitcher's hands has made the job simple, but I don't agree.

The American League manager still has to build lineups every day with the correct righthand-lefthand balance and with knowledge of his players' abilities against the opposing pitcher.

He still has to wince and send a .200 hitter to the plate because he needs his good glove in the field. He has to try to hide a defensive bozo in the field somewhere because the guy's going to hit thirty home runs a season. He has to divine somehow which member of his suspect bullpen is likely to be hot on any given day so he won't overtire his starters. He still has to act as a lay psychologist, den mother, and sergeant major to his players. He has to do all of this, and more, on a salary lower than most of the bums he leads, while spending half his time on the road in a period of his life when most men are starting to relax and settle down to the kind of rich family life they deserve.

Managers are as various in background and personality as the players they lead. There are glad-handers, front and centre show-offs like Tommy LaSorda, Sparky Anderson, and Whitey Herzog. These guys love attention, seek it out, and will talk as long as there is an audience around. They are much beloved by the lazy television reporters because they play so well to the medium. You'll never get dead air.

Others are more thoughtful, like Ralph Houk and Chuck Tanner. There is more solid baseball than grandstanding with this type of manager but you have to work a bit harder to get it.

Some managers are sweet and funny, like Jimmy Frey, George Bamberger, and Joe Altobelli (all out of the Oriole organization, which is probably no coincidence). They are the nice guys. Dave Garcia was one, too. They are a refreshing counter to gruffer managers like Dick Williams and Gene Mauch, the old guard. Ask them a stupid question at your peril. They seem rigid and bitter and have little empathy for the young millionaires in their charge. Coming along now are the young turks, Rene Lachmann, Tony LaRussa and Doug Rader, men who are more in tune with modern ballplayers. They are less concerned with a player's appearance and lifestyle than with what he does on the field.

Mercifully, most managers are quite agreeable to deal with because they understand that it is part of the job description to be co-operative with the press.

Some, like Frank Robinson and Harvey Kuenn, had long and successful major league playing careers. They are exceptions. It is far more common to find managers who learned their baseball in the minor leagues. The theory behind this is that the more a player struggled, the more he learned. The men with great natural talent didn't have to analyse what they did and try to improve and find it difficult to teach the less gifted. Ask a great natural hitter how to do it and he's likely to shrug and say, "Just swing at it. Easy."

The lesser players, on the other hand, had to try to take apart the components of the game and analyse them to survive. The best example of this was, of course, Earl Weaver. The Oriole manager for fifteen years never got out of the minor leagues as a player, but he went on to become one of the most successful managers in baseball.

I always suspected that Weaver's brain, could you peer inside it, would be something like Fibber McGee's closet, crammed to overflowing with wondrous bits of junk ready to come tumbling down on unsuspecting passersby. Weaver was a statistical pack rat, filing away baseball's equivalent of string collections, carpet slippers with holes in the toes, and broken toasters because they might come in handy someday. Open the door and duck.

Others might laugh at the clutter, but they couldn't laugh at how Weaver used it. There is nothing ludicrous about twenty-five consecutive winning seasons, fifteen of them in the major leagues. Insignificant as Weaver's information might have seemed, it was part of his success.

Weaver's attention to detail could be seen even in the uniform he wore. It had a secret pocket inside the jersey, over his heart. It was just the right size for a package of Raleigh cigarettes, the brand Weaver smoked for the gift coupons (joking that he was saving up to buy himself a coffin). Weaver, you see, could not be without his smokes, even during (perhaps especially during) a game, but he also took his image seriously enough to want to avoid setting a bad example for the young people watching. He never puffed when cameras were pointed his way. Considering the amount he smoked and his attraction for photographers, this was quite a feat. The secret pocket was sewn with great care, the thread colour changing to match the Oriole name and Weaver's number four on the front. The stitching changed from orange to black to white (or grey on the road) so that the pocket was virtually invisible.

Details were Weaver's meat. He collected them, hoarded them, admired them, and used them well. It has recently become fashionable for baseball teams to use computers with complicated programs to churn out data on any given player in any given situation, but Weaver had been doing it for years. The only difference was that the computer was in his head, aided by a clipboard full of charts on each team in the American League and a small, battered, blue card-box, the kind your Aunt Mabel keeps her recipes in, with three-by-five-inch cards on each of the opposing players. This was how Weaver avoided surprise. If a slugger had ever bunted against the Orioles, Weaver knew when and why. If a Punch-and-Judy shortstop had ever hit a home run off an Oriole pitcher, Weaver knew where and how.

What Weaver didn't know by first-hand experience, the kind he preferred, he got from other sources, his scouts, formal or informal. Even an opponent called up from the minor leagues only moments before the game began was never a complete mystery to Weaver.

"The first thing you have to understand about me is I'm intelligent," Weaver told me when we first met. "I'm probably one of the most intelligent people you've met, in terms of IQ. But that's not all. I've also got good baseball judgement.

"I can look at a player and know what he'll be able to do. I can build a balanced team: some guys that can pitch, some home-run hitters, some guys that can steal bases. That's what it takes to win. All the rest, the game strategy and all that bullshit, means nothing. If you haven't got a pinch hitter, there's no point pinch-hitting. If there's nothing in the bullpen and your pitching's tired out, it's tough.

"The last thing is preparation. Hard work. You can't play baseball or sell cars or lay bricks without hard work and preparation."

At that point, Weaver reached into the blue box and took out a dog-eared stack of cards held together with a rubber band. He pulled them out and ran through the Blue Jay lineup, player by player, with uncanny accuracy.

Weaver inevitably talked too fast for note-taking. I soon learned it was more valuable to sit back and listen to him, to the staccato cadences of his gravelly voice, and to watch the play of emotions on his weathered face. It was pointless to ask questions, unnecessary to prime the pump. Weaver loved to talk.

He also loved to argue, and his contretemps with players and umpires alike fuelled his legend. But his rages weren't malicious. Weaver always said that all he asked from umpires was that they followed the rules. If he knew the rules, they should, too, and he knew them well. He searched the thin baseball rulebook constantly for loopholes, for small quirks he could use to his advantage. As quickly as he could find them, the rules committee would eliminate them.

My favourite was the tactic Weaver used in 1980, when he began to put a pitcher in the designated hitter position on his lineup, then pinch-hit for him at his first at bat. Weaver came across the idea in a letter from a fan.

The strategy was designed to deal with the remote possibility that the opposing team's starting pitcher got knocked out of the game before the designated hitter came to bat and was replaced by a pitcher who threw from the other side. Weaver realized that if this happened and he had a regular designated hitter in the lineup, he might have to replace him with one who swung the other way, thus wasting a hitter he might want to use later in the game. So, halfway through the season, Weaver began to present lineups with the previous game's starting pitcher as DH.

At the 1980 winter meetings, the rule was amended so that the announced designated hitter had to have one plate appearance unless the starting pitcher was changed. Weaver pointed out that it was still technically possible to get around the amended rule. It all depended on the interpretation of a "plate appearance." Weaver maintained that if he sent his pitcher up to take one pitch, he could then pinch-hit for him. He was responsible enough not to try it, but enjoyed playing with the possibility.

Weaver was demanding of the umpires. He raged when they didn't play by the rules as he interpreted them and when they were lax in discharging their duties. After first reminding them of their responsibilities from the dugout, he would finally explode onto the field to take them on, toe-to-toe, but never head-to-head. Umpires tend to be large men. Weaver is not, and it was a splendid sight to see one of them wordlessly turning away from Weaver's wrath, only to have the manager race around him like a terrier, haranguing all the while, righteously but pointlessly.

When his rage wasn't directed at the umpires it could turn on one of his players, but in either case it was quickly spent. Elrod Hendricks, the coach whose association with Weaver began in the Puerto Rican League in 1967, was one of the manager's most loyal supporters. He explained the process to me one day. "Earl goes berserk after losses," he said. "He just rants and yells and says everything he's been thinking. But he only gets on you when it's necessary and then when it's over, it's forgotten. Earl doesn't hold grudges, and he keeps this team together, and we all know that Earl will go to war for us if necessary. Or to war with us if that's what it takes."

Weaver's belief was that his players had a responsibility to take full advantage of the talents that got them to the major leagues, and he had no time for slackers. He didn't think there was any need to baby them.

"Motivation?" he said. "These ballplayers have to have the desire to win or they wouldn't be here."

Beyond the gruff shell, Weaver did care, as anyone with eyes to see or heart to feel always knew. He cared passionately for the game and the players and most of all for winning. "It's no fun to lose," Weaver would growl. "It would be like playing Monopoly and saying, 'Here, you take Boardwalk and Park Place and I'll land on them.' That's no way to go about it."

No player without Weaver's passion lasted long with the Orioles and players with an equal fire, like Rick Dempsey, were the ones who most often clashed with him. They could hate him. They could also love him, usually at the same time. Overall, the Orioles seemed to view Weaver with the same affection they would accord a favourite, if slightly deranged, uncle.

The press, on the other hand, seldom had cause to dislike him. He was always ready to share his knowledge and opinions with anyone who sat still long enough to take them in. It was an education to sit next to him in the dugout. He was, of course, a tiny man in a world of giants, and he sat in the dugout like a leprechaun, with his feet barely reaching the ground, kicking at the floor as he talked. His cap sat on the back of his head and his grey hair habitually stood on end every which way. His voice was hoarse and grating as he talked. And talked. And talked, while not missing a thing the players – his or the opposition's – were doing on the diamond.

He held court every day of the baseball year, whether in Miami in the spring or at the World Series. It wasn't surprising that the press loved him, but perhaps he made it a little too easy for us. Our game stories too often focused on the man on the bench rather than the players on the field.

My favourite memory of Weaver was of a moment at once public and intimate. It happened after the Pirates won three straight games to beat the Orioles in the 1979 World Series. The Orioles, some were saying loudly, had blown it. Weaver, it was even whispered, had been out-managed.

An hour and a half after the game was over, some of us still sat in Weaver's office, still talking, going over the Series one more time. Most of the writers had left, to go to the festive Pirate clubhouse or back to the press box to file stories, but I stayed. It was partly out of curiosity to see how the genius-turned-chump would handle the loss, partly out of sympathy for a man I admired, and partly to find the image of the losers around which to write my story.

Jim Russo, the so-called "superscout," slumped in one corner, bleak and unconsolable. Weaver, looking drawn but not silenced, was still hoarsely analysing what had gone wrong when Rex Barney, the Oriole public-address announcer, came in.

"I'm sorry to interrupt, Earl," he said, diffidently, "but they want you to come on the field. The fans won't go until you come out."

"They're still there?" he asked. "Sure, sure. I'll go out."

Dressed in uniform pants, shower slippers, and his under-jersey, Weaver put down his beer, butted his cigarette, and grabbed his cap before heading down the runway with half a dozen of us in tow.

When he reached the dugout steps, the cheers began, eerie in the partially darkened stadium. Hundreds of fans were on the field, behind a cordon of policemen who outlined a no-man's zone as wide as the dugout and twenty feet deep. There was no pushing and shoving. Even the cops were smiling. They all just wanted to see their Earl. The field-level stands behind the dugout on the third-base side were filled, and some even lingered in the top deck, silhouetted against the haze. One bank of lights had been left on, and a television spot shone on the empty space.

When Weaver came out of the dugout, the cheers began – "Wea-ver, Wea-ver" – and the fans cheered and waved their hands. It was an extraordinary scene, happy and affectionate. Weaver turned slowly in the brightness, speechless at last, tears standing in his eyes. The pain of defeat and the joy of love combined for a moment on that field, and I knew I had my story.

After Weaver retired at the end of the 1982 season I occasionally saw him in his incongruous new uniform, the ABC yellow blazer, all blown-dry and smooth for the cameras, and remembered that night. In flashback, he stands in front of the dugout in the cold, hair wild, his hands cupped around his mouth to make himself heard over the cheers of the crowd. "1980! 1980!" he promised, but he never got back there again. By the time those Orioles won the big one, they were Joe Altobelli's.

Dear Ms. Gordon:
    Your near knowledge of baseball is finally no longer amusing. You have stretched your inability a long, long way, but finally, enough is enough. I wonder how receptive you would be to seeing yourself referred to in print as a "sleaze". Billy Martin, in many ways exemplifies what I love about baseball, its aggressiveness, fiestyness [sic] etc. He did not overload George Brett's bat with pine tar, but you are prepared to "tar and feather" him for it. Your "Blue Jay" bias is understandable, but I fear pennant fever has addled your pretty little head.
    Yours,

Gee, all I did was call Martin a "win-at-all-costs sleaze" after the infamous pine-tar incident in 1983. Next thing I knew, there was this letter, scrawled on lined paper, lurking in my mailbox. It was the type of screed I knew well, the only surprise being that the letter was signed. That wasn't typical of Billy Martin fans.

Martin, especially when he managed the Yankees, inspired fierce loyalty among the fringe of baseball fanatics who favoured anonymous ravings. Letters from Buffalo, Barrie, and even the Bronx came streaming in, calling me nasty names any time I questioned Martin's judgement, behaviour, or style. I had a lot of cause in the last tumultuous years of his managing.

Why a man so unsavoury was so beloved was always beyond me, but it was undeniable. I remember going to a B game one spring morning in Scottsdale, Arizona, in 1981, when Martin was going into his second season of managing the Oakland A's. There to check out some of the minor leaguers, he was dressed nattily in western wear, with alligator boots and a black cowboy hat with a feathered band, a pipe in his mouth. The moment he strolled across the grass from the parking lot, all attention was drawn from the action on the field.

"Look, there's old Billy," one retiree said to another with a chuckle. "Yep, that's old Billy, all right."

Martin, fifty-two at the time, signed autographs, posed for pictures standing next to one pastel polyester pantsuit after another, in which were clothed innumerable Mabels and Ethels and Maudes, and they ate it up.

During an exhibition game against the Japanese Taiyo Whales in the afternoon, Martin sat out in front of the dugout sunning himself. After the A's won (he had told his team to "remember Pearl Harbor") the Whales took turns having their pictures taken with Martin, a celebrity even in Yokohama.

Martin was probably happier that spring than he had been for years. The A's had just been bought by enlightened owners (Roy Eisenhardt and Walter J. and Wally Haas) who were determined to correct all the horrors Charlie O. Finley had wrought on the fans in the last few years. They had inherited Martin as manager and saw him as their most valuable asset. They built a promotion campaign around "Billyball," the scrappy, aggressive kind of game Martin loved.

If the owners liked him that spring, his players regarded him with an awe just short of worship. "Even when Billy's not around, mentally he's in everybody's mind," said Mike Norris, a pitcher whose best season was Martin's first at Oakland. "It's like a spiritual involvement with the Lord. You can't see him but you know he's there. That's enough."

That Arizona morning Martin was Dr. Jekyll, a mellow baseball genius for whom nothing could go wrong. The strike-split season even gave him a shot at the league championship, but the A's found their own level and dropped three straight to the Yankees in the playoffs. By the end of the next season, Martin had once again become Mr. Hyde.

He soiled his own bed in Oakland, betraying the owners' trust, and left hard feelings, a trashed office, and a bunch of burnt-out pitchers' arms behind him when he went. He also left any hopes for happiness and well-being when he once again put on the pinstripes for George Steinbrenner and, by the beginning of 1983, he was snarling again.

Martin was like the reverse of Earl Weaver's coin. They both were competitive, both liked arguing with umpires, both prided themselves on their knowledge of the game and used everything they could to get an edge. But there were serious differences between the two in their style and perceptions of the world. Weaver was motivated by pride, Martin by revenge. Weaver loved to win, Martin hated to lose. Weaver enjoyed life, Martin attacked it. Weaver never got into fights in bars.

Martin walked with a giant chip on his shoulder. When things were going his way, he was tolerable. After a win, in the good days with the A's, he looked young and relaxed, the kid again, and was almost charming. When he lost or when he thought the world was against him, which was often, he was nasty.

In the Yankee seasons, before and after his brief Oakland honeymoon, he looked older, drawn, and haggard, and his patience was wafer-thin. When he went back the last time, it was awful. From the beginning of spring training, paranoia rode his back like a trained monkey. First he issued a press release with short and sarcastic answers to a series of questions he didn't want to have to answer, about Steinbrenner and about himself. Then he hid.

He was the Howard Hughes of managers. Reporters he didn't know well and trust seldom got to talk to him outside of hasty postgame sessions, which he called "press conferences." (Other managers saw them as nothing quite so grand.) He referred requests for more far-ranging interviews to the team public relations director. When the meeting had been arranged, he wouldn't show. He was often vulgar and contemptuous, almost always faintly unpleasant.

The pine-tar incident my Barrie correspondent was so incensed about revealed Martin's nature as well as anything else, for better and worse. Martin had been lying in wait for George Brett after having noticed that the Kansas City Royal third baseman was using a bat with more stickum than the rules allowed. On July 24th, his moment came. After Brett hit a ninth-inning home run off Goose Gossage to give the Royals a lead in Yankee Stadium, Martin protested to the umpire that Brett's bat was illegal, that he should be declared out, the home run be disallowed, and the game be declared over with the Yankees the winners. The umpire, Tim McClelland, apparently didn't know the technicalities of the rules well enough to tell Martin that his interpretation, while attractive to the home team, was incorrect. He bought the line of goods completely.

Royals manager Dick Howser protested to the league that although the bat should not have been used, the rules did not stipulate that Brett should be called out. According to him, the home run stood and the game was still in the top of the ninth with the Royals up by a run. It was a complicated interpretation but the correct one, and American League president Lee Mac-Phail agreed. He said the game was to be resumed where it stood.

It was difficult to get the two teams back together again, since they had finished with each other for a season, but a mutual off-day was cancelled and the game was reconvened in front of a handful of fans and a mob of reporters.

It took twelve minutes to finish the game and take a win off the Yankees' record and give it to the Royals, but not before Martin tried to play his trump card. Because of scheduling, the same umpiring crew wasn't working the conclusion of the game, and Martin cleverly tried to use that to the Yankees' advantage. As the game resumed, the pitcher, George Frazier, threw the ball to first baseman Ken Griffey. Martin strode out of the dugout and claimed Brett had neglected to touch first base on his way around twenty-five days before, he was now out, and the game was over. Who could deny it?

It was a brilliant ploy, but up in the press box it made Bob Fischel beam. The public relations director of the American League just watched as the ball was thrown to second and then third and Martin made the same claim each time. Fischel had come prepared.

As Martin raged down on the field, Dave Phillips, the umpiring crew chief, pulled a piece of paper out of his hip pocket and handed it to Martin. Only then did Fischel, with a sense of drama of his own, walk to the press box microphone and explain that he had provided Phillips with a notarized affidavit signed by all four of the original umpires. The statement swore that not only Brett, but U.L. Washington, whom Brett had driven in, had touched all the bases.

Checkmate. It was a delicious moment. Fischel had beaten Martin at his own game.

There was a stampede to the Yankee clubhouse after the game to capture Martin's choice comments about the manoeuvring, but he wasn't in his office. Some talked to other Yankees, but they had nothing much to say after the anticlimax. Martin was the only man we really wanted to question. So we waited. And waited, standing like dummies in the middle of the clubhouse while the Yankees glowered. Martin was hiding out in the players' lounge. It was early, so none of us had deadlines to beat. All we could do was wait. We had no choice.

That was the difference between Martin and Weaver. Had Weaver been outsmarted by the league, he would have been in his office ready to laugh about it, accept congratulations for his cleverness, and give Fischel his due. Not Martin. All he could do was sulk.

One of the New York writers sent in a request to Martin with one of the clubhouse attendants. Nothing happened. After half an hour of this nonsense I asked myself why I was there, what I was doing hanging around a smelly dressing room waiting for a psychopath to talk to me. I left but a lot of others couldn't. If Martin talked to one New York paper and the others didn't have his comments there would be hell to pay. It was only after keeping them waiting for an hour and a half that Martin sent out a message that he had no comment, would have no comment in the future, and that the clubhouse was to be cleared.

Martin always seemed to me to be a seriously disturbed and unhappy man who was lucky to be making his living in baseball. He could never have lasted in the real world. I had nothing but sympathy for those who had to deal with him every day. He and George Steinbrenner deserved each other.

The managers I dealt with most closely, those who guided the Blue Jays, were not quite as charismatic as Martin and Weaver. Roy Hartsfield was the first, a minor league manager who found himself seriously out of his depth in Toronto. When I first encountered him, he was in his third, and last, season as Blue Jay manager. Hired by Peter Bavasi from the minor leagues when the Blue Jays were formed, he was not a man who inspired confidence or trust in his players or affection among those who dealt with him. Hartsfield was a good old boy, pure and simple, and his outdated authoritarianism didn't sit well with the new breed of ballplayer.

At first, Hartsfield's country homilies and down-home baseball philosophies had been quaintly charming, but they quickly grew stale. By the time I got there, the fans were sick of "looking on down the road a piece." Hartsfield was a bitter man, loathed by many of his players, ignored by his coaches, and the focus of the frustration of supporters who were impatient to win. It was not an enviable position, but he handled it badly.

He had given up all pretence of talking to his players or taking a direct hand in their day-to-day development. These basics he left to the coaches while he sat glumly in the corner of the dugout, lost in another world. On planes and buses he sat in the right-hand front seat, traditionally the manager's place, and puffed silently on his pipe, ignoring the eyes of all who passed. It was embarrassing and painful to watch.

Postgame interviews began to degenerate into monosyllabic grunts. He was fond of observations like "The other team is paid to play this game, too." A question about strategy would get a blank stare and a gruff, "I've been in this game a little longer than you have and that's why I'm where I am and you're where you are. Next question." We would look at the floor and hope someone else would speak next.

By July he wasn't speaking to me because I had written a story about the bad morale on the team. By the end of August, the team was in open revolt. Tom Buskey, a mild-mannered reliever, was the first to blow the whistle on Hartsfield in public, on an off-day in Anaheim. Hartsfield blew his top that night in the dressing room and the rest of the malcontents went public the next day.

The season was not only a lesson in bad managing, but a lesson in how not to run an organization. Peter Bavasi, then the Blue Jay president, sat back throughout the controversy, contenting himself with making flippant remarks about "childish" ball-players. He was in Anaheim for the mutiny and commented only that he "wouldn't want [his] daughter to marry a Blue Jay," a condescension that enraged the players, who were in no mood for jokes.

But he never supported his manager. He refused to fine or publicly chastise the players openly critical of Hartsfield, while denying that Hartsfield had done anything wrong. He also denied that the manager's job was in danger, but gave no further support.

Hartsfield was simply left hung out to dry until it was time for him to go. After the last game of the season, the team's 109th loss, after Hartsfield had left the stadium, the Jays announced that the time had come.

Hartsfield had served his purpose. He had wet-nursed the team through the first three losing years. He had acted as a lightning rod for criticism. He had become the scapegoat on whom the failure could be blamed. I can't say I ever particularly liked the man, but he didn't deserve to be treated so poorly.

A few months after Hartsfield's firing, the baseball winter meetings were held in Toronto. Hartsfield was there, job-hunting, and so was his wife, the saintly Alice. She was a southerner, too, a pretty little woman who spoke in honeyed tones. I had only met the lady briefly in spring training, but had heard nothing but good things about her, her kindness, warmth, and devotion. Even people who had nothing nice to say about Roy gushed over Alice, so I felt a bit badly when I encountered her chatting with friends in the ladies' room at the baseball banquet.

When you're trapped together by the basins and mirrors, a nod and smile won't quite do. I thought of ducking out, but she spotted me and rushed across the room in a flutter of chiffon to clasp both my hands in hers.

"Alison, I'm *so* glad to see you," she cooed. "I didn't want to leave Toronto without saying good-bye because I liked you so much when we met in the spring. I'm a God-fearing person, and wanted to tell you that I forgive you for getting Roy fired, and God forgives you, too. You do know, don't you, that you lost Roy his job? Why did you do that?"

She went on and on as I squirmed, her hands clasped firmly around mine as the knife twisted again and again, and the other lady wives sneaked peeks at the tableau in the make-up mirror.

Bobby Cox was the manager Pat Gillick wanted from the moment the team was formed, but he had to wait for him. Cox had managed the Syracuse team for the Yankees when Gillick was in that organization, and the two admired and liked one another. A couple of things put the appointment off. Cox was busy managing the Atlanta Braves from 1978 to 1981, for a start, but more importantly, the Blue Jays weren't ready for him for the first five years. His coming and their blooming coincided beautifully.

While waiting for Cox, the Blue Jays hired a babysitter, a sixty-four-year-old rookie named Bobby Mattick. Mattick had been a baseball man since he was in his teens in the thirties, but when he took over the Blue Jays his managing experience consisted of less than one season in the rookie Pioneer League in 1948 (he was replaced with a 29-40 record).

After his playing career was ended by a freak accident in 1944 (his skull was fractured by a foul ball during batting practice and left him with double vision), he became a scout all over the big leagues; no matter what fancy titles and job descriptions he picked up along the way, he was always a scout at heart. That was the source of his great charm. Mattick never looked as much at home in the dugout as he did in the hotel lobby, swapping scandalous stories with all his old cronies in their flashy Floridian sports clothes and laughing, always laughing.

Scouts are a breed apart, especially the older ones. They represent a kind of romance, an on-the-road mystique that predates Jack Kerouac and has more in common with Willy Loman than Willie Nelson. They are a link with baseball's roots in the small towns of America, where it is always 1935 and genuine phenoms lurk behind each tall stalk of corn.

Everything has changed in baseball, including the role of the scouts. The annual draft of high school and college players has democratized the selection process and made the scouts mere cogs in the machinery of drafting. In Mattick's heyday he had to move fast and talk faster to keep ahead of the opposition. He had to sweet-talk mothers into letting their sons sign a contract and lie to the other scouts about the prospects he was watching.

They all lived the life of commercial travellers on the back roads of America, staying in drummers' hotels, selling dreams instead of dry goods. It was a lonely life, with wives and families left at home, a life of blue-plate specials and sad small-town bars. But the scouts had each other and their stories, and there was always the chance of a touch of magic and an occasional payoff, that the greatest player in the sport was lurking undiscovered around the next leafy bend. To hear them tell it now, the scouts of old had the greatest life of all.

Now a scout has to carry airline schedules in his hip pocket to move him around the country. He assesses talent with a stop-watch and chart at organized games in high school and college, feeds the information back to his organization, and keeps his fingers crossed that the prospect will still be around when it's their turn to pick. There are no more surprises left, no absolute naturals discovered while wielding a pitchfork instead of a bat. Now the Central Scouting Bureau produces computer printouts of all the prospects ready to graduate from high school and college. The corporate reality of baseball has filtered down the line and taken the colour and soul out.

When Mattick was named manager, he was the Blue Jay director of player development, with some impressive credentials. In the past, he had scouted and signed such players as Frank Robinson, Vada Pinson, Curt Flood, Tommy Harper, Bobby Grich, and Darrell Porter. He had been responsible for developing the Milwaukee Brewer organization from the time the team started as the Seattle Pilots. He found Dave Stieb and Lloyd Moseby for the Blue Jays.

But he didn't know beans about managing in the big leagues. Mattick approached his new task with good humour and an irreverent spirit. The first thing he said was that he would only take the job if he could do it wearing street clothes. It seemed a remarkably sensible suggestion. Hockey coaches don't wear skates; football coaches don't wear helmets and shoulderpads; basketball coaches don't sit on the bench in their shorts. He was overruled, of course, and spent two seasons looking like an absent-minded professor at a costume ball.

Mattick looked his age but didn't act it. Older than Hartsfield by a decade, he got along with the players like a much younger man. He immediately revoked all existing rules forbidding beards, long hair, and drinking in the hotel bar. He lightened up all around and gave the players back the fun they'd been missing. He brought Hartsfield's enemies out of the doghouse and gave them a chance to play. He traded Rick Cerone and brought Ernie Whitt up from oblivion in Syracuse. He worked with Roy Howell on his fielding and gave Al Woods back his job. He worked as hard as any of the players and put the chance to fail or succeed back in their hands. In response, the team began to win, and in 1980 the Blue Jays had the best season they had ever known behind this rumpled old scout, whom they supported with a fierce loyalty. No wonder. He treated them like big-leaguers.

Mattick's accomplishments were being overshadowed all season by Billy Martin, who had taken the wretched Oakland A's and turned them into winners. To counter this, the team had T-shirts made up with Mattick's bemused visage on them, reading "Bobby's Amazing Jays." They laughed at him behind his back, but it was affectionate laughter.

And he did do some funny stuff. One day Alfredo Griffin stole third when the team was losing badly and there were two out in the inning. It was a dumb move, but when Mattick was asked about it after the game, he confessed it had been his fault. The steal sign that day had been for Mattick to cross his arms in the dugout. He had forgotten and was caught up in watching the game. Fed up with what he was seeing, he crossed his arms in a gesture of frustration. Jimy Williams, the third-base coach, was surprised, but he dutifully passed the sign along. Mattick, although embarrassed, laughed as hard as anybody about the gaffe.

He had peculiar theories about all sorts of things. Once, when Al Woods was being troubled by an ankle injury, Mattick had just the exercise to help him. He cornered Woods on the field during batting practice and began to demonstrate a rather peculiar little squat and bounce to him, while the rest of us watched and tried to hide our smiles. Trainer Ken Carson had never seen anything like it. When Woods came in later, he was still laughing. "I didn't understand a word of what he was talking about," he said.

He would also occasionally call players by the wrong name. Alfredo Griffin was always "Griffiths." He would call Willie Upshaw "Lloyd" or Lloyd Moseby "Woodsy" as he passed by the batting cage, dispensing encouragement.

"That's the thing. We all look alike," one of the black players would kid as soon as he was out of earshot.

For the writers, Mattick was a gift. Always quotable, he would never pull rank and would answer even the most basic second guesses. He had a cooler of beer in his office and loved to replay games for hours after they were over. He even enjoyed the second-guessing process. His habitual rejoinder was, "What would *you* do, Alison?"

He also had a way with words that was delightful. Once, to emphasize his veracity in relating an argument with an umpire, he said, "All I did was call him an arrogant son of a gun, in those words exactly, and that's the truth. You can dig up my mother and bury her again if I said anything else but that."

On the road he was always ready for a night out if there was no game to play, and hosted some killer poker games in his suite. He could, and often did, out-drink the most hollow-legged of us and be up and fresh for breakfast the next day.

Mattick's biggest fault was that he gave us too much. He would get so annoyed at losing that he would unload on a player to us without thinking about the consequences. Paul Mirabella complained that first season that he was being kept in the bullpen unfairly. The appropriate thing would have been for Mattick to talk privately to the pitcher about it, but that was never his style. In that particular case, he just snorted and said, "I'll tell you how he can get more starts. All he has to do is throw some zeros up on the scoreboard and he'll get all the starts he wants."

After a game in which Joey McLaughlin, who had pitched in the previous game, gave up a grand slam home run, Mattick was asked if he should have gone to another, more rested, reliever. "What do they need? Two weeks rest after pitching two innings?" he snapped. "That's their job. They get paid big league salaries and they should be able to get big league hitters out. They moan and groan about a chance all the time and then they come in and don't do their job."

That was good copy, but not necessarily good management. Players don't like to read criticism from their manager in the newspapers.

When the team began to lose in 1981, the honeymoon ended. What had once been quaint suddenly seemed incompetent. Players began to grumble again and question every decision. They got tired of reading his ill-considered jibes in the papers every day. The affection was gone, and Mattick lost control of the team. His time was up when the season was over. He went back into player development, back with his scouts and kids where he was happiest. He was refreshing while he was around. He may not be the best manager the Jays had, but he was the most fun.

The best manager has been Bobby Cox, a very nice man, but as bland as tapioca in his dealings with the press. He likes talking to us about as much as he likes losing games, and information is something to be hoarded. You can't prize a secret out of Cox, no matter how you try. Like Pat Gillick, he would deny to the writers that his pants were on fire until the press release had been issued.

According to Cox, all his hitters are "swinging the bat super" and all his pitchers "pitch super" every day of the year. This made for good press-box humour but didn't give us much colour for our stories. "Jeez, poor Clancy," we'd say upstairs after the pitcher had given up three home runs. "He's being 'flared to death' again."

Then we'd go downstairs and discover from Cox that Clancy had been just fine. "Aside from a couple of pitches, he pitched super," Cox would say, daring us to contradict him. "He pitched well enough to win."

This may not have endeared him to the sportswriters, but the players appreciated it after two years of turning to the sports section each day with an anticipatory wince.

Cox liked a closed shop. The fans and their press representatives were all very well, but baseball was a private thing. The Blue Jays were a family and they would iron out their problems without any outside interference, thank you very much. He was tough on players who messed up, but he was tough in private.

As a player for two years with the Yankees, Cox's scouting reports could have read "good field, no bat, great heart." He was a third baseman who played hard until his knees gave up on him when he was thirty. He started managing immediately and when he took over the Blue Jays at forty he had never had to leave the dugout. I sense that's why he likes tough players who give all of a smaller talent, players who remind him of himself. He certainly set the standard of toughness for his team when he finally had his knee treated in 1982. He was back in uniform the day after arthroscopic surgery.

Cox was happiest when he was at the ballpark. He got there early every day and liked nothing better than being with his players and coaches. The rest of the day was something to get through until it was time to go to work. You could see it when Cox was out in the real world, at a sports banquet or an award luncheon. Always cordial to the fans, he didn't feed off them the way some managers do. He wasn't Tommy LaSorda, who loved to work a room, soaking in the praise and giving back one-liners for change. Cox looked like he wished he was somewhere else, unsure in his street clothes.

In uniform, he was another man. I remember him always in the afternoon before a game, sitting in the dugout with one foot up on the bench and a chaw in his cheek. He and John Sullivan and Cito Gaston, the two coaches he brought from Atlanta, would talk about players long ago who could "flat hit" or "flat run" until it was time for batting practice to begin.

"Let's go!" Cox would say, with great joy, and grab his glove and limp out of the dugout. "Let's go!"

And sometimes, when he thought no one was looking, he would go out between second and third with a glove and field a hot grounder and throw it to first. Ahhh.

Chapter

4

The Playgrounds

With Will Rogers, it was men. With me, it's ballparks. I have rarely met one I didn't like, from tiny Grainger Stadium in Kinston, North Carolina, to the fanciest park in the big leagues. They are all magical places, from the great hulking structures that hold 50,000 fans to the little spring training jewels, each built around the diamond at its heart.

In every park there is a moment that I find electric, every time. It is especially heightened for the first game of the season or a first visit to a new park. It is the moment that comes after you've bought your ticket, gone through the turnstile, and stopped, perhaps, at the concession stand and the program kiosk. You walk up the ramp, be it wooden and old or new sleek concrete, full of anticipation. Suddenly the field appears, green and perfect, in front of you. In the cheap seats in a big stadium it's far away, the players tiny; in spring training or the minor leagues it's surprisingly close. The sounds come suddenly to the ear, the crack of batting practice, whistles from the outfielders, the cawing of the vendors down the rows.

At that moment, if you are a fan, your heart gives a little thump. The tension drains out of your body, worldly cares are shut off behind doors in your mind, slam, slam, slam, and you smile and sigh. It is a moment of homecoming, whether it be in cosy old Fenway Park, bland Exhibition Stadium, or riotous Comiskey Park. Outside the walls may be teeming streets or miles of parking lot, ferris wheels, or urban blight, but the ballpark is safe and familiar, wherever it may be.

The sensations are the same, but the parks are each unique. They have personalities of their own, partly because of the fans. I could tell a Kansas City crowd from a New York crowd with my eyes closed by the kind of fun they have, or Red Sox fans from Brewer fans.

I could recognize most of the American League parks in my sleep by now. I know both the public and private faces. I know how to get to the press box and the lunch room, where to find the visiting clubhouse and the dugouts, which parks have tunnels to the field, which have gates from the stands. I know where all the elevators and ladies' rooms are hidden. It was one of the joys of the job to see so many playgrounds. Almost every one became a favourite in one way or another.

I can't pass judgement on the National League parks because I only saw them during the World Series when their true natures and true fans were lost in the pomp, but they seemed characterless. One exception is Dodger Stadium. No matter what I think of that too-too Los Angeles team, the stadium they play in is breathtakingly beautiful and efficient. Another is Wrigley Field in Chicago, my kind of old-fashioned and iconoclastic park. Anywhere they only play in daylight is to be applauded.

But I have a special feeling for the American League parks in which I spent so many hours. They're worth a tour. Let's begin in the eastern division, where almost all of the best parks are found.

Memorial Stadium, Baltimore: opened, 1954; capacity, 53,208.
This is the ugly duckling of the American League. Outside, Memorial Stadium looks like it was designed by someone heavily influenced by public buildings in the Soviet Union. It's big and imposing, with a soldier in bas-relief on the facade.

Inside it is equally devoid of physical charm. The ramps are ugly and steep, the corridors grimy, the clubhouses tacky, the stands merely functional. There is an institutional look to the place, and everything could use a good coat of paint, preferably in a colour other than beige.

It also happens to be one of my favourite places to watch a game, warm and intimate despite its size. The fans are wonderful, friendly, and knowledgeable. The ushers remember you from year to year, kindly, helpful old gents with pride in their jobs. You can buy crab cakes in the concession booths and three different brands of very cold beer in the stands. The important part, the field itself, is perfect, a work of art with luxuriant green grass and an infield so smooth the ball hops true. It is kept groomed by groundskeeper Pat Santarone, who also grows monster tomatoes in the bullpen.

The mood of the park defies its ugliness. The Orioles fight the tawdry environment with a hokey, down-home spirit. There are scorecard giveaways and announcements of cars with their lights left on in the parking lot. Even the press box manages to overcome its ugliness. Although uncomfortable and clumsily designed, it is one of the most efficient in the league. The pencil sharpener is inside a huge old vault on the upper level, the ladies' room is in a broom closet, and the desks lie in wait to tear stockings and bruise knees, but it is always a cheerful place to be. Public-address announcer Rex Barney always has a friendly squeeze of the shoulder on the way by and Bob Brown's public relations staff is never at a loss for information. It is as if they all really care about making visitors feel at home.

The small-town feeling is everywhere. Every time a foul ball is caught cleanly in the stands, Barney says "Give that fan a contract!" and the fans all cheer. Barney even makes the call on fouls hit into the upper deck out of sight of the press box, a mystery to me until I watched him carefully one day. He's got a spotter in the upper deck, an usher whose job is to give him the thumbs up when a catch is made. After every announcement, Barney says "Thank you." He actually says "Thank yewwwww," drawling out the second word until it is almost a purr.

For years, Wild Bill Hagy, the mad cheerleader of Section 34, high in the rightfield upper deck, was, with his crazy cheer, as much a part of the park as the crab cakes. Bearded and pot-bellied, Hagy would lumber down the steps to stand on a seat at the bottom of the section, facing the crowd. He would plant his feet and wave his cowboy hat over his head like an umpire signalling a home run as the crowd howled. Then his cheer began, wonderful to behold as he spelled out the team name with his body.

Arms in a circle over his head formed the "O." For the "R," he put his left hand on his waist for the top curve and stuck out his left leg for the bottom bar. Hands straight up as if signalling a touchdown gave the "I," then the original "O" again. Sideways, one arm straight up and the other at right angles gave the "L." Then came the real challenge. The "E" involved sticking both arms straight, one above the other, with a parallel leg for the bottom bar. He formed the "S" like a Thai dancer, one forearm stuck out from his forehead, the other stuck out behind. It took some imagination to see it, but not nearly as much as it took to make it up.

Hagy was invited down to the box seats by the Orioles, the better to lead the cheers, but the cab driver insisted on staying up in the gods with his friends. Once a game he came down to the dugout roof and spelled the cheer for the whole stadium.

Hagy retired in 1983, but he lives on every time the anthem is played. There's no disrespect intended, but every time the anthem is sung, the crowd shouts out "O" for Orioles every time the singer comes to the lyric, "Oh say does that star-spangled banner yet wave." They do it whether the anthem is on a tape or an esteemed vocalist is on the field. They did it when the Baltimore Symphony Choir sang the anthem for the World Series. Some have even caught on to the Canadian anthem, and the last "Oh Canada" gets the same treatment. Maybe I'm just a silly person, but it never fails to make me giggle.

They've also got one of the most pathetic mascots around, a person in a bird suit who walks around the stands slapping hands with the fans. No San Diego Chicken or Phillie Phanatic, he doesn't have a routine, save dancing a hoedown with a ball girl on the dugout roof during the seventh inning playing of "Thank God I'm a Country Boy," but he suits the park.

None of this would be out of place in the minor leagues, and that's why it's so refreshing. It's good old unsophisticated family fun.

I can't leave Memorial Stadium without talking about the freight elevator by the press entrance, used to bring kegs of beer to the concession stands, reporters to the press box, and dignitaries to the owner's box on the upper level. It is old and temperamental and the wood on the side walls is full of splinters. It is summoned by a bell that clangs throughout the stadium, and is run by a courtly gentleman named Alan Anderson who does his job with great politeness, no matter what the circumstances

He always has a friendly word of greeting, and his face lights up with recognition when you arrive.

Ronald Reagan travelled in that elevator during the 1983 World Series on his way to sit with Oriole owner Edward Bennett Williams, ironically a staunch Democrat, but I'll wager that wasn't Anderson's most memorable ride. That came one night during the playoffs, just after the Orioles had lost the first game to the White Sox. The capacity on the elevator was supposed to be fifteen, but there were hundreds of reporters fighting to get down to the clubhouses. Anderson had to assert himself as much as he could to try to keep the numbers down, but when Williams began to get on an already full elevator with five friends, there wasn't much to be done.

I was on that elevator, along with my claustrophobia, mashed against one of the walls. There were twenty other passengers, none of us with room to scratch our noses, when it landed hard at the bottom of the shaft and stuck. We were there for half an hour while Williams tried unsuccessfully to make his cordless phone work to call for help. Sweat was pouring down all our faces, and we were all doing our best to keep calm, as deadlines ticked by. I could see the night desk at *The Star* getting more and more annoyed as my story didn't come in, but there wasn't anything I could do.

Williams had no deadlines, but he couldn't stand the affront to his power. He banged on the door. He shouted commands to the faint voices we could hear beyond it. "This is Williams here! You must get the fire department!" he finally shouted. "We're running out of air!" That was a possibility that hadn't occurred to the rest of us, who didn't much want to think about it.

Finally Williams made a practical suggestion. "I don't know what faith everybody here is, but I suggest we pray. I have something to say, and the rest of you can pray according to your faith."

Then he looked heavenward earnestly and began, in a booming voice, "Lord, this is getting serious!"

Half a minute later, the doors opened.

Fenway Park, Boston: opened, 1912; capacity, 33,465.
This is everybody else's favourite park, the most romantic of all the relics of the good old days, but it wasn't mine.

It's wonderful in many ways, rising all brick and quirky, in the middle of the city, with narrow streets all around. I love to be outside it just before the gates open, part of the throng, running the gauntlet of the vendors on a sunny day. You can buy big fat soft pretzels out on Yawkey Way, hot sausages with peppers on a bun, chocolate-chip cookies, or huge bags of bargain-priced peanuts, much cheaper than the ones inside.

Free enterprise flourishes. A store across the street stocks an incredible variety of baseball souvenirs from all teams: shirts, jackets, caps, socks, decals, ashtrays, dolls, key chains, wastebaskets, and posters are stuck up on the walls, hung from the ceiling, piled high on countertops, or displayed in a jumble in crowded cases. It's chaos, filled before every game with shuffling browsers and harried clerks. On the streets the freelancers take over, selling their own souvenirs. In the last few years of Carl Yastrzemski's career, anything with "Yaz" written on it somewhere was a sure seller, and anti-Yankee paraphernalia is always popular.

It's a carnival on Yawkey Way every game day, and if you turn the corner onto Landsdowne Street, you can see one of the game's most historic landmarks from an unusual point of view. The Green Monster, the thirty-seven-foot-high fence guarding Fenway's short leftfield, is massive and ominous from inside, but on Landsdowne, it's just kind of a funny wall with the netting billowing down over the top. It's a surprise to see its other face looking so prosaic above the street.

Inside, the stadium is wonderfully eccentric, all odd angles and bits. It's the only place I've ever been where a ball can bounce around in the centrefield corner, thanks to the bullpens, which jut out at an angle from the centrefield fence. The home team has a tremendous advantage because there is so much for a visiting outfielder to misjudge. Every time the Blue Jays went to Boston, the coaches hit fungoes off the Green Monster to help the outfielders learn to read the bounces, but it never did any good. Yastrzemski and Jim Rice learned to play the Monster like Yehudi Menuhin fiddles a tune, but visiting leftfielders can only guess and hope.

This makes for some exciting games, to be sure, but one of the frustrations of Fenway is that from much of the park it's hard to see what's going on. There are undoubtedly season ticket-holders who have never seen a catch in the leftfield corner. Sight lines are bad and pillars block a lot of the play. Too many of the seats are under cover, making it chilly even on warm days.

The press box is not a whole lot better. Cloudy Plexiglas windows obscure the field badly and the frames supporting them make it difficult to see home plate and the pitcher's mound at the same time without getting a kink in the neck. In the early and late season it's too cold to open the windows, and in midsummer they keep them closed to keep the air conditioning in. The box is also inhabited by the noisiest sportswriters and hangers-on around. They never shut up.

Inconvenience can be overcome by charm, to be sure, but the fans add their own chill. They are without question the most brutal fans in the league. They boo everyone and everything on the field, especially their own players. The Red Sox haven't given them too much to cheer recently, to be sure, but their rancour is out of proportion.

The Red Sox return the favour by being one of the least pleasant teams in the league to cover. It was one of the major disillusionments of my journey inside baseball to discover what a surly lot they were. Before I met them I had shared the impression with many that the Red Sox were the class of the league. It was nonsense. They were about as colourful and interesting a group as your average convention of morticians (and I may be doing morticians an injustice), and as friendly as your average customs inspector.

Sherm Feller, the Red Sox public-address announcer, fits right in. He's a laconic old guy who forms a wonderful counterpoint to the gung ho cheerleaders in the rest of the league. For that reason, if nothing else, I like his grumpiness. Feller doesn't crow out the names of "Your! Boston! Red! Sox!" He snarls them. No matter how exciting the game or crucial the situation, Feller leans into the microphone and mutters the batter's name the same way each time, as if begrudging the information: "Now batting. The leftfielder. Jim Rice. Number 14. Rice."

No inflection, no hype. Feller just spits out the names in his flat and gravelly Massachusetts accent, as much a part of Fenway as the Green Monster itself. It's a voice often imitated. I was there one day when Feller had a touch of laryngitis and was croaking even more than usual. In the middle of the game, the Red Sox play-by-play radio announcer, who was taking a break from broadcasting, wandered into Feller's booth and took over for him. Holding his nose to get the right tone, he did such a perfect Sherm Feller that the fans never knew the difference. Feller laughed as heartily as anyone in the press box.

Municipal Stadium, Cleveland: opened, 1932; capacity, 74,208.

There is a real sadness to the Indians' home field. Huge and usually quite empty, it is a place to sit and remember past glory. There isn't much in the present to enjoy, but there was a time in the late forties and early fifties when the stadium rang to the sounds of victory. Those were the years of Early Wynn and Bob Feller, Larry Doby and Lou Boudreau, the days when the seats were full. Now it's just a shell. The Indians have drawn fewer than a million fans in six of the last ten years, and just barely over that mark in the other four. The biggest ballpark in the league is the emptiest.

I've seen it full twice, and the sight was impressive both times. The first was for a game against the Yankees on the July 4th weekend in 1980, with fireworks scheduled after the game. The second time was for the 1981 All-Star Game, the one that brought baseball back after the players' strike. But for most Blue Jays games, it is a depressing place indeed.

It also holds several of the most irritating fans around.

Take the mad drummers in the centrefield bleachers – please! Every game, day or night, rain or shine, they're there, sitting in the top row, miles away from the field. And every game they beat their tom-toms, the boom, boom, boom echoing across the field. They sell a lot of Excedrin.

The stampers in the upper deck are particularly annoying in the press box, which is suspended below it. When they start pounding their feet in glee, it echoes in the press box like a drum. Old, dirty paint flakes and long-dead insects fall down on our heads. Bat Day, always a Sunday doubleheader, is particularly gruelling. If the Indians give any cause for celebration the bats never stop pounding. Saturday night celebrants feel more than their usual regret.

This is not to say there is nothing nice to say about Cleveland. On the contrary. The baked ham and fresh pie in the press dining room are the best in the league.

Like any old park, there are eccentric pockets in it. The public-address announcer sits right on the field, in a little box that he shares with a technician next to the visiting dugout. On nights that threaten rain, they put up a tarpaulin roof two inches over their heads. That's quaint. The anthem singer isn't. Rocco Scotti sings nightly, and nightly he threatens the record for the slowest anthems in history. He was the source of a great controversy when the All-Star Game was held there. The Indians decided to get a more famous singer for the grand occasion, but the public outcry was such that they hired Scotti instead. Rightly so. If the fellow comes out game after game to do his duty when there's nobody in the park, he deserves the chance to perform in front of a full house.

New ownership may well spruce things up, and I hope they do. It's a shame that the home of so much baseball history is such a dreary place. The field is treacherously badly tended and the visiting clubhouse is a disgrace. Even the press box hot dogs are atrocious.

Tiger Stadium, Detroit: opened, 1912; capacity, 52,687.
You want to talk hot dogs? I could live on nothing but the plump and delicious ones served in the Tiger press box, grilled golden with plenty of mustard and onions. They are quintessential ball-park dogs.

They make up for the box itself, which sways in a high wind and sits so high and so close to home plate that you have to lean forward to watch the game. It's neither good for the back nor helpful for vertigo.

The press box is like the stadium: old, a bit rickety, and decidedly good-humoured. The Detroit writers are a sarcastic lot, given to mocking the team that labours before them daily. It comes, I guess, with following a team when it promised so much for so many years without delivering, but if the players could hear what the reporters say about them in the privacy of the press box, they would never talk to a writer again.

Tiger Stadium is a wonderful blue barn of a ballpark that seems to bring out an urge to reminisce in all who visit it. The stadium is listed as being opened in 1912, but the field itself has been there longer. The Detroit baseball team has been playing at the corner of Michigan and Trumbull since the turn of the century, first in Bennett Park, which was expanded to Navin Field in 1911 and then Briggs Field in 1936. The final renovation was in 1961. All the new owners needed to buy to change the name from Briggs to Tiger was a "T" and an "E" for the sign.

The ghosts are always in Tiger Stadium, the ghosts of those great Tiger teams of the past. Lou Whitaker literally plays in Charlie Gehringer's footsteps, and Jack Morris throws from the same mound as Dizzy Trout.

A favourite pastime for visiting players is to sit in the old dugouts and recall epic home runs. The players remember their own best shots and marvel over stories about the feats of Mickey Mantle, Hank Greenberg or, further back, Babe Ruth. The great sluggers live on in the old parks as long as there is still someone around to keep the oral history alive, to point to the spot in the upper deck or to show where one flew right out of the park.

County Stadium, Milwaukee: opened, 1968; capacity, 53,192.

This is another brute of a ballpark, ugly and functional. County Stadium is blue-collar country, a rough-and-tumble environment for a rough-and-tumble team. It rises, prison grey, out of acres of parking lot in the middle of a residential neighbourhood. There's no finesse about it, and there are no pretensions at all, but it is a lively, vibrant place.

Arrive well before game time if you want to see the fans at their best. They're there already in the parking lot, tailgates down on their station wagons and pickup trucks, barbecuing bratwurst and drinking what made Milwaukee famous. These are good fans who come in from Sheboygan, Wawautosa, Oshkosh, and Cudahay to see the Brewers.

They continue the parties in the parking lot after the game as well, especially on weekends. When George Bamberger was manager, he used to stop off for a few on his way home, endearing himself forever to the fans, as did Harvey Kuenn when he wasn't manning the taps at Cesar's Inn, his wife's bar nearby. Managers without the common touch are out of place in Milwaukee.

Once inside, the fans sing "Roll Out the Barrel" and polka in the aisles, the blue and yellow and white of their lucky team colours brightening up the grey all around them. Bernie Brewer leads them. He's a fellow in bibbed lederhosen, a yellow shirt, and an alpine hat who lives out beyond the centrefield fence. He cheers on the team from the front porch of his cuckoo-clock house high above the bleachers and when a Brewer hits a home run he jumps off onto a long slide that deposits him in a huge beer stein. Blue and yellow balloons masquerading as foam splash out into the sky. It's corny, but easier on visiting pitchers than the fireworks in Comiskey Park, Chicago.

Everybody in the place seems dedicated to supporting local industry, but despite the huge quantities of beer consumed, it never turns nasty. The overall feeling is one of gusto.

Progress has ruined one small corner of County Stadium for me. The visiting writers are assigned to the back row of the cramped press box, and our desk sits under a low beam, waiting in ambush. Many an unsuspecting visitor has cracked his noggin standing up, and graffiti all along its length once detailed the encounters. It was a who's who of baseball journalism, written with more wit and colour than got into most newspapers, but when the Brewers won their division in 1982 and wanted to spruce up for the playoffs, some misguided soul ordered the press box painted, and a slice of history disappeared under a coat of greyish green.

Yankee Stadium, New York: opened, 1923; capacity, 57,545.
This was my first ballpark, so it will always hold a special place in my heart, but my most pleasant afternoon in Yankee Stadium came long after the games of my youth. On the day after Reggie Jackson's return, I went to the stadium early to meet with Lou Saban, the football man who briefly held a job as Yankee president. He had promised an old friend from Denver a tour of the monuments behind the centrefield fence, and they let me tag along. I had never seen them up close before, these most hallowed of baseball's icons. It was a bright, softly warm May day, and I was filled with the furtive excitement of a trespasser as we approached the gate in the fence.

The first thing I saw was the pinstriped Toyota used to ferry relief pitchers from the bullpens, parked hard by Miller Huggins's stone. In new Yankee Stadium, class and crass collide. But still, standing in front of the big stones and plaques of Babe Ruth, Lou Gehrig, Casey Stengel, and Mickey Mantle, I felt a few chills. I was also amused to see plaques commemorating the visits of two popes (Paul VI and John Paul II), who held masses in the stadium. (This has given rise to one of my favourite trivia questions: what two former Cardinals have plaques behind the centrefield fence in Yankee stadium?)

On our way back across the centrefield grass, as our feet trod the same spot where Joe DiMaggio and Mantle once roamed, Saban spoke quietly. "Every time I walk on an athletic field I think of the other people who have walked there," he said. "I can almost hear their footsteps."

It is a fine, proud ballpark, and I can't separate it from the Yankee Stadium of my childhood, but it is not one of which I am particularly fond anymore. It is still beautiful. Renovated after the 1973 season, it keeps the old majesty and adds modern comfort. The attendants are colourful, the vendors cheeky and fun. Some have been there for decades.

Despite all this it is a cold place now, businesslike and professional. There's too much difference between the rich fans in the box seats and the poverty on the other side of the wall, too many cops with guns patrolling in the cheap seats, too much drunkenness and vulgarity. I wouldn't want to go there with my grandfather these days. The mood of the players and fans alike is chippy and arrogant; vainglory has replaced joy. George Steinbrenner has put his stamp on the place and made it less than it once was. Every game ends with the playing of his smug anthem, Frank Sinatra's version of "New York, New York." More appropriate would be "My Way."

Exhibition Stadium, Toronto: opened, 1977; capacity, 43,737.
My home field is hard to admire. There are too many bad seats in the stadium, and the sight lines are atrocious. But it isn't a baseball stadium. It's a football field, with baseball tucked into one of the corners, covered with odious artificial turf.

It has all the warmth and charm of an airport departure lounge.

The ushers are teen-agers with the mentality of Moonies. In the seventh inning of a rain-delayed game they're still rousting people back to the cheap seats if they dare to move down to where they can see the game. That's the rules. Whatever would happen if a season ticket-holder arrived at 10:30 and wanted his seat? Heavens.

The seventh-inning stretch, with earnest athletes from Fitness Ontario leading exercises from the dugout roofs, has to be seen to be believed. That the exercises are presented is strange enough; that two-thirds of the fans do them is really peculiar.

The working facilities are good. The elevator is modern and quick. The press box is big and comfortable, but miserable on a hot summer night. After the first season, during which reporters froze and chased their notes in the wind, the press box was glassed in. That's fine, except the windows don't open. All sounds come through a speaker into the hermetically sealed box. The heaters are welcome in April, but there's no air conditioning for July and August. The afternoon sun beats in and turns the place into a hothouse.

The scoreboard, big and modern as it is, presents less interesting information than any other I've seen in the major leagues. Everything about the park falls just short. The mascot, with the unimaginative name of B.J. Birdie, is still amusing to the kids, but he hasn't added a new shtick to his repertoire since he was hatched in 1979. The food is awful. It was the last park in the league to allow beer in the stands, and they have imposed restrictions on how many, where, and when you can buy them, making it all seem somehow tawdry. Of course, many adolescent yahoos manage to get sloppy drunk despite the restrictions.

Ah, it's unlovable, but it's all we've got, and the fans and the team are doing their best to change things. The underdog spirit has given the place an energy that is undeniable. And it's still got the prettiest sunsets around, against the lake and the gingerbread Exhibition buildings in the gap between the leftfield stands and the bleachers.

The sad thing is that the Babbits of southern Ontario think they will solve the problem of an inadequate stadium by building a dome. They will take away the sun on a summer Sunday or the cool breezes on an August night and call it progress. They will take threatening rain clouds or a gale blowing out to rightfield and eliminate them, poof, like that, and claim it improves the game. They will destroy the heart of the sport and send it out on picture postcards to the States.

I say phooey to all of them with their accountants' souls.

With the exception of Chicago, the western division of the league is afflicted with new ballparks, much duller than the ones in the east.

Anaheim Stadium, California: opened, 1966; capacity, 67,335.

This used to be a lovely spot with a gap in seating in centre-field framing the big haloed "A" that held the scoreboard. In 1980 they closed the stadium in to give more seating and took the character away. Now the "A" sits in the parking lot uselessly and the stadium has become just another modern ballpark.

Anaheim is antiseptic and surreal, like Disneyland down the road. Gene Autry owns the team, and they show his old film clips on the scoreboard screen before games. The fans are more interested in playing with Frisbees and beachballs than in watching the ball game, and they leave in the seventh inning. My most memorable visit was in 1979, when Richard Nixon came to an Angels-Jays game and sat in Autry's box on the press level. I shared the feeling of most of my generation about Nixon, and having that symbol of venality in the flesh not fifty yards away both fascinated and repelled me. I could barely keep my attention on the game.

Nixon was a big Angel fan, and he rooted wildly all game. He had a big red handkerchief or napkin that he waved in circles over his head when the Angels were doing well. He danced like a manic puppet in glee. Then the Blue Jays started a comeback. Aghast, he put the handkerchief in his mouth and chewed on it. At one point almost the whole thing disappeared into his mouth before the crisis passed. When the inning was finally over, he pulled the whole soggy hanky out and waved it in the air again.

The Secret Service agent posted outside the box was wearing, somehow appropriately, a necktie printed all over with little Snoopy dogs. Ah, California.

Royals Stadium, Kansas City: opened, 1973; capacity, 40,635.

During the seventh-inning stretch in this jewel of a modern ballpark, the fans all turn and look up behind home plate, anticipatory smiles on their faces. They are soon rewarded when a glass door slides open in the private box area and owner Ewing Kauffman and his wife Muriel lean on the railing and wave. All that can be glimpsed from the press box is their hands, fluttering at the ends of their wrists, and glimpses of their faces from time to time, smiling sweetly. They are the King and Queen of Royals Stadium, and their subjects are truly loyal. From the box seats behind home plate they wave back with genuine affection for the self-made multi-millionaire and his Toronto-born wife.

There's a lot of Mom and apple pie in this place, an old-fashioned innocence and healthy heartland feeling that reflect Kauffman's style. The man who built a major pharmaceutical company out of his basement, using profit-sharing to motivate company loyalty, has the same attitude toward his fans and the team.

Take the Royal Lancers. The group's name raised a lot of giggles during George Brett's well-publicized haemorrhoid problems during the 1980 World Series, but they are an extraordinarily efficient business support group that keeps season ticket sales the highest in the league year after year. In return, the Royals give them perks like trips with the team during the season.

Physically, Royals Stadium is as close to a perfect modern park as you can get. It is clean and cheerful, and a wonderful place to watch a game. That's what it was built for. Not football, not soccer, not tractor pulls or rock concerts – nothing but baseball. Each of the 40,635 seats, rising in tiers of maroon, orange, and gold, faces second base. There's not a bad seat in the house. It shares a vast parking lot with the Kansas City Chiefs football stadium in the Harry S. Truman Sports Complex on the outskirts of Kansas City.

The scoreboard, twelve storeys high and topped with a crown, rises out of a grassy slope behind centrefield. It is surrounded by thousands of lights, which flash and twinkle around it for moments of celebration. Above the slope, on which home-run balls sit in silent testimony after they have been hit, the fountains play. They are spectacular, especially the ones that run from centrefield to the rightfield corner. The fountains are lit by spotlights, which change colour during the nightly water show.

The only drawback is the field, the first artificial turf in the American League. The only explanation I can think of is that at the time the stadium was built, turf looked to be the wave of the future and an "everything's up to date in Kansas City" mentality took over.

It was a terrible mistake. The weather doesn't warrant it and the field doesn't have to be protected against football spikes or other indignities. The irony is that groundskeeper George Toma, generally acknowledged to be one of the best in sport, has to spend his time cutting and sewing plastic grass instead of building a truly great field.

The Metrodome, Minneapolis: opened, 1982; capacity, 55,122.
The Kingdome, Seattle: opened, 1977; capacity, 59,439.
I lump these two together because they deserve each other. I hate domes. They are horrible, sterile places that take away all the charm of baseball. In Minneapolis, signs caution against smoking "in the arena." Arena? Hockey is played in an arena, not baseball. But then, neither of these two teams can be accused of playing baseball. My theory is that the space makes it impossible to play well. Who can play baseball depressed for eighty-one games a year?

Balls get lost in the fabric ceiling in Minnesota and stick in the speakers in Seattle. The artificial turf is rock-hard in Seattle, bouncy as a trampoline in Minnesota. Fly balls in another park turn into home runs indoors. The very parameters of baseball get skewed, somehow. There is none of God's own sunlight to get in the eyes or God's own wind to carry a ball wildly or God's own rain to slow it down.

There are also very few of God's own baseball fans who come out to these two parks, and who can blame them. It might be because both teams are playing badly, but I suspect there's more to it than that. If you lived in Minneapolis or Seattle (or Toronto), where cold or rain keep you inside for too much of the year, summer is a time to be cherished outdoors. The only place domes make sense is in hot climates where people need to escape the heat.

If you come early to a dome, the main sound you hear is the air conditioning. Voices echo in the space like in a gymnasium. You can hear fungoes bouncing across the artificial turf. The lighting seems gloomy and dim. There is nothing more unpleasant than coming in from a bright sunny day to the fluorescent haze of a dome.

Everyone who wants a dome in Toronto should be sent to watch a series in one of these horrible places.

And think for a moment about what happened in Minnesota when they moved from their funky old park in Bloomington. Now the real baseball fans organize bus trips to Chicago and Milwaukee where they can watch real baseball being played, no matter what the team.

The Coliseum, Oakland: opened, 1968; capacity, 50,219.
I can never figure out why it is so cold in this park. Sunny California may be going on all around it, but the Oakland Coliseum is chilly even on a July night.

The first year I went there, it was the most depressing place in the league, a big concrete horror that Charlie O. Finley was letting run down, just like the team that played in it. Crowds were small and bad-tempered. Since the Haases and Roy Eisenhardt bought the team in 1981, the old place has been transformed. New seats replaced old ones, facilities were improved, and most importantly, the fans came back through good promotion.

There's nothing like a full stadium to brighten things up a bit. Now Crazy George leads fans in waves of cheering that flow from one side of the stadium to another, or around the circumference in wild circles. It has become a happy place.

I was there for a home-plate wedding in 1983. The couple had met as season ticket-holders at a game. The bride, wearing a full-length ruffled white gown, waited in the visiting clubhouse for the ceremony to begin. As she walked to home plate, all I could think of was the tobacco juice through which she was dragging her train. When the minister asked for the groom's "I do," the crowd shouted "No! No!"

A good time was had by all.

It still doesn't rival Royals Stadium for comfort or Comiskey

Park for charm, but it's not bad. And they have the best sound system in the league and the best choice of music. As is appropriate for the state, of mind and geography, they lean heavily to California sixties rock and roll.

On my last trip there I had one of those moments I will long remember. It was a long trip, the last of my career. I was feeling lonely and depressed about some bad news from home when I went to the stadium before a Saturday afternoon game. Some A's were taking early batting practice, but the field was otherwise deserted when I walked on the field. It was sunny and warm, a perfect day for baseball. I leaned against a rolled tarpaulin and just listened to the sounds, smelled the air, and felt the sun on my face. The sound system came on, playing an old Grateful Dead tune, and I opened my eyes to see a Monarch butterfly dipping and dodging like a knuckleball. I suddenly felt very much alive and glad of it.

Arlington Stadium, Texas: opened, 1964; capacity, 41,284. This park is so bad, it's almost good. It was originally built as a minor league park to hold 10,000 for the Dallas-Fort Worth Spurs, then expanded twice for the Rangers. The original park is still obvious within the outlines of the new add-ons. The scoreboard is shaped like the map of Texas.

It's hot all summer long. The Rangers don't play any day games at home from early June until well into September, even on Sundays. The sun bakes the infield clay hard and treacherous and the humidity hangs heavy over the field. This place could use a dome.

The clubhouses are minor league and the press facilities are laughable. I hate to think what would happen if the Rangers got into a championship series. The press box itself is fine. There are enough electric outlets and plugs. The view of the field is good. They bring nachos to your seat mid-game, and the beer and Doctor Pepper are always cold. The company's the best. But try getting a story done on deadline here and you'll get ulcers.

Baseball and morning papers don't go together. The basic and unavoidable fact is that night games and early editions are incompatible, especially when the game is being played in a later time zone. So if the sports desk at *The Star* would like my story to them by 10:30 and the game starts at 8:30 Toronto time, there's a problem already. Farther west it isn't as hard because they just write off the first edition. We file an early standup story to fill the space and hope for the best in later editions. But just one time zone away, we can always hope. If the game isn't too long and if the deadline can be padded just a bit, the story can make it to every edition.

The usual procedure is to file a story immediately after the game ends, race down to the clubhouse for a few player quotes, then back to the press box to file the next story. In Texas, forget it. There's an elevator near the press box, but it doesn't go to the basement where the clubhouses are. It goes to the top of the grandstand, from where we fight our way against the traffic down the ramps the fans are crowding up. At field level, it takes a leap over the railing (skirts are a hazard in Arlington) to get to the dugout.

Then there is the dirt tunnel under the stands (rats, scorpions, snakes lurking in every shadow, it was said) to the clubhouse where, unfailingly, the player you need a quick line from is either in the shower or in the trainer's room.

Then it's back up through the stands (the lights are turned off by then) to the press box in time to file the second story and miss the team bus.

My third season on the beat I found a pay phone near the clubhouse to file quotes, but I don't think I wrote a good first-edition game story from Arlington in five years. That's with the kind of small crowd the Jays and Rangers drew, too. With the kind of mob a playoff attracts, I'd still be trying to get to the clubhouse.

There is one attraction unique to Arlington. Bobby Bragan was for years a special assistant to the general manager and he made the park a wild place to visit. For a couple of seasons he set up a piano in the press dining room and played and sang cocktail music during pregame meals and incongruous accompaniment to barbecued beef and press notes.

I'll not soon forget the night the Lone Ranger made a visit to the stadium to ride around the outfield before the game. Bragan wandered into the press box, sidled up next to me, took the cigar out of his mouth, and said, in a W.C. Fields kind of voice, "Well, it's not often you get to see the Lone Ranger and Toronto on the same night."

Comiskey Park, Chicago: opened, 1910, capacity, 43,651.

I've saved the best for last. Comiskey might be my favourite stadium anywhere. It is the most exuberant park in the league. Comiskey is a great sprawling park, old and funky with a cheerful exuberance that reflects itself in the fans. The soft green of the trees showing through the arches in the leftfield stands gives a sylvan feeling that masks its rough neighbourhood.

Nancy Faust will never play Carnegie Hall, but she is a splendid musician nonetheless. Seated at her ballpark organ right in the middle of the upper deck, young, blonde, and attractive, she leads the fans in raucous response, smiling and waving and rocking on the bench.

Comiskey is probably the worst park to play in as a visitor if you happen to lose the game. Every time one of the White Sox hits a home run, fireworks explode from the old centrefield scoreboard capped with pinwheels. The home team rubs it in badly. Dave Stieb told me after the 1983 All-Star Game that it was the first time he had ever enjoyed the fireworks. The American League was the home team, and the pyrotechnics were for his side for a change.

Should the visiting pitcher be taken out of the game, the White Sox fans have worse in store than just fireworks. With Faust leading them, they sing and chant a derisive, "Na na na na, na na na na, hey, he-ey, Good-bye!" over and over again, the song recently picked up by Montreal Forum fans. It's good fun.

The best seventh-inning stretch in the league is also at Comiskey, though it's not what it was before Bill Veeck sold the team and crazy Harry Caray, the long-time White Sox radio play-by-play man, crossed town to the Cubs. Caray used to lead the fans in singing "Take Me Out to the Ball Game," standing up in the radio booth and using a beer can as a baton. The fans loved him and sang their hearts out.

They weren't the only ones. At his seat in the press box, Veeck would put down his inevitable cigarette and get up on his peg leg and sing along, quietly. His grizzled face under the crew cut wore a quizzical smile. Every night he would do it, with no embarrassment at all, and when it came to the lyric, "and there's one, two, three strikes, you're out," Veeck would raise his right hand into the air with one, two, then three, knobby fingers outstretched, then thumb the imaginary player out of the game. Veeck didn't call attention to himself there in the back row. It was kind of private, and it never failed to make me smile. I miss him in Comiskey.

Now different people, designated fans (one night, I remember, it was a priest and a nun, in full habit), lead the seventh-inning song. Veeck has defected to the bleachers of Wrigley Field with the Cubs fans, unhappy with new owners Jerry Reinsdorf and Eddie Einhorn. You can't take a spirit that strong out of the ballpark, though, and something of his childlike enthusiasm and zany democracy lives on.

Each ballpark, even the domes, has its own character and its own sense of family. I watched a game from the box seats in Minneapolis one night, smack in the middle of a group of season ticket-holders who had become old friends. They missed their old ballpark sorely but were getting used to the new one, slowly. What struck me was how friendly they were, how their humanity fought the coldness of their surroundings. I guess no place can be all bad on game day.

Chapter

5

The Fans

Baseball played privately in empty ballparks would no doubt be amusing for the participants, and possibly would lose none of its charm and excitement, but it would be like the tree that falls in the forest when no one is around. Would it make any noise?

Of course not. The spectators are as much a part of the sport as the players. If people didn't buy tickets, owners couldn't meet their payrolls. If fans didn't watch television, the networks wouldn't have to shell out billions to baseball for the rights. If they didn't show up at the ballpark and cheer, there would be no point in playing the game.

Corny as it may seem, the fans matter to the players. They get an extra jolt out of playing in front of the friendly home crowd or sticking it to hostile thousands on the road. The ones who understand how the game works see the fans as allies. It is the selfish and stupid players who see them as a nuisance.

The same is true for that small proportion of spectators who report the games to those who can't be there. Like it or not, and a lot of players don't, those of us who act as eyes and ears for the rest of the world play our role, too.

Baseball fans are an amazing group, opinionated and obsessed with the workings of the sport. They can debate for hours the merits of a trade that is nothing more than a sportswriter's hallucination. They laugh at discomfort and will sit in the rain or snow because they know they are part of the game. They don't want to miss an inning. It is said that hard-working ballplayers "come to play." There are fans who "come to watch" with as much fire.

Baseball is participatory because all the fans can believe that they understand what's going on. They boo the umpire because they saw the close play or outside pitch at least as clearly as he did. They can form an opinion about players' skills on the basis of the evidence of their own eyes, not because of what they have been told. If a tackle isn't doing his job in a football game it's difficult to see. If a shortstop drops an easy ground ball or a hitter doesn't hustle to first it's obvious.

Most fans are ardent democrats with a love of taking authority down. Listen to the names they call the umpires or the opposing team's manager when he comes on the field. They secretly root for the ones who can bend baseball's rules. Gaylord Perry could always draw a crowd to see him throw a spitter, and he played to the folks, touching his cap bill, belt buckle, and various parts of his body as a ritual before each pitch.

The democracy combines with a love for the underdog that is at the heart of rooting for the home team. Even the wretched Mets had staunch fans when they were the worst team in baseball. Look at the Chicago Cubs, the Seattle Mariners. Fans root for these teams because they know how quickly things can turn around in baseball. The Toronto Blue Jays drew a million and a half fans when they were lucky to finish fifty games out of first place.

The most obsessed fans tend also to be collectors. Some only do their collecting in their minds. They worship trivia, numbers, batting averages and earned run averages, odd plays they have seen, loopholes in the rules. They know the ten ways to score from third base. They bring their collections out constantly for perusal and admiration, like a lepidopterist with his moths. They love sports hotline programs and are happiest when they are stumping one another with obscure and meaningless questions. Sometimes they don't even bother to watch the game.

Others collect ballparks. They plan vacations around minor league schedules, so they can see as many games in as many parks as possible. Some never even go to a major league game. They lose interest in the players just when the rest of the world has started to recognize their names.

Still others collect bats, uniform jerseys, ticket stubs, autographs, and, of course, bubble-gum cards. For most, it's a casual hobby, each item a souvenir of a particular game or trip, but for others it's an obsession. These are the grown men and women who can be found lurking outside team hotels all afternoon waiting to get autographs, any autographs, from players on their way out the door. A lot of them are in it as a business, and players who don't hesitate to sign anything for kids at the ballpark gate, genuinely nice guys, shy away from these people. Some of them have elaborate albums or cross-indexed boxes, and ask each player to sign stacks of his cards. The autographs eventually make their way to dealers.

When Early Wynn travelled with the Blue Jays as a broadcaster, he would simply refuse to sign anything for anyone he suspected was a collector or dealer. As a member of the Hall of Fame he knew his signed cards would be worth a fair bit of money and he didn't see why he should help someone else get rich. He couldn't stand the lobby rats.

Card collecting is a huge subculture with its own jargon and communications network. There is even a biweekly magazine for collectors with the latest word on which players will sign autographs and which won't, which players will sign one card only, which will only sign an autograph for a kid, which have mail requests signed by someone else. The magazine is crammed full of ads from dealers all over the continent.

New York and Chicago are the prime spots for the dealers and their agents. A small group of them hang around in front of the hotel every afternoon carrying boxes of cards. These are grown men, mind you, some dressed in shirts and ties. Most of them are fat. Many of them have funny haircuts or shifty eyes. These are grown men who spend most of their afternoons in baseball season waiting for baseball players to come out and sign a bubble-gum card. These are weird grown men.

I have never really understood the impulse for autograph seeking in anyone over the age of fifteen. I enjoy an inscription from a friend in a book maybe, as a souvenir of a meeting. But standing outside a hotel and collaring a ballplayer or movie star is something that holds no appeal. But listen, it helps keep the weird grownups out of trouble, right? And some of them look like they could use all the help they can get.

I fully understand the impulse to collect. There are people

who think we have some pretty strange stuff in our house, souvenirs from several leagues that we cherish. We are always delighted to come across more baseball esoterica in our travels, but not if it's going to break the bank.

Only one item offered in the collectors' magazine tempted me, just a bit, because it was so rare. The lineup card for the one-inning completion of the Yankee-Kansas City pine-tar game of 1983 was up for auction, signed by the players involved. Just the thing to hang over the pinball machine. But the opening bid specified was $700: even baseball collecting has gone through the roof. You'd have to be making major league minimum to afford it.

This doesn't bother the fanatic collectors, who are willing to spend fortunes. Some would rather collect than eat. Others turn their basement rec rooms into virtual clubhouses, with uniforms hanging all around and bats in elaborate racks, with rows of seats from demolished ballparks instead of chairs. All these things are available through the collector magazines and at the dozens of sports shows and auctions all over the continent. The going rate for a Ted Williams road uniform from the late fifties is $2,500, but there are some bargains. For a paltry $115 you could have Mark Wagner's Texas Ranger road uniform hanging in your own closet.

Want the Kansas City Royals banner that used to hang in Baltimore's Memorial Stadium? Yours, for $75. A mint condition Reggie Jackson bat? Sold, for $125. A used but uncracked Dave Goltz bat? A bargain at $5. What a deal!

The ultimate collector could be Larry Luebbers, a Kentucky realtor who made a deal with the demolition company that took down Crosley Field when the Cincinnati Reds moved out in 1970: he put it up on his farm. Shades of Ray Kinsella, hero of W.P. Kinsella's splendid novel *Shoeless Joe*, but Luebber didn't build an outfield so that the ghost of Heinie Groh would come to play. According to reports, he just stuck up the scoreboard and fences and dugouts for the ghosts, then let weather take its toll. What a splendid fancy, just the same.

Most fans keep their particular lunacy slightly more tightly under wraps, but their dedication is no less. Some are simply passionate fans of baseball, but most prefer to follow a team and identify totally with it.

Listen to them talk about it: "We won today" or "We lost." (Except in more fickle towns, like Boston and Philadelphia, where the team is "we" for a win, but a loss is blamed on "the bums who blew it.") None of the fans played an inning of the game, but their spirits rise and fall with the fortunes of the team.

The idea that fans are a part of the game isn't ludicrous to me because I have seen them affect outcomes as directly as any player. I remember the third game of the American League playoffs in 1979, played at Anaheim. The Angels' theme that year was "Yes We Can!" and the Angel fans still believed it, even though the team had lost the first two games.

The third one was close. The stadium was full and every person there was chanting the three words. The din was deafening by the bottom of the ninth inning, when the Angels were down by a run and two outs away from being out of the playoffs altogether. With men on first and second, Bobby Grich lined a ball to centre-field. ("Yes we can!") Al Bumbry, who couldn't hear the crack of the bat over the noise, raced in ("Yes We Can!") and watched as the ball dribbled off the end of his outstretched glove ("YES WE CAN!") and the game was tied. Larry Harlow's double, which won the game, was an anticlimax.

The fans won that game by their noise and by the emotional energy of 43,000 people directed toward Bumbry. Five years later, facing another playoff series, Ken Singleton of the Orioles still remembered that night. The Angels unfortunately lost the next game, and the Orioles in the clubhouse splashed around champagne, chanting "Yes we did!"

It happened again, in another eventual losing cause, in Milwaukee in 1982, when the fans woke up the Brewers in the seventh inning of the fourth game of the World Series against the Cardinals and willed them to win it. The 56,000 filling every available space in the stands were the people who had been there all season, faithful Brewer rooters who wouldn't let the team quit. After they stood up for the seventh-inning stretch, they didn't sit down. They clapped, they cheered, and they chanted "Here we go Brewers, here we go," as the Cardinals called in three different relievers. They helped the Brewers score six runs in the inning to win the game.

"I don't know if the noise bothered the Cardinals, but it sure helped us," said Paul Molitor after the game. "They had been fairly quiet, with good reason, because we weren't playing well. But they came to life and got things going."

"Our fans are great," said Charlie Moore. "It doesn't matter if they're 10,000 or 50,000, they know how to make noise. There is a lot of pride involved and we were pretty embarrassed until then."

There was something refreshingly old-fashioned about those Brewers, their fans, and their attitude toward each other, an attitude I fear might soon disappear.

In most places, baseball crowds are extraordinarily cheerful and friendly, even after a loss, but there are bad signs popping up here and there, particularly in the urban east. Yankee Stadium can get very nasty, as can Shea, home of the Mets. Philadelphia and Pittsburgh crowds are ugly. Obscenity and violence have become commonplace, a trend that has players worried. When Dave Parker got pelted with batteries in Pittsburgh, other outfielders began looking over their shoulders between plays, scanning the stands for wackos. Some believe it is inevitable that a player will get shot at in a ballpark some day.

By and large, the ballpark is still a gentle haven for a whole range of sporting humanity: the strange lonely people who sit absolutely quietly, marking plays meticulously in a score-book; the old people who ramble on about games played fifty years ago, making comparisons between old favourites and the young ones on the field; mildly eccentric middle-aged women who stretch team T-shirts over their ample bodies and giggle like schoolgirls; courting teen-agers in skin-tight jeans; little boys with eyes like saucers, gloves at the ready for foul balls; beer-bellied softball players roaring approval or despair. The ballpark is still, in most places, a wonderful, funny, happy place to be.

For baseball fans, winter is cruel. Not only is the weather miserable outside, there's no baseball anywhere. They know they are playing it in the Caribbean, but that is small consolation for most. It costs too much to get there, and the games aren't reported in papers north of Venezuela. There has to be another way to fill the void.

APBA is one. Pronounced ap-bah (the letters don't stand for anything), it is a game involving a cardboard diamond, two dice, and a separate card for each player in the league.

Ah, yes, it's a game. Just a game. So is baseball, remember?

APBA is also a way of life. It is an obsession, a rich fantasy that makes winter go away. There are other forms of table baseball, too, but APBA was my first madness.

Table baseball players are a little bit strange. Well, we're actually very strange. When it comes to our teams, we're almost certifiable. All table baseball players share two traits, a love for the game of baseball and a well-developed imagination. You need the former to understand the game and the latter to believe in it.

What an escape it is. By day, we live humdrum lives as sportswriters, lawyers, civil servants, students. By night, we are transformed into rich, powerful, dashing entrepreneurs of sport. George Steinbrenner and Ted Turner have nothing on us.

We are the Boys (and Girls) of Winter.

For me, the APBA experience began in 1978. My friend Bryan Johnson and I were feeling the usual baseball withdrawal symptoms that set in after the World Series when we decided to send away for the game, which we had seen advertised.

Once we played it, with the teams that came with the game – the Orioles against the Yankees, for example, or the Mariners against the Blue Jays – we decided to form a league. Bryan recruited his friends Hal and Warren Quinn, I brought in Ken Becker and Marty O'Malley, and the Fireside APBA League was born.

Most of us, as it turned out, were roughly in the same business. Hal was sports editor of *Maclean's* magazine; Bryan was drama critic for the *Globe and Mail*; Ken had just spent a year covering the Blue Jays for the *Sun*; and Marty and I were freelance, writing for anyone who would pay us. Warren was between engagements.

The night we met as a group for the first time was for the draft, around my dining-room table, a bit warily. After pulling numbers out of a hat to determine order of drafting (in subsequent years we drafted in reverse order of finish the season before), we announced our team names.

Most were chosen in relation to the streets on which we lived. I was Owner and Chief Operating Officer of the Simpson Avenue Studs. Bryan's team was called the Chateau Neufs of Pape, Ken's the Hudson Rivers, Hal's the Roselawn Undertakers, Warren's the Quebec Avenue Separatistes, and Marty's the North End

Greens. He took a lot of abuse from the rest us about the prosaic name, and when he drafted Manny Sanguillen in the tenth round, when many good players were still available, the first Fireside APBA tradition emerged: O'Malley became the league scapegoat.

That was the beginning of something that has become part of all our lives since then. As O'Malley once said, "In the beginning it was just a way to get through from the World Series to spring training, but now it's the real thing." More real to us than anything that happens between March and October, in what some call "real baseball." (We call it "other baseball.")

We hold our draft each year just as the "other" season begins. Since the game we play is based on the statistics of two years before (in the winter of 1983-84, we were playing with cards based on the 1982 season), this is how we avoid having advance knowledge of an unknown player suddenly becoming a star. Each of us protects up to twenty of our existing team (to encourage loyalty) and fills in the roster with rookies, new arrivals in the league, and our rivals' unprotected players. (A practice to be indulged in at your peril. Since we are allowed to reclaim unprotected players for the future, we get quite annoyed if one of them is stolen. The drafter can expect retribution from the previous owner.) We spend long hours in the days before the draft with our heads buried in the previous year's statistics, looking for sleepers.

This does not mean we always draft intelligently, and beer-induced over-exuberance can be costly. Hal Quinn phoned around the league the morning after one year's draft to inquire how he had managed to wake up with five first basemen.

You want a team? Forget the Tigers or Twins. Try the 1983 Simpson Avenue Studs: Willie Aikens at first base (with Don Mattingly waiting in the wings), Damaso Garcia at second, Alan Trammell at short, Carney Lansford at third, John Wathan behind the plate. In the outfield are Harold Baines in right, Dwayne Murphy in centre, and a platoon of John Lowenstein and Gary Roenicke in left. (What's good enough for the Baltimore Orioles is good enough for the Studs.) I have some problems, like any owner, but I like my team.

My designated hitters are Don Baylor from the right and Reggie Jackson from the left. I'm not keen on the latter's influence in the clubhouse, and he doesn't get along very well with management, but we were having terrible attendance problems, and he can put the meat in the seats. I didn't pay him the attendance bonus he got from the Angels. I have some principles, after all. I dropped him after the 1983 season, with some relief.

My starting pitchers are Dave Stieb, LaMarr Hoyt, Larry Gura, and Tommy John, with Goose Gossage leading the bullpen crew.

As in "other" ball, we owners have to worry about good years and bad years. Was Gura's bad season a fluke? Should I protect him in next year's draft or let him go? We have a farm team, on which players who had a bad year can spend a season, then come back up when they have regained their good form (and good card). Gura and John went there for rehabilitation after the 1983 season. I had faith that they could come back.

Trades or free agent moves in "other" ball can also be vexing when the move is into the National League. When Gossage went to San Diego after the 1983 season, it was a disaster for the Studs, and we couldn't even claim compensation. (I tried to trade him to the Riverdale Rogues, the National League APBA franchise owned by my husband, for Phil Niekro, but the inter-league trade was soundly vetoed by the other owners.)

From the end of the World Series to the beginning of the regular season, we meet weekly, rotating the venues, the Quinn-dome one week, Green Stadium the next, the Riverdale Zoo, new home of the Studs, the next. Once together, we play ball.

The game is quite simple. The managers announce their starting pitchers, and lineups are written out accordingly. After the anthems are sung (or hummed), the visiting team (we alternate home and away games with each team) is up.

The 1983-84 Studs, for example, led off with Garcia, who batted .310 in the American League, .306 in APBA, against lefthanded pitching, and Murphy, who walks a lot, against righthanders.

After putting the token representing the player up at home plate (Some use pennies. I use dimes. American dimes. Canadian dimes are sissy – who wants the Queen up to bat?), we roll two dice. The ones that come with the game are uneven sizes. A large red one always represents the first number. The smaller, white one is the second number. Some of us have our own dice, though. Marty O'Malley started it off when he found a green die to match his team name. The rest of us followed suit. Particularly deadly for me are some I bought in Baltimore in honour of Roenicke and Lowenstein: black with red dots for the first number, ivory with black for the second.

After rolling the dice, I consult Garcia's card. Listed by each of the double-digit possibilities is another number, representing the outcome of the at-bat, whether it be a single, a double, a strikeout, a flyball to left, a groundout to short, a walk. Each player's card is designed with the help of a computer fed the previous year's statistics and reflects the type of offensive player he is and the season he had. The cards are updated yearly. Garcia, for example, has fewer home runs on his card than Jackson. He also has fewer strikeouts, and fewer walks than most other players since he rarely walks in "other" baseball.

To determine the outcome of the roll, there is a series of large cards with results listed for each number, one card per situation: bases empty, runner on first, on second, on third, on first and second, first and third, second and third, and bases loaded. Each card has listings for three levels of fielder and for specific plays that the manager calls: hit and run or sacrifice bunt play on offence; holding the runner on base, playing the infield deep or close for defence.

The opposing pitcher has a bearing on the outcome, too, with the results also listed on the cards. If Garcia's roll was 31, for example, the outcome on his card would be an 8, which is a hit against some pitchers, an out against others. A control pitcher strikes out more batters, a wild one gives up more walks.

Some rolls also depend on the fielders. Each has a number rating. A low rating will lead to an error. A fielder with a higher number will get to the ball or turn a double play.

There are two versions of APBA, the basic game and the Master Game, with which we have been playing since we discovered it in the second year.

What is complicated in the telling is less so the more you play. For most of the standard rolls, we don't even have to consult the charts. We do have to check the rare-play cards, though. These are a separate series of cards, printed in red instead of black. When a roll produces a 39, 40, or 41 on the player's card, it means something odd is afoot. It's time to move to the RP boards.

Mayhem lurks on these cards. Errors are here, and injuries,

wild throws, player ejections, and inside-the-park home runs. All the off-beat permutations of basic, three-strikes-you're-out baseball are waiting in RP land.

Let me take you through a couple of plays. Say I have runners on second and third with nobody out and decide to try a squeeze play. I roll for my batter, and the result is a 41. Checking the regular boards, I discover it is a rare play. Then I roll again. If, in this instance, I roll a 32, the corresponding number on the rare-play chart is 26.

Now my opponent rolls for his team fielding. If he is Fielding One, the best, the result is a triple play: the bunt is popped up, the third baseman catches it, tags the runner coming home and throws out the other runner trying to beat it back to second. Not nice for me.

If he rolls a higher number, though, and his team drops to Fielding Two, things look up. In this case the catcher fields the bunt and throws wildly to first, allowing the runner to score. The other runner is out trying to score and the batter goes to second on the throw home (unless he is slow, in which case he is out).

If my hapless opponent should chance to roll a really high number to drop to Fielding Three, watch out. The pitcher tries to field the bunt but bobbles it and the first runner scores. The pitcher tries to get the batter at first but throws past the first baseman, letting the other runner score. The first baseman scrambles after the ball, picks it up, and tries for the batter, who is now heading for second. He throws the ball into leftfield as the batter heads toward third. The leftfielder picks up the ball and heaves it home, wildly, and the batter scores. That's three runs and four errors, two to the pitcher, one to the first baseman, and one to the leftfielder.

This play is particularly pleasant if you are the home team, listening to your fans scream with glee, although the joy of the embarrassed silence from the stands if you happen to be on the road is also quite sweet.

My personal favourite, although I have never seen it come into play, is RP 18 on the card for runners on first and second, Fielding Two. It is also a bunt play. The third baseman fields the bunt but bobbles it, so all hands are safe. *But*, if the runner who ends up on third will not reach the age of twenty-three during the season being played, he will be caught in the dreaded hidden ball trick and be out. And with what embarrassment will he return to the dugout and avoid the manager's eyes while his teammates stifle their smirks behind their hands.

And don't think for a minute that we can't see it all, in our minds. The "other" baseball season takes care of that. We go down to Exhibition Stadium to watch our players and see how they perform. Summer baseball is simply research material.

None of us is quite as bad as J. Henry Waugh, the proprietor of the *Universal Baseball Association* of Robert Coover's fine novel. Mr. Waugh invented a baseball game that took over his life. His game had options that included sudden death on the diamond, and his players finally became more real to him than the people he dealt with every day.

But I have to admit that sometimes we come close. We talk to our players. When my pitcher is in trouble I call time out and trot the catcher's card out to the mound to consult with the pitcher's card. We talk about problems in the clubhouse and worry about drug use. One player, in another league, used to line up his team, the Philharmonics, before every game and play them Beethoven's Fifth Symphony. I have tried Aretha Franklin singing "Respect" to get the Studs out of a slump. It didn't work.

We have talismans and superstitions, lucky hats, dice, even lucky underwear. Just after our first season began I took a trip to Egypt, and all the Studs came with me. I surreptitiously brought their cards into the Great Pyramid for the magical emanations. It worked, but not the way I expected. They ended up playing the season like mummies.

Over the years, the league has changed. When Bryan became the *Globe*'s correspondent in China (refusing, despite our pleas, to rename the Neufs the Peking Ducks), he became the Commissioner in Exile. Marty's son Sean took over the team for him (although there was some argument from those of us who felt that someone who had homework to do had no place in the league). When Becker left Toronto to seek fame and fortune, the Rivers moved to Pickering under the guidance of Gord (Duke) Shank. The Undertakers moved from Roselawn to Wheeler and changed the team name to Dealers.

The league expanded. When Bryan came back to take over the Neufs, Sean got his own team, the Avenue Road Runners. When Ken came back, having discovered, like Dorothy, that Oz was overrated, he established a new franchise, the Expatriates. Finally, in 1981, a new league spun off ours. It plays with National League players. We call it the junior league. They are a more dramatic league than ours. They shout more, and talk more to their dice. They have even had special rare plays of their own.

Take the suicide-squeeze broken-glass play. Riverdale Rogues owner Paul Bennett invented that one the first time the two leagues played simultaneously, in the recently renovated Riverdale Zoo. (The co-tenancy of the stadium stemmed from the first inter-league marriage in Fireside baseball. The other owners, appropriately, gave us a ceiling fan – stadium improvements.) With two out and Ozzie Smith on third base, Bennett intended to call a steal of home. In the heat of the moment he shouted "squeeze" instead. The sacrifice worked, but was, unfortunately, the third out of the inning.

When Paul realized his stupidity he threw his dice through the window, which, unhappily, was closed at the time. From the next room, we American Leaguers stared in amazement at the two holes neatly punched in the glass. Such a feat has never been duplicated, in either league.

Over the years there have been marriages, separations, and births in the league. Some hair has turned greyer; some has disappeared altogether. But APBA remains the same.

The National League changed when Steve Reid, one of the original members, was killed in an accident. His friends made sure that Mike Schmidt's APBA card was buried with him. The league has since expanded, but Reider's favourite player belongs only to him. The best player in the "other" National League will never again play in the Fireside League. And no table-top baseball player I've ever told about it finds it strange.

Chapter

6

Ink-Stained Wretches

The press box, behind and above home plate, with a splendid panoramic view of the field, is the worst seat in the house. All of the joy of the ballpark is outside the home of the working press, where cynicism lurks in the murk from cheap cigars. There the only good game is a fast game. There star players are the butts of cheap one-liners by pot-bellied former jocks whose dreams have turned sour. The press box is a place in which it is hard to remember the joy of the game. It is, paradoxically, a very cosy private club.

There is a camaraderie among baseball writers because we all have many of the same problems, face the same deadlines, deal with the same people. We help each other out, exchanging information or anecdotes about the teams we know best. We talk a lot during games, wandering around the press box to ask a question or tell a story, not always paying strict attention to what goes on down on the field.

Most of us must write while the game is going on, filing stand-up stories for early editions, and the rhythms of play are second nature. We know when it is crucial to watch carefully, and when one eye will do. We have all learned to keep our ears tuned to the crack of the bat, which brings our eyes off our computer terminal and back to the field, but we still have to ask a neighbour what happened from time to time.

"Six-three?" (Was that a groundout to short?)

"No, four-three." (No, the second baseman.) – "With an asterisk." (Good play.)

The redeeming feature of the press box is that it is a very funny place. There are a lot of eccentric people covering baseball, people with biting wit. Most of the humour probably falls into the "you-had-to-be-there" category, but it usually centres on the personality quirks of the players or on their self-image.

Reggie Jackson was always a popular target. I was in Anaheim his first year with the Angels shortly after his fifty-cent attendance bonus for each patron over 2,400,000 had kicked in, and the writers were having a lot of fun with it. First we figured out that he had made $12,506 for an infield hit, two fly balls, and a walk the night before.

Then someone (always referred to in print as a "press-box wag") grabbed the internal microphone to make an announcement: "Attention, ladies and gentlemen. Please have correct change ready. Reggie will be passing among you after the third inning." Later in the game, the wag was back: "Attention, please. Would the person who gave Reggie a Canadian quarter please identify him- or herself and pay the exchange."

Another favourite tactic was to quote a player's excuses for poor play. A pinch hitter who had complained about not getting enough at bats might hit into a double play, prompting a wag to yell, "Jeez, if he had more A.B.s he coulda made four outs."

Second-guessing of the manager was another favourite. The Tiger writers loved to get on Sparky Anderson about over-managing, especially when a move backfired. The most original press-box wits were in Arlington, Texas, where Randy Galloway and Jim Reeves set the style for a band of iconoclasts who played by their own rules. They even let the style carry into their writing. For years Galloway led a campaign against former owner Brad Corbett, whom he habitually called "Chuckles the Clown" in print. It was gonzo sports journalism. They even gave a new name to the Shah of Iran when he stopped briefly in San Antonio in his dying trip around the world. Now that he was a Texan, Galloway and Reeves reasoned, he deserved a new name. They called him "Billy-Bob Pahlavi" until the day he died.

Of course, none of this carried down to field level. The same writers who had mocked a player or manager unmercifully upstairs would approach him with appropriate reverence after the game was over. We all pretended that each loss was as life-and-death serious as the players did – who would dare behave otherwise? – even if it was nothing but a charade on both sides of the notebook. The press box was a release, a haven from the offensive obsequiousness we were forced to adopt face to face, often with men for whom we had little respect.

It was a ticklish business, a tightrope we writers walked in our dealings with the men on the field. Personal feelings had no place in our professional contact with the players, but they were difficult to keep out. Because beat writers spend so much time with the team they cover, it is impossible to be neutral about the twenty-five men that make it up, especially when some of them are bozos or brutes.

I don't know about other writers, but there were times when I would find myself interviewing a self-important pitcher after a game, listening to him making excuses for a loss, and let my mind play with what I really wanted to say to him.

While my lips said, "Tough game, what went wrong?" my secret self ranted: "You have just kept me waiting half an hour on deadline because you weren't in the mood to talk to the press. Did it ever occur to you that I am never in the mood to talk to you? I'm older than you, nicer than you, both smarter and wiser and a lot more interesting and worthwhile. Admittedly, I can't throw a slider for strikes, but today, honey, neither could you. How dare you treat me like a piece of dog waste on your shoe?"

The internal monologue was possible because it took less than half a brain to listen to the habitual postgame prattle from most players and keep track of it with a kind of baseball shorthand: "dn s w/ s," for example, was the ever popular "I didn't stay within myself" and "h b gd, rt a/ p" stood for "I was hitting the ball good, but right at people." "110p" stood for the mythical 110 per cent that players swear they give every day. If I had been paid by the clichés I was forced to endure, I could have retired early.

These are the kind of remarks a player tends to make when surrounded by a scrum of print and radio reporters with their microphones stuck in his face, precisely the remarks I tried to keep out of the paper at all costs. Usually when the scrum moved on to the next player, I could get more thoughtful comments. Writers can also get better interviews from the players they cover all the time because they have a perspective through which they can ask more challenging questions. This means the beat writer gets the best stuff and leads to co-operation among sports-writers.

Ideally, after a game, the beat writer goes to both teams for quotes, first to the winning clubhouse, then to the losers. In practice, there is often not time for both, and informal pools are set up. Say the Blue Jays were playing the Royals in Kansas City at night. If the Blue Jays won, I went to their clubhouse after filing my initial, "game over" story with the bare bones of the game for the early editions. Then it was time to rush back to the press box to write my next story. When Tracy Ringolsby, from the *Kansas City Star-Times*, came up from the Royals' clubhouse we quickly compared notes and shared quotes. He would give me the Royals side of, say, a controversial play, while I gave him the Blue Jay response. Typically, I would give only one reporter the best quotes and he would do the same for me, so they would be "exclusive" to my paper and his. The other beat writers made their own sharing arrangements.

Cheating? Maybe, but I prefer to think that it was simply making the best of a difficult situation. When circumstance allowed, I went to both rooms. With limited time, I preferred to do a complete job in one clubhouse as long as I knew I could rely on my colleague who followed the other team. There were some writers I simply didn't trust.

The practice could raise very interesting questions. In 1983 in Baltimore I was writing my story in the press box when I was approached by a radio guy I didn't know. He was filing a report to the CBC network and thought I might like to hear one particular exchange. Cliff Johnson, the Blue Jay designated hitter, had made a flippant but fairly inflammatory remark to this guy, not realiz-ing it would be broadcast in Toronto. Asked if he was looking forward to a change of scenery (the team was leaving for Califor-nia after losing three of four to the Orioles), Johnson said that he looked forward to a bigger change of scenery within the next week, referring to the upcoming trade deadline.

Here was my dilemma. I couldn't get back to Johnson for clari-fication because the team was already on the way to the airport. I was returning to Toronto and my colleague Al Ryan was picking up the team on the coast, but other reporters were on the plane. If Johnson was really asking for a trade, the other papers would get a story *The Star* didn't have, which would get me in trouble. Johnson, a big complainer, was obviously in a foul mood, so something could blow up on the flight.

The source for the quote was not somone I knew, so I wouldn't have gone on his hearsay, but he had the whole thing on tape and I knew Johnson's voice. Just in case, I went with the quote, playing it low-down in the story because it might mean nothing. I explained the situation to my editor and put in a call to Ryan in Anaheim to alert him.

Poor Ryan almost had his head bitten off by Johnson when he asked him about it; two days later, the *Sun's* John Robertson ran a column full of Johnson's denials, scoffing at the unnamed writer who had fabricated this nonsense.

When the team got back from the trip, I confronted Johnson in the dugout before an audience of gleeful players anxious to see the big guy do me in, but they were disappointed. As Johnson started in on his rant – "I don't want to hear any of this hearsay, he-say, she-say . . ." – I explained to Johnson that anyone who listened to CBC had heard his remarks. He backed off that time, but it didn't stop his habitual bitching about the press he received. I guess some guys are just frustrated media critics.

Another was Doyle Alexander. I remember one day in 1983 when I stayed after the scrum to ask Alexander a few more questions, even though I had noticed him glowering at me throughout the session. As I approached him, the pitcher made shooing gestures at me with his hands. When I asked him to elaborate, he muttered that he had nothing to say to me because "I don't like the way you write." I wondered initially if I had offended him by splitting an infinitive or dangling a participle, but on reflection I realized that he was reacting to the fact that I had dared to report his five previous consecutive losses.

Sportswriters must get used to being treated like villains for transmitting bad tidings. If a hitter strands five teammates on base in a one-run ball game, he's going to be the goat of the game whether I report it or not, but the boos the next day always seemed to be my fault. I usually dealt with the bad feelings by pointing out that the alternative would have been to have lied and said the player had actually won the game with a home run but that the readers might have found out the truth from another source. I was fortunate in the team I covered, because Blue Jay intimidation was seldom overt or extreme (a Toronto player has never swung at a sportswriter or stuffed one in a garbage can, as has happened in other cities), but even being glared at constantly can take its toll.

The players who amused me were the ones who claimed they never read the newspapers. If you believe that one, stroll into a team hotel lobby some afternoon. You'll find dozens of papers lying around the lobby with the sports section missing.

In the face of distrust or hostility from players, writers tend to band together, either for commiseration or for mutual assistance. There is nothing like a late-night bitching session in a hotel bar to cheer one up, and an attitude like Alexander's is harmless as long as another writer will share quotes. (It is obviously preferable to straighten out problems with players, but in the short term, colleagues are invaluable, and even competing reporters will help out in the face of blatant antagonism like that.)

Although writers have a bond almost as strong as that among the players, there are definite cliques within the general collectivity. The variety of baseball writers calls out for an Audubon to classify them all, from the pot-bellied stogie-sucker to the press-box grouse, but most fall into one of eight groups.

The Old Guard

These are the men who fit all the old sportswriter stereotypes. The Oscar Madisons of the profession, they chew on cheap cigars and wear clothes that range from marginally unattractive to truly hideous. Some are hacks, some aren't, but they all seem to prefer the good old days. There's no question they know the sport backwards, but they are uncomfortable with baseball today.

My colleague Neil MacCarl was Old Guard. His love of baseball went back to the start of his career when he covered the International League Maple Leafs in the years when the Havana Sugar Kings were still in the league, and he seemed happiest with his cronies from those days. He always had the inside track with people like Sparky Anderson and Dick Williams, whom he had covered as players decades before, but had less rapport with today's players. It made for a nice balance on the beat.

Red Foley and Jack Lang from New York epitomize the Old Guard and run the Baseball Writers' Association of America like a personal fiefdom. The BBWAA has a policy of rotating the chairmanship among chapters annually, but Lang hangs on as secretary-treasurer year after year, with Foley as recording secretary. A short, overweight, pugnacious guy, Lang is guaranteed to take over every meeting from that year's chairman. One of the high points of the sessions is to watch the new guy struggle to keep control.

Two stories exemplify Lang and the BBWAA. In my first two years on the beat, my membership card in the all-important organization read "Mr. Alison Gordon," the title being a permanent part of the card, printed to the left of the space for the member's name. I asked Lang at the end of the 1979 season when the "Mr." was going to come off the card. We were on a fairly boozy World Series writers' charter from Philadelphia to Kansas City at the time, and he gripped both arms of his seat, leaned forward, and spat out one word: "Never." Change is not the favourite occupation of the Old Guard.

At the end of the same charter, some of the sportswriters misbehaved badly, creating a scene about luggage at the airport, and Lang heard about it the next day. One of the miscreants was an Old Guardsman with whom Lang had been feuding for years. "I've got a good mind to give him a higher number next year," he said, pronouncing the ultimate threat.

It is safe to say that no one but an O.G. gave a hoot whether his BBWAA membership number was high or low, but within that fraternity it was a chilling threat indeed. You show 'em, Jack.

Other O.G.s could be counted on to keep the meetings lively, which took some doing: we dealt mostly with really exciting stuff like Hall of Fame voting procedures and World Series accreditation. Some of the O.G.s, like Dick Young from New York and Jerome Holtzman from Chicago, got into screaming matches over policy or procedure every time we met, dignified members of the profession calling each other assholes as the rest of us watched in delight. There were three meetings held annually, at the All-Star Game, World Series, and winter meetings. I could only stand one a year, and usually arrived late, but the Old Guard just can't wait for the next one to roll around.

The reactionary machinations of the BBWAA would just be funny if the organization didn't have so much power. The BBWAA members vote on the Cy Young, Most Valuable Player, and Rookie of the Year awards each season and elect members to the Hall of

Fame. They also control all baseball press boxes. In theory, if not always in practice, the BBWAA could bar anyone without a membership from watching a game in the press box. The hitch is, there are people who make their living covering baseball but who are not eligible for membership in the association, which is only for newspaper journalists. Consequently, the likes of Ron Fimrite, Jim Kaplan, and Steve Wulf from *Sports Illustrated*, who write only baseball from March to October, can't become members, and the Old Guard refuses to expand.

One footnote: "Mr." was deleted from the membership card after a vote at the 1980 winter meetings, but my membership category remained "men whose principal duty is to cover major league baseball on a daily basis" until I left the beat.

The Young Turks

These writers are a refreshingly iconoclastic breed, the New Journalists of the Toy Department, as the sports section is called by scornful news-side types. Peter Gammons of the *Boston Globe* is the unchallenged leader of the pack, overseeing his territory with a lot of help from Ma Bell. Gammons is the only person I knew who can put you on hold on his home phone to take another call and is paged a dozen times a night in every press box he visits.

A greying blond with a slightly rabbity face, Gammons would not look out of place as a master in a good private school. He wears preppy sweaters and tweeds with his blue jeans and has a slight stoop and a perpetually interested expression on his face. He is extremely hard-working and has the best contacts in baseball among writers, executives, and scouts.

He also floats some of the most outrageous rumours going, a by-product of a basic gullibility that general managers aren't loath to exploit to their own ends. A rumour printed in Gammons' voluminous Sunday *Globe* column or his weekly "AL Beat" in *The Sporting News* is a very effective trial balloon. It also makes the columns a great read.

Gammons hooks up with writers all around both leagues in a network that includes Galloway in Texas, Terry Pluto in Cleveland, Peter Pascarelli in Philadelphia, Murray Chass in New York, Kit Stier in Oakland, and Tracy Ringolsby, wherever he is. (Ringolsby moved from covering the Angels to the Mariners to the Royals in the five years I knew him.) Gammons didn't need a Toronto media connection, not when he had Pat Gillick and Bobby Cox. Through his sources, he had the most comprehensive information possible to get.

Tom Boswell is the other outstanding Young Turk, but he lacks the basic jockishness that binds the rest of them together. I have a memory of Boswell leaving Memorial Stadium in Baltimore one chilly spring night that sums him up perfectly. He was wearing an old man's raincoat, the kind of trench coat that buttons right up to the chin, and an Andy Capp flat tweed cap. His binoculars were hung on a strap crossing his chest one way, a small bag on a strap crossing it the other, with his computer in one hand and an old-fashioned briefcase in the other. He looked like a grown-up version of the nerd in high school that got good grades and knew every batting average in baseball, not the kid that was head jock of the block. He also writes rings around almost everyone else in the profession. He is national baseball writer for the *Washington Post* and is a bit of a loner, travelling all over both leagues, although his home team is the Baltimore Orioles.

Boswell is a real character. He can't keep quiet for more than two minutes in the press box and he has more twitches than a horse's tail in fly season, but he is a pleasure to be around because of his passionate love for the game. Boswell is known for his Total Average, the first well-known challenge to baseball's traditional measurements, and has one foot in the camp of Bill James and the Sabremetricians; but he isn't totally obsessed with numbers. He takes as much delight in the form of baseball as in its content.

The Young Turks differ from the Old Guard in their basic approach to the game and to writing about it. O.G.s report the facts, the whats and whens of baseball. Y.T.s are interested in the whos, whys, and hows. Y.T.s are as well versed in the baffling complexities of reserve clauses and free agent compensations as in the infield fly rule. O.G.s figure if it didn't apply in the Babe's day, why bother with it. There were members of both groups who were able to cross over, and others who fell between the two camps, but they generally left each other pretty much alone. The younger ones think the older ones are past it. The older ones wonder why the new guys take everything so seriously.

Just One of the Guys

The writers with whom I had the most difficulty were those men who identify so strongly with the team that they forget that there is a line drawn between players and the press. These are the ones who chew tobacco, shag fly balls, play cards with the players, and call them all "Champ." These types are looking for the inside track, but they have a hard time criticizing their good buddies when they deserve it because they want desperately to be liked. They don't get a lot of respect from their writing peers. A writer's loyalty has to be to his newspaper and readers, not to some jock who calls him "good buddy" and gives him a nickname all his own. This is a principle that "just one of the guys" seems able to ignore.

This type exists all around the league, but the one with whom I was most in contact was Kevin Boland of the *Globe and Mail*, also known as "Baretta." He joined the beat in 1983, a big macho guy with greying hair, and soon the press box was filled not only with cigar smoke, but with the sight of Boland spitting tobacco into a plastic cup. He spent more time in the clubhouse than the bat boy, playing cards and shooting the breeze with the rest of the team. He would have watched the games from the dugout if they'd let him, and he treated the other sportswriters with a player's disdain.

Boland was probably better liked by the players than the rest of us, but I'm not sure what advantage that gave him or the readers of the *Globe*. The "inside stuff" he got was pretty trivial. (A writer for another section of his paper once complained that it was hard to understand why, whenever a Blue Jay put shaving cream in someone else's shoe, it became the lead story in the sports section.) And I can't remember a critical word he ever wrote.

There are writers who go to the other extreme, the "I-can't-stand-the-bastards" writers who remain completely aloof from the players, the better to criticize them, but they lose out because they have no sources in the clubhouse. They seldom break a story of their own.

Most of us walk the line somewhere in between, developing

friendships and contacts within the team, but reporting accurately no matter who must take the heat. I think that we earn more respect from players, peers, and the public.

Gentlemen of the Press

Standing out from the mob are the class acts, the columnists who have been covering sports since Man O' War was a colt, and the magazine writers, who have time to put things in perspective. They wear trench coats and view things with a quiet detachment and seem immune to the rough fuss and hullabaloo around them. They've seen it all before.

Milt Dunnell of *The Star* and Trent Frayne of the *Globe and Mail* are two Toronto gentlemen. Dunnell is tall, elegant, thoughtful, and perpetually tanned. In the office he lurks at his desk waiting to entrap passersby in one of his endless series of sporting wagers. He has even been known to catch *The Star*'s austere publisher, Beland Honderich, in his web from time to time. On the road, Dunnell goes his own way. It was always difficult to cover the same event because I was never sure his column wasn't covering the same angle as my story and I couldn't always find him to check what he was writing.

Frayne is a sheer joy, a small, mischievous man with wonderful wit, who refuses to take anything, including himself, seriously. He is also a wonderful writer, with none of the pomposity of others in his journalistic generation. He calls me Alistair, which for some reason always makes me smile.

Red Smith of the *New York Times* posed for the mould out of which all the other gentlemen were formed. I'll never forget the first time I met him, nor will I stop being embarrassed by it. It was on a press bus on a ride from the airport to the hotel in Kansas City after one of those hellish BBWAA World Series charters. It was close to dawn, we were all tired and half drunk, and I was staring out the window when an elderly man sat down next to me. The World Series brought out a lot of people from small papers and I assumed this was a sports editor from the sticks. I graciously decided that I would be nice to him. He looked sort of lost. We chatted all through the ride, me babbling on in an attempt to make him comfortable. We didn't introduce ourselves until the ride was over, and when we did I wanted to crawl under the bus. I had just spent forty-five minutes in conversation with one of the finest living sportswriters and had never shut up. Smith, bless his heart, didn't seem to mind.

My personal hero among the gentlemen is Roger Angell of *The New Yorker* magazine, baseball's most elegant chronicler. I had such a literary crush on him before I ever met him that I was almost afraid to meet him. I didn't want him to turn out to be a jerk, which would spoil my enjoyment of his work. That had happened to me before.

I needn't have worried. Angell is as gently courtly in person as he is in print. He is also one of the few people I've met who looks exactly as he should. A tallish man, he wears professional horn-rims and tweed jackets and is balding, with salt in the pepper of his moustache. He has the light of humour in his eyes.

He always looked slightly ill-at-ease in the crowded World Series clubhouses, as if he would prefer to be in the stands. His class shone out among the squalor; it was like finding Katherine Hepburn in a mud-wrestling emporium. My lasting image of him finds him standing on the fringe of one of the pushing mobs, an expression of faint bemusement on his face, straining to hear the ballplayer at the centre, writing it all down in his notebook, then wandering off to the fringe of another crowd.

The best remark I ever heard about Angell was from B.J. Phillips, former sports editor for *Time*. Late one night during the 1979 World Series, she turned to Angell and said, with feigned belligerence, "Every time I read something you've written I want to cut off my hands so they will never touch a keyboard again!"

The Talking Dogs

I can't take credit for this description, which is pure Galloway. In Texas parlance, a talking dog is a television sports reporter. To say that print reporters don't think much of the blow-dried pretty boys that decorate your home screen would be to understate drastically. These guys tend to report superficially and steal all their insights and analysis from the newspapers, and they wouldn't know a scoop if it came up and bit them on the knee. On top of that, they make more money than we do.

Of course, they are not all the same. Toronto has some who don't take themselves too seriously and aren't arrogant and rude. But an amazing number of them, especially in the States, would make Ted Baxter look like Henry Kissinger in brainpower and make Henry Kissinger look like Mother Theresa in humility.

There is no question in their minds that they are the most important people in the media. They walk into the middle of an interview and demand that the player or manager come to the camera immediately. "Just for thirty seconds, guys," they say to the writers, flashing all thirty-seven teeth. After fifteen hurry-up-and-wait minutes the player or manager is so fed up he decides that he doesn't feel like talking to the rest of us anymore.

A rare moment, sweet enough to savour, came during the 1983 World Series, when half a dozen of us were sitting in the dugout talking with Oriole manager Joe Altobelli. There was a television reporter standing on the field, microphone at the ready, hair freshly combed. He sent a nervous flunky over to get Altobelli to go live to air. Live to air! Big deal.

The flunky came over, barely waited for Altobelli to finish a sentence, and asked him to do the interview. Altobelli looked at him slowly, then asked, "You mean you want me to disappoint, let's see, one, two, three . . . six people to go and talk to your camera? I think I will finish the discussion we're having here, thank you." I could have kissed him.

He is rare, though. Most players, who grew up in the television generation, consider television to be far more important than newspapers and believe it gives them some sort of legitimacy if people can watch them at the neighbourhood saloon. They realize, too, that it is difficult to be misquoted in a thirty-second clip and love the fact that the talking dogs will never ask them a challenging question. The more experienced players know exactly how to manipulate the medium. Watch Reggie Jackson with Howard Cosell if you think I'm wrong.

The television play-by-play men are exempt from the blanket criticism. They tend to be people hired for their knowledge of baseball rather than for how good they look in a blazer.

I always enjoyed it when we were joined by the Blue Jay television crew. Don Chevrier is a very pleasant man, and Tony Kubek always brought along the juiciest rumours in town. He would pass them along, glancing over his shoulder to make sure he wasn't being overheard, and warn me not to tell where I had got the tip. Then he would go on the air and spill the beans himself. Some tip!

One of my funniest encounters with the media was with Cosell. Very early one morning, after a very late New York night, the phone rang. After a drop-the-phone-and-put-the-mouthpiece-to-my-ear comedy turn, I agreed with the caller that I was indeed Alison Gordon.

Then the man at the other end identified himself. "*This is Howard Cosell of ABC Spohts,*" he said.

Yeah, sure. It was a passable imitation, but I wasn't in the mood for practical jokes. He explained that he was doing a feature on women sportswriters and wanted to interview me. I'm a very gullible person, and I hate it. I said that I would check with one of the other participants, who was a friend of mine, and if it was really going on I'd be glad to be part of the show. "Let's face it," I said. "Cosell is the most imitated man in North America, and I want to make sure this isn't a bad joke."

Cosell would have no part of it and told me to call him back at ABC so he could confirm that he was "the authentic *Howard Cosell of ABC Spohts.*"

Not me. I wasn't going to fall for that one. You've got to get up even earlier than that to catch old A.G. I decided I would sleep on it and call my friend at her office when I woke up. I had just drifted off again when a slightly hysterical ABC assistant called to ask why I hadn't called Howard back.

The funniest thing about this whole episode for me was that Cosell didn't seem to find it funny at all. When I showed up for the interview, he was decidedly chilly. I thought it was a hoot, myself. That's what he gets for doing such a bad imitation of himself.

The Microclones

Radio play-by-play men, who are cheerleaders (one Blue Jay used to call Tom Cheek "the tallest groupie in the American League"), are all right to get along with and know their stuff, but the radio reporters are even worse than their television equivalents because there are more of them around. They invariably ask dumb questions, when they bother to ask any questions at all. Often they just walk up to an interview in progress and stick their microphone into the middle of it.

Nothing is more annoying than trying to develop an original story angle or being in the middle of an exclusive story when one of these jerks sidles up and records it. So much for your scoop if it's going to be on the sports in a fifteen-second clip an hour after the game.

Radio reporters are also a press-box nuisance. Right after a game, when writers appreciate some quiet for writing a story, the radio guys are either fast-forwarding their cassettes at a high-pitched gabble or filing game stories at full volume over the telephone. ("In three . . . two . . . one . . . The Toronto Blue Jays had their hopes for a pennant dashed tonight at Exhibition Stadium when Dave Stieb fell down delivering a pitch and injured his ego. It is not known how long he will be on the disabled list . . .") Groan.

They are also pushy and insensitive. I remember a game in Kansas City in 1983 when one of them came into Bobby Cox's office after a tough loss. The final score was 7-1, but the real damage had been done in the five-run fifth inning, and Cox was furious. Jim Acker had come in with the bases loaded and walked the first man he faced, gave up a single to the second, and walked the third to score three more runs. Then Mike Morgan relieved him and got out of the inning.

Cox was never a good-humoured person after a loss, and he really got mad after a game like that one. The signs were all over the place. If you didn't notice that his uniform was strewn all over the room in a rage, you couldn't miss the expression of anger on his face. We were all treading very softly in our questions.

In came Mr. Radio, bustling and important. He stuck his microphone two inches from Cox's nose and said, "Of course, hindsight is twenty-twenty, Bobby, but do you wish you had brought in Morgan instead of Acker in the fifth?" As Blue Jay writers shifted away, ready to dive for cover, Cox stared at the man as if considering which form of murder was most appropriate. He finally managed a civil, if noncommital reply.

"Thanks, Bobby," chirped Mr. Radio, and bustled back out of the room. He hadn't even noticed.

My very favourite of this breed was in a large World Series scrum after the Kansas City Royals had tied the 1980 Series with the Phillies at two games apiece. Willie Aikens had hit two home runs for the second time in the series and was standing in a crowd of about twenty-five reporters, talking slowly. Aikens had been a big hero, and most of us had already written about him before. Now we needed a new angle. Very gently and politely, someone asked Aikens about his speech impediment, which was quite severe at the time.

He talked about it frankly, telling of being "afraid and ashamed" when he was a kid, of how everybody had made fun of him, and about how he had worked to overcome his fear. It was good stuff. Aikens had earned our respect by the dignity with which he had behaved all series. While the Phillies had refused to show up for some interviews, Aikens, whose painful stammer gave him an understandable excuse to hide, never had. He stood with all the cameras of all the world on him and stumbled through his replies.

It was as moving a moment as it could be in the crowded push and shove, and we all strained to hear him. Suddenly a voice from the back of the pack cut in: "Can we get off the stuttering," snapped the radio man. "We've been on it for seven minutes already."

The Number Crunchers

There is a new breed growing in the sportswriting profession like fungus on a tree stump. These are the spiritual progeny of Bill James, the statistics guru from Lawrence, Kansas, and they would quantify all the joy out of baseball if they could. They are "sabre-metricians," a remarkably pompous name for a group of loonies, derived from the acronym for the Society for American Baseball Research. They just love numbers and aren't satisfied with the already existing multitude of quantifiers of the sport.

James is the author of the annual *Baseball Abstract*. When I first encountered the publication in This Ain't the Rosedale Library, a small Toronto bookstore that specializes in rock and roll, obscure poetry, and baseball, the *Abstract* was a mimeographed hodgepodge, obviously typed on an ancient machine that could use a good cleaning. It had all the design qualities of the *Barney Park Reporter*, the first paper I worked on (as publisher, managing editor, reporter, literary critic, and distribution manager) when I was ten. It was splendid opinion in the guise of statistical analysis, a quaint and contentious ranking of all the teams and players in the big leagues based on James's own formulas.

Here you could find things like "the Victory-Related RBI," the "Power/Speed Ratio" or "Bobby Bonds Effect," "Runs-Produced

Averages," and "Production/Age" ratio. It was a wonderful and eccentric publication, easy to get lost in if you had flunked trigonometry. It was the work of a man fascinated by baseball and by numbers, an Arthurian quest to define the undefinable.

In 1979, the *Abstract* was sold mainly by mail order, and James sold fewer than a thousand copies a year. By 1983, in its seventh year of publication, the *Abstract* had gone glossy, published by Ballantine Books and sold in every bookstore. And that's the problem. Sabremetricians are everywhere now. I have one correspondent from California named Joseph M. Wayman. Every year he analyses each player in terms of unearned runs scored as a result of errors he made and numbers of games lost as a result of those errors. Now he's trying to develop a new formula to rank relief pitchers.

My friend Bryan Johnson is similarly afflicted (and to think we bought the first *Abstract* together!) and writes a weekly column in the *Globe and Mail* in which he proves repeatedly that the Blue Jays are overrated. He even had a mention in the 1983 *Abstract*, a theorem named after him by James that demonstrated why the Blue Jays should win fewer games in 1983 than 1982. The mention was nirvana for a sabremetrician, perhaps, but the theorem had to go back to the drawing board.

And that's the problem. Individually, working away in their little warrens, communicating only with each other, the number crunchers are a harmless and amusing group of folk. Once they enter the mainstream, once people start taking them seriously, they become a danger to the sport, because it means that there is a growing belief that baseball should make statistical sense.

But it shouldn't. Once it starts making sense, we might as well punch batting and earned run averages into a computer every April and give out the World Series trophy on opening-day afternoon.

Thank goodness it is only the laymen who have followed the sabremetric piper. When ballplayers borrowed my copy of the *Abstract*, the inevitable response was, "That guy's full of shit." Could you imagine what would happen to the sport if players began believing in the percentages? Can you imagine baseball with no surprises?

Let the number crunchers play with their computers. I'd rather go to a ball game.

Women on the Beat

Tolerated by the Young Turks and ostracized by the Old Guard, the handful of women baseball writers exchanged chauvinist alerts, warning each other about players and managers who had it in for women, but sisterhood was not an overriding impulse. I was always glad to see other women sportswriters. Women in other male-dominated professions could understand some of the problems we had and male sportswriters could understand other sportswriters, but only another woman sportswriter understood it all.

The one I was most comfortable with was Claire Smith, who began covering the New York Yankees for the *Hartford Courant* in 1982. She had a refreshingly matter-of-fact approach that I liked and a warm sense of humour. Claire, who was black, was a double token but refused to let it intimidate her. Jane Gross, on the other hand, was a tiny, nervous person who seemed intimidated all the time – by the players, by deadlines, and by the awesome significance of working for the *New York Times*. She was a nice writer, but she never relaxed. Other women occasionally dropped in and out of baseball beats, but the field hasn't opened up. I think, though, that each of us proved in different ways that a woman can do the job and do it well, and that opening the clubhouse doors didn't lead to the end of the world or of baseball as we know it.

Women aren't rare in sports departments any more, but they are too often used to cover "soft" sports: tennis, figure skating, amateur sports. The next step is to get them onto traditional men's beats, covering the gritty professional sports, if they show the talent and desire.

One of the nicest letters I ever got came from a young teen-ager in a small Ontario town. She told me that she wanted to become a sportswriter but everybody laughed at her. She thanked me for being there so she knew she wasn't crazy and that her ambition wasn't impossible. I was her counter to the naysayers who told her that sportswriting was no job for a woman.

I was very moved by her letter and answered it with some encouragement. Six months later she wrote to tell me that she was writing a school column for a local paper and that the basketball coach had asked her to write about his junior boys' team. Most of her relatives still thought that it was no job for a woman and that it would destroy her reputation, but her mother had been won over. Even if five years on the beat hadn't been fun and rewarding, that letter would have gone a long way to making it worthwhile.

And maybe I've changed a few minds in baseball, too, convincing some sheltered players that feminists are not the ogres they thought, and some hidebound sporstwriters that new blood might actually be good for the profession.

Chapter

7

Token Broad

Madam — I see where you don't seem to mind male nudity in athletes shower rooms at sports arenas. Well, neither would any whore.

There is too much of this atmosphere in society today. It is not conducive to anything of higher motive or conduct, respect or constructive thought, to say the least for any level of humanity.

(signed)
Male Senior

This letter, which I received in response to an article I wrote after my first season, hangs framed in my bathroom, below a photograph taken in the clubhouse by a *Star* photographer. The photo shows me in mid-interview, oblivious to the fact that behind me Rick Cerone is cavorting madly in the nude. It's a very funny photograph. So is the letter, now.

I didn't start the job with any stirring sense of historic destiny. I was no brave pioneer on feminism's cutting edge. I was just another scared rookie on the way to my first spring training, playing a new game at which I would have to make up the rules. I wasn't only new to baseball, I was new to newspapers, and there were more than several people waiting for me to fall on my face.

The battle of the clubhouse had already been fought and won the year before I started the job. Time, Inc. had sued baseball Commissioner Bowie Kuhn for refusing to allow Melissa Ludtke, then a reporter for *Sports Illustrated*, into the dressing rooms at

Yankee Stadium during the 1977 World Series. Time claimed that her exclusion had been based on her sex, in violation of the Fourteenth Amendment of the United States Constitution. Kuhn, defending the integrity of baseball, argued that "to permit members of the opposite sex into this place of privacy, where players who are, of course, men, are in a state of undress, would be to undermine the basic dignity of the game."

The female federal district judge who heard the case was not moved by the Commissioner's eloquence. Judge Constance Baker Motley quite reasonably suggested that privacy problems could be taken care of by the players involved and ordered the doors open as of September 26, 1978.

The day may have been semi-historic, but it was also a mess. Coincidentally, the Blue Jays were playing at Yankee Stadium when the barrier crashed down, and the reporters who were there remember the scene as a zoo, with the Yankees doing everything they could to embarrass the women. Sparky Lyle brought in a phallus-shaped cake with pink frosting and posted a sign next to it: "for women sportswriters only." The Blue Jays, mainly younger players, were simply embarrassed.

Technically, the judgement applied only to Yankee Stadium, and the Commissioner tried unsuccessfully to appeal it, arguing that women in the locker room would threaten baseball as a family sport. Judge Walter Mansfield of the Second Circuit Court of Appeals didn't buy that line of reasoning, commenting drily that "The last I heard, the family includes women as well as men."

Just before the 1979 season began, Kuhn realized he was licked, dropped his appeal, and issued a carefully worded memorandum to all twenty-six major league clubs suggesting that they do all they could to "minimize problems in this area" and "to afford identical access, in one way or another, to all reporters regardless of sex."

The Blue Jay response was commendable. Once they realized that they were going to have a real, live, full-time beat woman knocking on their door, they made sure that I would have no problems with their organization. They even gave their players a lecture during the annual spring training public relations briefing on the way they would be expected to treat me. I should be accorded the respect, the players were told, that they would like their wives or sisters to have in the same circumstances.

I knew all of this as I sat in my hotel room in Dunedin, Florida, on the eve of my first day on the job, full of doubts and an apprehension bordering on terror. All the friends who had wished me well and buoyed my confidence were back in Toronto. It was now just me, and the interesting legal precedents weren't much help when I was about to go out and do it. It felt like I was on the front lines, and I wasn't sure if I was a foreign correspondent or a soldier in one of the armies.

Unable to handle the dining room in my state of panic, I ordered room service and turned on the television. I tuned in Lou Grant – I had to learn how to be a newspaper reporter somehow, didn't I? – and there he was, that vastly reassuring fictional editor, slightly off-hue on the cheap set, railing at a woman sports editor about locker rooms.

Oh, Lord. Even Lou Grant was against me. What had I got myself into this time? I wanted to go home.

By the next day I had my game face back on, albeit precariously. When the taxi stopped in front of the training complex, I had to speak sternly to my feet to force them to get out and walk through the gate.

The players were all in centrefield getting the team picture taken while the reporters hung behind the photographers kibitzing, but I couldn't cross the seventy-five yards or so to join them, I felt so conspicuous. When the session was over and the players picked up their gloves and jogged off the field, I found it wasn't so. I was not conspicuous. I was invisible. Even the players I had interviewed the season before pounded past me, part of the herd, with no sign of recognition. There were glances, oh yes, out of the corner of every eye, all day long. Every one there was aware that the dreaded woman had arrived, but nobody stopped to say howdy.

Even the sportswriters ignored me those first few days, something I would become less surprised about the more I learned about that particular breed of gentleman. Alan Abel of the *Globe and Mail* came to offer a condescending "welcome to the big leagues," and for that I was pathetically grateful.

Mike Cannon, the iconoclastic travelling secretary who held neither the sport nor its practitioners in the awe usual among his kind (he called the players "mutts" and complained constantly about their demands), took me under his wing. I think it amused him to aid and abet the enemy. One day he equated me to Jackie Robinson, rather a grand comparison, for my role in the latest revolution. The next, he presented me with a T-shirt, reading "token broad beat writer." The jersey was, of course, pink.

Cannon helped, and so did several of the players, then and throughout the long first season. One was John Mayberry, the team's first baseman and leader, particularly among the black players. He was a big man, menacing to opposing pitchers when he scowled out toward the mound, but off the field he was a sweetheart with a twinkle in his eye.

Mayberry is a man of great kindness and is generous with his experience and talent, as the younger players could testify. He isn't an intellectual, but he is a teacher of baseball. Mayberry didn't hesitate to accept me and make his acceptance obvious. He had a smile for me daily, and I can still hear his rumbling baritone – "Here she comes, *sweet* Alison Gordon. How are you today?" He made it clear from the first that I was fine with him, just another writer, and made it easier for the others to accept me, too. Mayberry was a good man to have on my side.

The other was Tim Johnson, a journeyman utility infielder who was a bit of an outlaw. Older than the rest, just putting in his last major league season, he was a hard-nosed jock who raced motorcycles in New Mexico during the off-season, but he was also an acute observer. A real character around the dugout, he was the subject of the first feature article I wrote on the beat.

"You don't have to be worried about the clubhouse," he told me during a lull in the interview. "I don't want to tell you how to do your job, but if you could avoid coming in until after the roster has been cut down to twenty-five, it might be better. There are a lot of rookies in there who have enough to worry about just trying to make the team."

Johnson was like that all season. Sometimes it would be oblique criticism that would be helpful if I had the ears to hear it. Other times he was my pipeline into both the Blue Jays and the world of men who saw things differently from any man I'd ever known. If I was the foreign correspondent, he was my interpreter, my double agent behind enemy lines.

I also met less savoury types that spring, one in particular whom I never will forget. His name is irrelevant, since only his mother remembers him, but he confirmed my most lurid fears about the new life I had chosen. He was a washed-up pitcher who had never amounted to much, but he still yearned for a comeback. After playing for a while in Japan, he had come to the Jay camp for one last tryout. He was my age, an elderly thirty-six at the time, and when I met him I kidded him that the eyes of the old folks were on him, that he had to do well for all of us.

I thought nothing more of it until a couple of nights later, when I ran into him in the hotel restaurant. He'd had a few. He signalled me over to the table and told me, with the earnestness that comes from the bottle, that he had an offer for me too splendid to pass up. It seems, as he told it, and I was never able (or, perhaps, willing) to confirm the story, that the guys had taken to calling him grandpa and had taken up a collection for him. All he had to do to get $500 was to take me to bed in front of witnesses.

He offered me $200. Without discussing the insult of the implication that he deserved the bigger share, I politely declined. He couldn't believe it, and in a stage whisper clearly audible for several tables, he asked, with disbelief, for clarification.

"Do you mean y'all wouldn't even let me eat your pussy in front of witnesses for $200?" he said.

He was cut from the team within the week, either for lack of talent or lack of manners, but not before I compounded the problem with a stunningly stupid move of my own.

I'm not too bright early in the day. The morning after the encounter in the restaurant, I wasn't thinking and made the mistake of pulling back the curtains to check the weather. I wasn't clothed, and at the precise moment I appeared at the window, the pitcher and two coaches, who were walking through the parking lot four storeys below, turned and looked directly at me.

The pitcher had no less restraint that day at the ballpark than he had had the night before in the restaurant, and everyone had already heard the story, with embellishments, I'm sure, by the time I arrived. It speaks well for the rest that they let me forget it.

It wasn't only players I had run-ins with. Some male reporters did their best to make me feel uncomfortable, too. Early Wynn, the redneck Hall of Fame pitcher, was one of the Blue Jay broadcasters at the time. He joked that he saw no reason why I couldn't be a sportswriter. "All she's got to do is learn how to do two things," he said. "Stand up at the bar and buy a round of drinks and stand up at a urinal and piss."

Then there was Clem Kealey of the *Toronto Sun*, who eventually became a good friend and delightful press-box companion. He and I got into a wrangle one night. Kealey's theory was that I wouldn't last a season, and he spent an evening trying to convince me that he was right, in an increasingly hostile manner. He wanted to bet $100 on it. I agreed. Then he upped the bet: $200 said I wouldn't cover eighty-one games, half the number played. I refused that bet, since the way the beat was split was my editor's doing, not mine. Finally, the bet was raised to $1000 that I would have a nervous breakdown before the season was over. I was ready to go for it, but he backed out of the deal. I lasted longer than he did on the beat.

Once the roster was cut and the season started, I finally had to deal with the big problem, the only problem in most people's eyes, the locker room. I had followed Johnson's good advice and stayed out in Dunedin. It seemed to me wiser to spend my time and energies learning my way around the team and how to cover them, and the relaxed atmosphere of afternoon games free of deadline pressure made it possible.

By the time I covered my first regular season game, the jokes and hostility were mainly out of the way, at least with the Jays. They were glad I had held back, had come to respect me as a person doing a job, and the threat inherent in the circumstance had diminished.

That didn't make the first time any easier. They knew I was coming in, I knew I was coming in, most of us wanted to make the situation as natural as possible, but no one had told any of us the rules. The Blue Jays beat the Royals in their home opener, and I headed downstairs. I swept into the clubhouse like it was my living room, looking definitely cool. At least until I had to ask somebody where the dressing room was. Shown the proper door, I sashayed calmly in and looked for Rick Cerone's locker. The catcher was to be my first victim. Cerone was a kind person, and he stood there, mainly clothed, and answered my questions patiently. There wasn't any heckling to speak of. I began to relax.

In the middle of the interview I sensed, rather than saw, a great pink mass move to the locker next to Cerone's. It was Roy Howell, fresh from the shower without a towel, putting me through my trial by flesh. He took longer to get dressed than any person I have encountered, before or since. He patted on aftershave, blew his hair dry, stood around waiting for me to react.

Damned if I would, I kept asking Cerone questions long after I had enough for my story. We discussed the fine points of the game, inning by inning, while I kept my eyes on my pad and pencil, taking notes.

Howell finally put on his jeans. I thanked Cerone, turned and nodded coolly to Howell, and went back to the press box. When I got there, I couldn't read a word I'd written in the last ten minutes, but I knew I had passed some kind of test.

After that, with most of the Blue Jays, everything became routine. Some players stayed in their uniforms until after I had left the room, others wrapped themselves in towels, and they all realized that if I was talking to a player in the other part of the clubhouse I was unlikely to whirl around with an "aha!" to catch them in the act of dropping their gotchies.

Call it a truce.

With other teams things weren't quite that smooth, especially the first time around the league. Until they encountered me, most players' experience with women writers had been during the first week of the season, when editors looking for sensation had sent women down to report on the opening of the locker room doors. I had tremendous sympathy for these women, thrust into a room with a bunch of half-naked strangers to ask them how they felt about it all; but they, or their editors, did a great disservice to women on the beat. The reporters, mainly assigned by the news desk, knew little about baseball and were as uncomfortable as most sportswriters would be at a cabinet briefing. All they did was confirm the athletes' prejudices. Women reporters? What did they know?

My first road trip was at the end of April, to Arlington, Texas, the Dallas suburb that is home to the Rangers. That's where the trouble began.

When Commissioner Kuhn was trying to force an appeal, Judge Motley gave him a clarifying order: teams could bar *all* reporters, male and female, for a period long enough for the players to dress, or they could bar them from the locker room altogether if a separate interview room was provided. That was just the kind of loophole some teams were looking for.

The Rangers had returned home from New York, where there had been considerable interest in Sparky Lyle (he of the pink phallus cake), who had been traded to the Rangers between seasons. He had just published *The Bronx Zoo*, his exposé of Yankee life, and the reporters in New York were anxious to talk to him, including Jane Gross, then of *Newsday*, and Kathy Andrea from *Sports Illustrated*. When the women tried to go into the clubhouse there, the Rangers claimed that they had decided in spring training to close the clubhouse to all reporters after games. Then they had waived that decision for the first eleven games of the season, invoking it only when a woman appeared.

The Rangers had set out to make the male sportswriters blame women for their barring. Now that they were on their way home to face the Blue Jays and me, I was sure that the tactic would work with the rednecks who undoubtedly covered the Texas team. I knew I was in for a rough three days.

That was before I discovered that prejudice works both sides of the street. When I got to the ballpark I met the gentlemen of the Dallas-Forth Worth press, in the persons of Randy Galloway of the *Dallas Morning News*, Jim Reeves of the *Fort Worth Star-Telegram*, and Paul Hagen of the *Dallas Times-Herald*. Galloway epitomized all that I feared. Tall and thin, wearing blue jeans and boots, drawling his words out of one side of his mouth, spitting tobacco out of the other, this man was no feminist. He was, however, as were his colleagues, a believer in freedom, and that was how they saw the issue. Although they saw it as an "us against them" battle, I was part of the "us" and the Rangers were very definitely "them." They assured me that I had as much right to be there as they did.

After the game, which the Rangers won, we all headed down the tunnel under the stands to the Ranger clubhouse. The door opened and Jon Matlack, the team player representative, stuck his head out and said the clubhouse was closed. After a brief shouting match, he offered to bring out any player we wanted.

"The hell with 'em. Let's go write," roared one of the surly scribes, and we all stomped back up the tunnel. There have been more eloquent rallying cries in the history of humankind, but none ever sang so sweetly in my ears.

And write they did. Columnists editorialized unmercifully –

"Heaven forbid that the Rangers should recognize that this is the twentieth century," said Reeves. Even the game stories took a mocking and sarcastic tone, calling them the "bashful Rangers." They reported all games from the visiting team's point of view because the Blue Jay clubhouse "is open to any accredited member of the media. That's male, female, black, white or any color. And that's the way it should be."

For my part, I was so distracted by the confusion and by the logistic complications of filing to deadline from another time zone on a telecopier I couldn't work, I got the score wrong in my first night's game story. When I was curtly informed of this by my editor the next day, I was humbly apologetic. I hoped that I might be forgiven, or preferably forgotten, but that night I got a call at midnight from the overnight desk.

"You know you got the score wrong in last night's story, don't you . . ." growled Dave Perkins from Toronto.

"Yes, I'm sorry, it will never happen again," I interrupted.

". . . well, that was no reason to leave it out entirely, which is what you did tonight."

The Rangers' behaviour became a big story that week, and my confusion was increased by being interviewed myself by every two-bit paper and television station in the Dallas-Forth Worth area. To my great amusement, I was even phoned and interviewed by Barbara Frum for the CBC radio program *As It Happens*. Eight months earlier, I had been lining up off-beat stories for the show. Now I had become one. The players began to complain, only half in jest, that I was getting more ink than they were.

Eddie Robinson, then Ranger general manager, called the local writers in on the third day of the controversy to clear the air, but the meeting descended into a desk-thumping argument. During the first inning of that night's game, the last of the series, I was summoned into Robinson's office. There I found the man joined by his old friend, Blue Jay vice-president Pat Gillick. In fact, Robinson had given Gillick his first baseball job when his playing career ended, as assistant general manager in Houston. Now Gillick had flown in to help his buddy talk some sense into me.

Robinson, summoning as much charm as he could muster, told me he understood and sympathized with my plight and would open the clubhouse if I, as a personal favour to him and to Gillick, would promise to stay out. Seeing as how I didn't have any particular feelings of kinship with either of the two, I pointed out that I was unfortunately in a competitive situation with two other Toronto writers on the trip and would be unable to do them that little favour.

The Rangers won that game in extra innings, and the Texas writers pulled out their trump card. They suggested that we stay in the press box and see what happened next. Soon there was the startling sound of baseball spikes clicking down the corridor. Ferguson Jenkins, the starting pitcher, and Al Oliver, who had scored the winning run, sauntered in, sat down, and held a press conference of their own. The Rangers' last stand was over. The next time I saw them, in Toronto, the clubhouse was open.

I guess there is nothing strange about the locker room being a contentious issue, but I got awfully tired, that first season when it was still "news," of answering questions about it. No one wanted to talk about what the job was like, what the real challenges were. They didn't want to talk baseball. All they wanted to know was whether I saw lots of naked men.

It was actually fun, each time I was "discovered" by another radio station or columnist, to watch the discomfort as the interviewer tried to get me to talk about naked men without asking the question right out.

"Tell us about the problems you have on the job," they would suggest. I would talk about deadlines.

"Aren't there some unique problems you have *as a woman* doing this job?" would be the next try.

I would talk about the attitudes of male sportswriters, or the advantages I had as a woman. If they weren't going to ask the question, I sure wasn't going to give them the answer. I suffered from a sense of humour inappropriate to my station, and there were times I longed to lean forward and say, "Gee, Harry, I guess you could say that my favourite thing about this job is all the naked men I get to ogle. I just can't get enough." I never had the nerve.

When a man of macho bent would find out what I did for a living, I could count on two things. First he would make a joke about wanting to go into Chris Evert Lloyd's locker room; then he would want the most graphic anatomical details I was willing to give him. I was actually asked, more than once, by relatively sophisticated and intelligent men, whether black men really had bigger penises than white men. I was never asked the same question by women, and my friends are not bashful or reticent about sex; but a small boy of my acquaintance did once ask me, when his father told him I had seen players without their clothes on, whether Cliff Johnson had a big belly button.

Yes, women reporters go into locker rooms. Yes, if the players are out to embarrass us, they make sure they're naked when we get there. Yes, there are those who express their hostility toward the press and toward women by behaving in a particularly gross fashion. With some teams, like the Detroit Tigers, there was always a lot of foul language and gratuitous farting and belching when I was around; but it was always background noise, the adolescent show that happens when immature men get together.

And I have to credit one Tiger, who had the imagination to find a new name for women sportswriters. I walked in one day to a shout of, "Watch out, here comes the pecker checker!" (It was a lot nicer than their usual greeting, which was "Meat!") I tried for years to find out who had coined the phrase, but failed.

The acting up usually took place in the background. A player being interviewed by a woman reporter generally treated her with respect. It took more nerve than most of them had to hand out the insults face to face, especially where there was good or bad press on the line. And besides, that came with the territory. I never asked for special treatment. In truth, most players had the class and decency to treat women reporters like human beings.

Reggie Jackson was another story. There was evidently some exhibitionist streak in the slugging superstar. The minute a woman reporter hove into view, Jackson would be the first to strip and the last to dress; and he did everything he could to draw attention to himself. He may have been "Hi, Mom" on television or humble and God-fearing with Howard Cosell, but in the locker room, where the public doesn't go, he showed a different, uh, face.

One typical incident happened in Toronto in 1983 when, as a California Angel, he had beaten the Jays with a dramatic home run. A handful of us waited to talk to him in the dressing room, but when he came off the field after the postgame radio interviews he brushed past us and went into the trainer's room, which is off-limits to the press. He stood in the doorway, in full view, doing calf exercises for twenty-five minutes while we waited and his teammates, who would have preferred to be alone, got more and more annoyed.

I was talking with another reporter about Jackson's arrogance when I realized that something was missing from the act. "I'll make you a side bet that he'll get naked before he comes out here," I said.

And won. Just before he finally favoured us with his presence he turned his back to us in the doorway, bent over and touched the floor, then peeled down his longjohns in one swift move of utter contempt.

The locker room isn't the Ritz. Generally, it is a fairly spacious room with a wooden cubicle for each player, with a stool or folding chair set in front. There is usually a table for card-playing in the middle of the room, and another table for baseballs to be autographed or postgame meals. When the players arrive before the game, the locker room is spotless, kept so by clubhouse attendants. The fresh uniforms they have washed hang at each locker and polished shoes wait by each stool. Clubbies, as they are called, are like manservants of old, charged with making everything pleasant for the athletes in their charge. They arrange restaurant reservations, tee-off times at golf courses, and fishing trips. They also run errands.

Each player's stall has his name over it. At home, the name is often a gag nickname. Lloyd Moseby had his name in Japanese all through the 1983 season because he was trying to "sneak up on the league" and didn't want anyone to notice him.

Players personalize their spaces in other ways, too, through the full spectrum of taste. It's not unusual to find a locker with scriptural reminders next to one with pinups. George Brett's had an extraordinary collection of photographs: semi-pornographic self portraits sent to him by female fans with more than auto-graphed baseballs in mind.

Visiting clubhouses are less homelike. The names over the lockers are written on surgical tape and the furnishings aren't as nice. I've always thought that the relative luxury of the two clubhouses was a form of psychological warfare: in Cleveland, it's warfare in the trenches. The clubhouse there is the pits, espe-cially for a woman sportswriter. It is tiny and cramped, with the smell of generations of sweat imbedded in the walls, and the small cubicles force the players into unwelcome intimacy. The route to the manager's office for a postgame interview is an eyes-front path with showers on one side, urinals on the other. Charming.

Working conditions aren't the best for the press in the locker rooms. By the time the game is over, the clubhouse is a slum, with clothes and cigarette butts and empty beer and pop bottles strewn all over the place. As the players undress, they hurl their sweaty socks and underwear in the general direction of the clothes hampers in the middle of the room. In time, reporters learn to duck. There is absolutely nothing titillating about the experience. Anybody who thinks there is should try doing interviews after a doubleheader in August. Especially when the players are in foul temper after a loss. Even the novelty quickly wears off.

The obsession with the locker rooms completely ignored the most serious problem of being a woman reporter in those early days. For us, the real challenge of the job was having to do it better than anyone else or risk failure on behalf of the whole female sex. An inexperienced male reporter could ask a dumb question and get away with it. An eyebrow would be raised here and there, perhaps, and some might think him awfully dumb. If a woman asked the same question, it would be further proof that broads didn't know anything about baseball.

Paradoxically, any success we had was not similarly extrapolated. A woman doing the job well was considered an exception.

Just before my first season, Roger Angell wrote a long and thoughtful piece in *The New Yorker* called "Sharing the Beat," in which he looked at women in baseball. He spoke to nine sportswriters: six women and three men. The man who took the middle position, intellectually recognizing our right to do the job, but emotionally believing that we just didn't belong, was Jerome Holtzman, then with the *Chicago Sun-Times*, and one of the senior journalists in baseball. Among other things, he talked about being bothered by what was happening to his sport.

"I suppose the fact that this was an all-male world was what made it so exciting to me at first," he said. "And now that it's being invaded and eroded it's much less attractive. Maybe I'm a male chauvinist, I don't know. The press box used to be a male preserve. That was its charm. I'd rather not have a woman as a seat-mate in the World Series game. It wouldn't be as much fun."

In October of 1979, I walked into the press box at Memorial Stadium in Baltimore for the first game of the American League Championship Series. There were eighteen inches reserved for me at the long desk in the third row. In the next chair, puffing on a big cigar, his bushy eyebrows beetling at his computer screen as he pounded on the keys, was Holtzman, looking like a slightly more attractive Ernest Borgnine.

I sat down next to him and began to go over some notes, but soon he introduced himself, and we chatted briefly before going back to work.

After a few moments, Holtzman turned to me again, taking the cigar out of his mouth.

"Did you read Roger Angell's article in *The New Yorker*?" he asked.

I said I had.

"What did you think?" he pressed.

I said that I had found it interesting, and we went back to watching the game, working on our stories and occasionally exchanging a comment or two about a player or an umpire's call.

After a few more innings, Holtzman couldn't stand it. Taking his cigar out of his mouth one more time, he glowered at me.

"You know the Angell article?" he said. "I was the heavy in it."

"I know," I said, and went back to my story.

We spent the first two games of the series cheek to cheek in the crowded press box, and when it was over, Holtzman had something to tell me.

"You know, you're all right," he said. "Not like the rest of them."

Same to you, Jerry.

If the truth be known, women sportswriters have an advantage over men. The players who treat us badly generally treat all reporters badly, but the players and managers who have some sympathy with our plight go out of their way to treat us better.

I also found that players were more willing to open up to me about problems on the field, perhaps because they are more used to letting their guard down with mothers or sisters or wives. But with male reporters, who are members of the very male, very macho club that is the sport of baseball, they cover more up.

Increasingly, readers of the sports pages are looking for the human side of sports; and women, who often began their careers as feature writers, are particularly good at finding it. With some notable exceptions, too many men are caught up in the old-fashioned school of reporting: "Garcia singled through short, stole second and scored on Upshaw's double to right."

I was lucky, too, in the team I covered. They were young and struggling in the early years, and walking pretty softly. Once Mayberry and Johnson set the tone, I was treated wonderfully by the Blue Jays. There were times that first season when I felt as if I had inherited twenty-five kid brothers. They teased me a lot, but they were protective of me, too, and proud of treating me right. Other women writers marvelled at how pleasant and helpful the Blue Jays were to me.

The Jays also did a bit of public relations work for me. There are very few strangers in baseball. Most players have friends on other teams, former teammates in the minor leagues or in winter baseball in Latin America. In each team's first encounter of the season with the Blue Jays, players would ask their friends on the Blue Jays to tell them about me. The reports were usually laudatory and helped smooth my path.

One day in Kansas City I overheard Mayberry, formerly a Royal, talking to Frank White, their second baseman. They were talking about me, and when Mayberry spotted me, he called me over.

"Frank wanted to know what you were like," Mayberry said. "so I told him. I told him you're my *main* person."

The two laughed, and I joined them.

There were holdouts. In Cleveland, the Indians would only let me into the manager's office. He would then call the players I wanted to talk to out of the clubhouse for me. That wasn't very satisfactory, because the other reporters had quicker access to more people; moreover, what a player will say in front of his manager is not necessarily what he will say when alone. It was awkward, for the players and for me.

Oddly, this changed in Toronto, where there was no separate entrance to the manager's office. I explained this to Jeff Torborg, then the Indian manager, their first time in town, but he didn't see a problem.

"Oh, you can come into the clubhouse when we're on the road," he said.

This strange double standard was finally resolved in 1981 when Len Barker, then an Indian pitcher, threw his perfect game against the Jays in Cleveland. Facing screaming deadlines, I raced down to the manager's office with everybody else. We were talking to Dave Garcia, Torborg's replacement, when a great commotion began in the clubhouse. Barker had obviously come in. The other reporters headed out of the room and I looked at Garcia, helplessly. I didn't even have to ask.

"As far as I'm concerned, Alison, I'm not going to stop you tonight," he said, and held open the door.

The first person I ran into, almost literally, was Gabe Paul, the old-style team president who most likely had been behind the closed clubhouse policy all along. I don't think he even noticed me in the excitement. I stepped around him and followed the ceremonial carpet of towels to Barker's locker. Once the Indians realized that my foot in the clubhouse didn't immediately cause the earth to open and the team to be plunged into a bottomless pit below, they opened their clubhouse for good.

There are still a couple of holdouts left, both in the National League: the Montreal Expos and the straight-arrow Cincinnati Reds. Only the Expo ban affected me, since Canada's other team was also big in Toronto, especially when they were in a pennant race.

Despite the good wishes of their public relations people and despite their co-operation in all things short of opening the clubhouse door, I was always at a disadvantage with the Expos. In 1981, the year of the baseball strike, I was in New York when the Expos clinched the second-half division championship. This was the first time a Canadian team had won a major league championship, even one with an asterisk; and it was as much a story in Toronto as it was in Montreal.

Champagne flowed inside the locker room: I could hear the corks popping and the hoots and hollers of joy. There was, I was sure, tremendous emotion in the room, players embracing and saying wonderful, funny stuff, all good copy. I knew what was going on because I'd been in other locker rooms during moments of great triumph and joy, but I couldn't report it. I was outside the door like a supplicant, waiting for the jubilant players to be brought to me, dragged unwillingly from the party. Not surprisingly, they were more subdued when they came outside, content to speak in clichés for the leper. I even got a boring interview from Bill Lee that day, perhaps the only one he ever gave.

It was one of the most frustrating days at work I ever had, watching the New York press with no angle on the story rush past me while I eavesdropped outside, under the baleful gaze of a large uniformed guard with a pistol, who was presumably waiting for me to make a break for the door. It was at moments like that that I wondered what I was doing trying to make a living among people who saw me as the enemy.

Isolation is always part of the job for a writer, who is always on the outside, hanging around the fringes; but the woman has an added barrier. There were times when the hostility and loneliness combined, usually after I had been on the road for a while, and I would have to fight back tears. Just to maintain the facade of being immune to their barbs took more effort than I could muster. Luckily, those times didn't come often, and inevitably they would be followed by some small gesture of sympathy from a player or fellow writer and I'd decide they were all princes after all.

It was on a late charter back from Cleveland one night in 1982 that I hit bottom. I was sitting near the front of the crowded plane, since I didn't like to infringe on the players' privacy; but when the equipment manager got on after supervising the loading of the bags, he told me I was in his seat and would have to move. Barry Bonnell, across the aisle and one row back, chimed in with the suggestion that I get off the plane altogether. Considering the source, the suggestion wasn't a joke.

I made my way to the back of the plane, past players using the empty seats beside them to hold their cassette machines, but no one offered to let me sit down. Several tried to send me back to the front. Finally I came across a rookie who didn't dare say no, took a seat, and opened my book.

It quickly became obvious why the players didn't want me around; they began to pass a lurid skin magazine back and forth across the aisle in the rows ahead of me. I did my best to ignore the giggles over explicit photographs of bondage and anal sex, while the poor kid next to me squirmed in embarrassment.

Just behind me in a separate section, Bobby Cox and a couple of the coaches took the whole scene in without protest. It wasn't hard to read their minds: "That's what she gets for wanting to run with the guys." They were right, of course.

After we landed, about 1:30 in the morning, I had just one

more hurdle. During the road trip, I had written about the pitching troubles being experienced by Roy Lee Jackson, a born-again reliever, and suggested that he might be consulting the Book of Job in his hotel room Gideon. It had been meant as colourful writing, not as an attack on his faith, but his wife, who met Jackson at the airport, didn't take it that way.

Moments after we cleared customs, the pitcher stopped me angrily and accused me of having written "trashy" things about him. It was the last straw. I told him we would talk about it another time and escaped outside, where my fiancé was waiting in the car. I waited until we had pulled away from the curb before I fell to sobbing and cursing most of the way home. Only the determination that I wouldn't let the bastards drive me out of the game kept me from resigning the next day.

Bonnell was my particular tormentor, as, in his terms, I was his. When he was traded from the Atlanta Braves in 1979, the first thing I heard from the Atlanta reporters was all about the temper tantrum Bonnell had thrown when a woman reporter came into the clubhouse.

With a whole year under my belt, I figured I could handle the situation pretty well, and so I set about converting him the minute he arrived in spring training. I talked to him about both of us trying to make a difficult situation easier, establishing routines that would make it possible for me to do my job without offending his sense of propriety.

He was an intelligent man and an otherwise reasonable one, and I was convinced that he would see that compromise was possible. I even tried humour, presenting him with a bathrobe. It had a name on the back, sewn on in purloined official Blue Jay letters by a couple of nimble-fingered friends: Bashful. (I figured it was better than Dopey, though Grumpy might have been more appropriate.) He, in turn, gave me a bell to ring when coming into the clubhouse. It was all fine, I thought. The crisis had been averted. I was wrong.

It got worse as time went on. In 1982, just after John Mayberry was traded to the Yankees, things got completely out of hand. Bonnell, who was then among the top hitters in the league, decided that he would step into the leadership vacuum created by the team captain's departure, and the first direction he would lead would be against me.

The cold war turned hot. A day didn't go by without some sort of harrassment. He took to shouting at me when I came into the clubhouse.

"What are you doing here, Alison?"

"My job, if you'd shut up and let me," I would shout back, all patience and pretence of civility gone.

Previously he had taken his clothes into the trainer's room to change, but he began to detour to wherever I was to make a sarcastic crack on the way. He refused to be interviewed inside the clubhouse, accused me of trying to spy on players in the shower, and wouldn't ride on the same bus with me if there was a choice. Once, in Boston, he even refused to get on an elevator with me and some of the other players at the hotel. We're talking major league childish, here.

One day in Toronto I became aware of a commotion while I was interviewing Lloyd Moseby by his locker after a game. I ignored it, since I suspected it had something to do with me – Bonnell was ranting about something – but Moseby cracked up and told me to turn around and see for myself.

Bonnell, in a rage, was building a barricade around his own locker with clothing racks and equipment trunks. Since he hadn't done anything in the game worth talking about, I didn't really understand what he was protecting himself from. While the other players laughed, Bonnell kept at it, helped by Damaso Garcia and Alfredo Griffin (as usual after games, naked as a newborn), who brought towels for him to drape over stools piled atop one another.

After a while the joke wore thin, and the rest of us went back to our business, but Bonnell kept on moving furniture around, shouting that I was "sick."

If Bonnell was sent to try me, there were others who made the job a joy, like Earl Weaver. I met him in 1979, shortly after he had announced that women sportswriters could come into his locker room only with a note from their fathers. He was very gruff when I found him in his office, several hours before game time, complaining that he was sick of interviews and that he hoped I had something new to ask him; but once we settled into it he generously gave me an hour and a half of his time. He loved to talk. He tested me during that first interview, but once I passed, he was solidly on my side.

He complained constantly about having me around, but it was all show. He would stand in his office after a game and yell, "Where's Alison? Tell her she can't come in now because I'm getting dressed. She's always trying to catch me with my pants off!"

During the first World Series I covered, between the Orioles and Pittsburgh Pirates, Weaver repeatedly singled me out from the crowd and asked me for information or an obscure fact out of the season's statistics. "Where's Alison, she'll know," he'd rasp. In truth, we all had the numbers with us, but Weaver was trying to make me look good.

Before one game he noticed a group of male writers sharing quotes and anecdotes for their stories that night, standard practice at big media events. I stood by myself twenty feet away.

"Can't you guys do your own work?" he called to them. "Look at Alison over there. She's the best reporter in the league. She doesn't need anybody's help." (Weaver was never averse to hyperbole to get his message across.)

He was also responsible for one line I'd be glad to take as my baseball epitaph. It was spoken at a party in Pittsburgh, laid on by the home team after the fourth game of that same World Series. The hosts were subdued because the Orioles had just won their third game, and it looked (wrongly, as it turned out) as if they had a lock on the championship. Weaver, who doesn't know what low-key means at the worst of times, was having a ball. He hailed me warmly, the latest gin and tonic gripped firmly in his hand, and dragged me across the room to meet his wife.

"Marianna, this is Alison," he announced, in his gravelly voice. "She ain't no pecker checker, she's okay."

Chapter

8

The Winter Game

The small plane banked sharply to the left, leaving the beaches and breakers of the Caribbean coastline behind, and headed toward the interior of Venezuela, across the coastal range.

It was a beautiful flight, the sunshine welcome just hours from the grey slush of Toronto. Bumping over the thermal currents rising from the landscape below is a nightmare to all but those who enjoy the sensation of really flying, and has filled many a manly ballplayer's heart with terror over the years.

My destination on that January afternoon in 1980 was Barquisimeto, an agricultural town of 600,000 in the state of Lara, home of Los Cardenales de Lara of the Liga Venezolana de Beisbol Professional.

When baseball is only a memory in the north, a rumour ringed on the calendar in red, it is thriving in the Caribbean. There are leagues in Venezuela, Puerto Rico, and the Dominican Republic that play a three-month season at approximately the Triple A level, meeting each February for the Caribbean World Series. Most teams in these leagues employ a handful of foreigners, American professionals from the high minors or low majors, "requested" by their parent organizations to spend the winter working.

They sign on for various reasons. Some young players get a leg up for the jump to the major leagues here. Pitchers can work on a new pitch, trying it out in game situations. Marginal veterans can try for an edge to keep them in the bigs for another season.

Career minor-leaguers go there for the paycheque of $2,000 to $5,000 a month. Some, unknowns in North America, enjoy being stars far from home.

I had timed my trip to correspond with the end-of-season play-offs, and left for the ballpark as soon as I had checked in to the small hotel the Blue Jays had recommended, a cozy pensione in the heart of the town. Barquisimeto is not Rio de Janeiro. It isn't even Caracas. Cut off from the tourist mainstream by the mountains all around it, it has very little to offer visitors, and non-Spanish-speaking guests like myself were rare. My Spanish phrase book and the friendliness of the hotel staff broke through the barriers, and I was soon on the way to Estadio Barquisimeto in a cab.

The streets were narrow, the sidewalks almost non-existent. The small stucco houses were painted in cheerful pastel colours, with windows shuttered to keep out the sun and rain, and ornately grilled to keep out uninvited guests. Political slogans were chalked on the walls, remnants of a recent election.

It is a rule of thumb that in any small town the best way to find the ballpark is to look for the light standards, and this was no exception. They were visible from the taxi window before the stadium came into sight, a small park surrounded by a forbidding wall, covered in stucco and studded with broken glass on the top to make sure only those who had bought tickets would come inside. The atmosphere, though, was warm and festive, and the fans were in the plaza outside hours before game time.

While waiting to get in, "los fanaticos" made themselves at home. Vendors strolled by selling food or tickets for that night's pool. For two bolivars (worth about a quarter each) you could guess which player from either team would score the first run. The payoff was ten to one. Families gathered around charcoal fires to cook up their *pinchos*, South American shishkebobs – a tailgate party, Venezuelan style. The air was full of fragrant smoke.

Inside the players were warming up as they do anywhere, the Cardenales and the visiting Tiburones (sharks) from LaGuaira, the Caracas seaport, playing pepper and fielding fungoes, bunting two in batting practice and shagging fly balls. Dozens of little ragged kids "helped," and the field was patrolled by corpulent, gun-toting policemen wearing mirrored sunglasses.

139

The scoreboard was being put through its paces, too, a dress rehearsal that only proved how international is the language of baseball. There were permanent spots to record "bolas," "strikes," and "outs" on the scoreboard. Commercial messages were flashed for Seguar de Lara, an insurance company, and Cervesa Polar, a beer with a bear on the label. Then came the game messages: *Flash* ... NUEVO PITCHER ... *flash* ... DOUBLE PLAY ... *flash* ... JONRON ... *flash* ... JON ... *flash* ... RON ... *flash* ... JONRON ... *blink blink flash.*

No matter how you spell it, it's still out of the park.

Once the gates opened, the playoff tempo started to build. The locals shouted encouragement to their favourite players and heckled the Tiburones. Groups settled into their seats and ordered up cold Polars from the vendors, some of them tiny children, selling bottles out of buckets full of ice. Some had brought picnics, others hailed vendors selling *arepas*, corn meal buns stuffed with meat or tuna or cheese. *Tostones*, banana chips, were also popular.

José Jimenez was a local favourite. A very old man, he sold individually wrapped *pastelitos*, small cheese or meat tarts, tossing them dramatically and accurately rows away and making spectacular catches of coins thrown his way. He joked with the regulars, chiding the ones who wouldn't buy his wares that day. They insulted him back, to great laughter all around. I was told that Jimenez had seven daughters, no sons, and that he had sent each of them to university. They are now doctors, lawyers, and teachers thanks to their father and his *pastelitos*.

The stands were divided between the cheap seats and the expensive ones, each section served by a separate entrance outside the park. Prices ranged from sixteen bolivars for reserved seats behind home plate to three bolivars for the centrefield bleachers (students, half-price). Unlike common North American practice, there was no sneaking up from the cheap seats into the boxes. To discourage moving, there were ten-foot-high chain-link fences between sections, with four strands of barbed wire on the top.

The real elite didn't sit in the stands. For them there was a special box, a concrete bunker at field level, slightly to the left of home plate. Here, sealed behind glass in air-conditioned chill, sat the owners and their guests, mostly men, in two uncomfortable rows. They filled their big bellies with copious amounts of scotch, even during the Sunday games that began at 11:30 a.m. In the middle of the game, they could open the door and talk to the players or the manager on the bench. Wouldn't George Steinbrenner love that?

In the major leagues there is sometimes too much formality. In Venezuela there was hardly enough. Players complained that there were so many well-wishers in the dugout they couldn't find room to sit down. A cute little kid named Enrique used to hang around and generally behave like the team mascot. During a game he could often be found either sitting between manager Vern Benson and pitching coach Bob Humphries on the bench or on one of their laps.

I watched some of the games from the radio booth, a tiny plywood structure at the top of the stands, no more than four feet deep and a dozen feet wide. I shared the space at various times with six announcers, a technician, and, occasionally, a small black cat. It was chaos. Each function, except the technician's, was doubled. Two men alternated play-by-play; there were two commentators; and two announcers just to read commercials. No cartridges with pre-recorded jingles in this studio. And, most assuredly, no dead air.

Every time there was a brief pause in the action, when the batter stepped out of the box to check a sign, when the pitcher went to the resin bag, or when an umpire called for new balls, one of the two announcers would jump in with a message. There were thirty separate sponsors for each game, and 400 commercials to work in. The messages were written in a loose-leaf notebook, one to a page. The notebook was three inches thick.

As is true anywhere in the world, the announcers had deep velvety voices, their Rs rolling like thunder across the airwaves. When play resumed, the other broadcasters would take over. If a commentator had a bit of colour or analysis, he simply snapped his fingers for attention, then said his piece.

Here, as in the dugout, there was none of the North American feeling of sacred ground. The fans turned and shouted at the announcers if they didn't agree with them. There was no hermetic sealing or fancy protection for the equipment. There was hardly any equipment.

The technician appeared to do very little work. He didn't ride levels or fiddle with dials. He had just one job. When *El Himna Nacional* was played in the stadium he took a microphone and stuck it out a hole in the studio wall to pick up the music for the radio audience. Other than that, he cracked jokes.

The din was marvelous, and the game not that hard to follow even if I closed my eyes, what with references to "un bouncer rolling foul," or "el centrefielder." A double was a "tubeyes," or two-base hit.

During the first game I watched from the press box, Ruben Mijares, the genial commentator who eventually became my interpreter, driver, and host, turned suddenly with his microphone and interviewed me at length about the playoff. In Spanish, translating my replies. All that was expected of me was to speak with all the authority of a major league beat writer about the skills of two teams I had watched for a total of two innings. I still wonder what I said.

Sitting in the stands, when I could find a seat, was an even more splendid experience. There was as much to watch up and down the rows as there was on the field, which was obscured by another chain-link fence, fifteen feet high and angled in at the top to discourage climbing.

When a foul was popped up behind the plate, it rolled up the netting over the stands, a cue for the kids, who would race up the fence, fitting their sneakers into the holes in the mesh, and fight to grab the ball through the netting before it could roll back down. Then, to great cheers of encouragement, the successful one would work the ball gradually down the outside of the fence, moving it from hand to hand stuck through the links, until he found a hole big enough to pull it through.

When people found out who I was (I was welcomed on the scoreboard each game and my picture was in the local paper) they would come and chat. Many were English students or simply teen-agers with a great fascination for all things North American, wearing sweatshirts from U.S. colleges that sold for small fortunes downtown. My dictionary became dog-eared from searching for phrases in both languages. The friendliness was almost overwhelming.

The music in the stands between innings was *salsa* and the patrons danced on the benches. There was no seventh-inning stretch, but that inning, and the fifth, were considered lucky. It was explained to me that the fifth inning is lucky because in bullfighting, the fifth bull is never bad.

Fan reaction to play on the field was hysterical and characterized by ear-piercing whistles and vituperative shouts. In the game against the Tiburones, the underdog Cardenales took an early lead and were up 4-0 by the fourth inning. Each time the Tiburones came to bat, the fans chanted "Uno-dos-tres" as the Sharks went down one-two-three. They turned and faced the visiting radio booth and shouted the numbers, waving the appropriate number of fingers in the air, laughing and stamping their feet.

The object of this derision was the LaGuaira announcer, a smooth gentleman with grey hair and a David Niven moustache, called Musiu, a variation on Monsieur. He was the local equivalent of Harry Caray in Chicago, a colourful character who rooted mightily for his home team, and was as well known as any of the players. The Cardenales fans revelled in his discomfort, and he cheerfully waved back at them while pulling faces of dismay.

By the ninth inning, it was "uno-dos-tres" from the first pitch and when the last out was made, the crowd went nuts. With great whoops of joy, not one, not two, but dozens and dozens of fans threw full cups of beer into the air. It ran in cascades down the steps. As the happy crowd milled around celebrating and the announcers read their final commercials and wrapped up the game, the final word was flashed on the scoreboard: "Recoge tu sardena muerta, Musiu," – pick up your dead sardines.

The exuberance of the fans turned into adulation on the streets of Venezuela's baseball towns, where followers of the teams have tremendous loyalty and long memories.

Benson, who first came as a player, told a story about one man he encountered during the 1979-80 season. "I was the shortstop on the 1953 champion Pastorias of Maracaibo," he recalled. "This year we were in there playing a game and I went out for a walk. Suddenly a man ran out of his house shouting 'Ben-son, Ben-son – Pastorias champion!' You can't tell me they don't have some fans here!"

Benson, who had come back to Venezuela year after year, had an obvious affection for the country and the fans, but most of his American players didn't share his attitude. For them, winter ball is simply a place to work on their skills and further their careers. The fact that they play for a team is almost irrelevant. Most of them can't wait to go home. The adulation wears thin, and the Americans are homesick for people and things they understand. They get tired of being followed by laughing, cheering children on every street in town. What was an appealing novelty at first wears badly. Many players left before the season was over, claiming illness in the family or heavy business commitments. This led to a great deal of distrust on the part of the owners. The year I was there, two American players had simply gone AWOL, refusing to return after the Christmas break.

The American players are not particularly sophisticated, and very few appreciated the opportunity of spending time in a different culture. There are exceptions, of course, but most players resent having to get through their day without a McDonald's takeout around every corner and a television with all the soaps. Frustrated by inefficiency and slowness all around them, by the foreigners who perversely refuse to speak English, the athletes are less than model ambassadors at times.

One night I was going out to dinner with several of the ballplayers: I walked into the bar at my hotel in time to hear one of them cussing out the waiter for bringing the wrong drink. The waiter spoke no English, but he couldn't mistake the tone of the abuse. Worse still, unbeknownst to the ballplayer, sitting at the next table were two American couples, consultants at a local bottling plant, who knew exactly what "Go fuck yourself" meant. The Americans were appalled, in part because the attitude of the players went so against what they were trying to do in the country. They had been through orientation sessions before they even left the United States, and worked very hard at being model guests, unofficial ambassadors for The American Way. The player's rudeness offended them personally.

The only orientation the Cardinales ballplayers got was a short lecture from Benson, suggesting that they would have to adapt to Venezuelan ways and try not to get into any trouble. But no one told them how to deal with loneliness, living in a compound run by the army, with motel-like accommodations and carefully screened access to visitors. The only telephone was in the compound office, where every homesick conversation could be overheard by the officer on duty. "I know they can't understand what I'm saying," one ballplayer told me, "but it still bothers me to have them listen."

Players complained that there were too many silly rules they had to conform to. One told me about an impromptu basketball game broken up by the army because it was against regulations to play in shorts and no shirts. This was with temperatures heading into the nineties.

I went to a big end-of-season party given for the players by the owners and supporters of the team. It was held in the courtyard of a fancy mansion, and invitations were issued only to the best-connected people in town. Guests were let in through a gate; outside dozens of people waited for a glimpse of the players, trying every con in the book to get in. There was a touch of Fellini to the scene. Inside the gates, three bands alternated to supply music for dancing. The players sat uneasily at three or four tables, joined by giggling young women in their early twenties. Whisky was the drink, but it wasn't free; players bent on offering hospitality paid 200 bolivars per bottle, about $50. The young women mixed the scotch with cola and shared it freely with friends at nearby tables.

I remember Garth Iorg in particular. The clean-living Mormon with a wife and children at home in California was a particular favourite with the fans, even if the pronunciation of his name ("Orge") was beyond them. At the ballpark, he was announced as "Gar Iiiorrrrg", with a hard "g." At the party, they settled for one name only.

"Iiiorrrg, tu gusto salsa?" asked one teen temptress.

"Si," Iorg nodded agreeably, "mi gusto mucho."

"You want dance with me, Iiiorrrg," she continued. Iorg assumed an expression of great sorrow as his tablemates wondered how he was going to wriggle out of this one. "No, gracias," he said. "Y no possible dance. My knee is malo, much malo."

Others didn't share his reluctance to mingle with the señoritas. Daniel Boone, a diminutive lefthander then with an Angels' minor team, had recently arrived and spoke a hilarious mixture of Spanish and English with no embarrassment at all. As he danced by he paused at the table.

"Look at this girl," he said. "She is so beautiful I'd like to take her home with me – her and about ten of her friends. But I bet she's got a father here somewhere, and I bet he's got a forty-five."

Yes, indeed, they were a long way from home.

The married players sent to Venezuela faced a quandary. Although they would prefer to have their families with them, they were worried about their children getting sick in a foreign country, or how their wives would react to the experience. One wife told me she hated Venezuela because people always wanted to touch her blonde hair. Her husband went back several seasons because it was important to his career, but she only went once.

Jesse Barfield was an exception. He and his wife Marla had their first child, Joshua, in Barquisimeto in January 1983. Other players and their wives thought they were nuts, but the Barfields, born-again Christians, put it all in God's hands. Barfield joked that all he had to do was look at Luis Leal, the Blue Jays' chubby righthander, who was a home-town player, to know they could deliver healthy babies in Barquisimeto.

Jim Gott also brought his wife when he went south. Clenice spoke fluent Spanish and had spent her eighteen-month Mormon missionary assignment in Guatemala. The two spent every off-day seeing as much as they could of the country, and took advantage of all it had to offer. But they were rare.

Perhaps because my visit lasted just ten days, I loved Barquisimeto. The last day of the season, a sunny Sunday, was Fan Appreciation Day, Venezuelan style. After the game, a stage was built on the field and awards were handed out to worthy Cardenales while musicians set up their instruments all around them.

Oscar d'Leon, one of the country's most popular *salsa* stars, gave a post-game concert. The first thing he did was invite the fans from the centrefield bleachers to come onto the field, which they did, racing across the grass toward the stage. Quickly, a section of the fence over the home dugout by third base disappeared, and those fans swarmed onto the field as well. There was no sense of violence here, though. I have felt more nervous in Yankee Stadium in mid-season. The fans did not have vandalism or destruction in mind; they simply wanted to get closer to the music, closer to the fun. As the afternoon wore on, ice-cream carts appeared in the outfield, and the beer vendors moved through the dancing throngs. Little kids rolled around in the dust. The sun beat down.

In the middle of it all were the players, some still in uniform, some with small children on their shoulders. Some danced; some took pictures; others stood back and watched in amazement. They signed autographs on scraps of paper, fuzzy pictures torn out of the newspaper, plastic cushions, even an arm and leg or two.

After a few hours, d'Leon packed it in and told them all to go home. Quite cheerfully they left the field and danced out of the park. All in all, it had not been a bad January afternoon.

Chapter

9

The Spring Game

Highway 19 crawls up the gulf coast of Florida, a congested, malodorous six-lane road that travels through the suburban fringes of America's playground: mile upon mile of Denny's and Red Lobsters and Steak and Ales and Steak and Shakes and Steak and Cakes; billboards advertising the wonders of Disney World and Busch Gardens next to sad and seedy bars offering incongruous happy hours morning, noon, and night; discount shoe factory outlets and waterbed stores; gas stations with signs painted in their windows offering bargains on six-packs of beer. The cars that ride 19 are driven either by cautious senior citizens who haven't passed a driving test since 1953 or by reckless redneck yahoos, tossing their empties out the window.

A few miles north of the Clearwater turnoff to the beaches of the travel agency brochures, diagonally across from the sprawling Countryside Mall, squats the Ramada Inn Countryside, a four-storey motel set among some brave palm trees, yellowed by exhaust fumes. For the Toronto Blue Jays, this is where the big leagues begin.

Like most spring training homes of major league baseball teams, the Countryside is no vacationer's paradise. The pool is tiny, the tennis courts seldom used. The beaches are nothing more than a rumour, half an hour's drive away. The rooms, done in mock-Hispanic decor, are a horror of green shag rugs and matching flowered drapes and bedspreads. Clothes hang on a small exposed rack on the wall. One of three pictures dominates each room. Depending on the luck of the draw, tenants spend their springtime staring at a matador flapping his cape, a dancing señorita, or a sleepy village square.

Unlike many major league headquarters, though, the hotel is clean and friendly. The staff is the same year after year, always ready with a cheerful greeting or a helping hand. They have seen the players come and go, one season's nervous rookie the next season's swaggering star, and treat them the same. Over the years they come to feel like family and every spring is a reunion.

The baseball fans and other tourists who choose the Ramada hoping to mingle with their favourite stars are disappointed. They don't find Dave Stieb and Willie Upshaw hanging around the lobby because most of the established players opt for six-week rentals in condominiums near the beach. The players bring their families with them and have one last domestic fling before the season begins and they belong again to baseball.

The players in the lobby are the rookies, the new kids in town, cashing their expense-money dollars for quarters with which to establish supremacy over the aliens in the video games.

The fans retreat to the bar, where the players are forbidden to drink: they huddle in groups, shouting to be heard over the relentless disco music and the sparkling inanities of the meat-market singles around them.

The fans aren't there to cruise. They want to talk ball and play at being general manager. They make hypothetical trades and send players to the minors for more seasoning, only to be embarrassed an hour later sharing an elevator with a player they have just coldly "released."

The fans aren't necessarily well-heeled. They hitchhike to Florida, share drives, or take the bus and stay in low-rent motels or campgrounds. This is not a luxury trip – it's a necessity. They're in Florida only for an early baseball fix, and it's probably their one holiday of the year. In the summer, who wants to travel? The team's playing at home.

There is a magic in spring training. There is a sense of sin watching baseball when winter still rules Toronto. There is something iniquitous about sitting in the stands with a beer and a dog and the players so close, while at home people are punching the time clock and waiting for real spring to come.

And in springtime it's possible to get close to your heroes in

149

the most relaxed atmosphere of the season. The fans lean against the chain-link fence dividing the bleachers on the first-base line from the area around the Blue Jay clubhouse in rightfield foul territory, keeping one eye on the game and the other open for their favourites. The fans call out, "Hey, Alfredo, how're ya doin'?" . . . "Ernie, over here, would ya sign one for my boy?" They are rewarded by smiles and waves. The players stop and chat because in the springtime they've got all the time in the world.

In the stands behind home plate, the wives sit with babes in arms and toddlers in strollers while the older kids race around under the affectionate gaze of the senior citizens sitting in the shade. And on top of it all, there's ball, even before the exhibition season starts.

In the middle of the retirement bungalows, along Solon Avenue, past Socrates Drive and Dinner Bell Lane, is the Cecil B. Englebert Recreational Complex, named after the mayor who enticed the Blue Jays to come to Dunedin. There are bonus-money muscle cars in the parking lot next to pickup trucks and luxury vans with love goddesses rising out of flames in silhouette on the sides. There are old junkers, too, and the disposable rental compacts with which sportswriters are afflicted at Tampa Airport.

Inside the gates, guarded zealously by the same amiable retiree who is in charge of the Blue Jay clubhouse door all summer, the season has begun. When the first players report, even though the calendar insists it is still February, spring has arrived. There are a couple of four-row backless bleachers set up behind the screen on the main diamond and down the third-base line. The early fans sit here, as do the scouts with their sunhats, stopwatches, and charts. In recent years, radar guns have begun to show up, but they are thought a bit foppish.

The pitchers and catchers report first, given a few extra days to work the million-dollar arms carefully into shape. (The buck-ninety-eight ones are accorded the same respect.) Along with the established players and high-level minor-leaguers who have a chance to make the team are a number of kids who have been invited to camp merely as bodies. They are the extra catchers, from all levels of the minor league system, who ensure that Luis Leal and Jim Clancy will always have someone to catch the pitches they throw. Their status is as clear as the numbers on their backs.

Major league uniforms seldom have a number over 50. Some minor-leaguers, the sure prospects like Tony Fernandez, who was assigned number 1 the day he made the forty-man major league roster, also have good numbers. The rest, those whom baseball people cruelly call "suspects," are stuck with embarrassingly high numbers. They do their best to appear unconcerned, but the springtime is hard on them.

Dave Shipanoff wore number 32 in the spring of 1983, a sign that even though he was not yet close to the big leagues, he had a future. The twenty-three-year-old pitcher brought an unusual background to his first major league camp. The eldest of five children of a carpenter in a suburb of Edmonton, Alberta, Shipanoff was one of very few Canadians to play professional baseball. He had a built-in handicap. While young Californians and Texans can play organized baseball virtually year-round, Shipanoff's Little League season in St. Albert lasted two months. Coaching is unsophisticated in Canada and Shipanoff was years behind other players his age. Fortunately, the Blue Jays have always been willing to give their Canadian prospects more time.

"There are always doubters," he said that spring, looking around at the coaches and scouts who held his future in their hands. "You find them everywhere, but if every player here had quit when someone told him he didn't have it, this place would be empty."

It is this kind of determination that characterizes the spring in baseball, especially among the rookies. They know that their big league exposure will be brief this time around and they want to make sure they make an impression. It could cut half a season off their minor league career.

That's the other way you can spot the rookies in camp. Rookies run everywhere, from the practice diamond to the workout mounds, from the batting cages to the sliding pit. Veterans stroll. Rookies run to the bathroom and back.

"Look at me," the youngsters gallop. "See how hard I'm working? I've got the good attitude. No problems here."

"I've been here before," the veterans amble. "I don't need to prove anything. You all know what I can do. So I reported a few pounds overweight. Don't worry about it. I'll be ready when the bell rings."

They all talk about that bell, the mythical one that rings when the umpire shouts "Play Ball" on opening day. The ones who have heard it know that what they do before that moment doesn't really matter. The rest desperately want to prove themselves so they can finally hear it.

Lloyd Moseby or George Brett can go hitless in an exhibition game, shrug, shower, and go home, but a rookie takes it to heart, because he has to. To him, every meaningless spring game is the seventh game of the World Series, because it is the most important he has ever played. Too often, the pressure leads to disaster and the pitcher who can't get his curveball over the plate and the hitter who swings for the fences and falls on his ass go home and stare at the matador on the wall and reflect on failure. There are more tears shed in spring training than the young players would care to admit. It is those moments that the doubts come crowding in and they feel scared and alone.

Spring is a happier time for veterans, a return to the identities they hung up in their lockers the autumn before. Athletes, like most of us, are happiest doing what they do best, and it's a rare ballplayer who enjoys his off-season. After the first few weeks of rest, the novelty of being at home wears thin. Somehow, building a rec room in the basement or working out at the nearest Nautilus centre with a bunch of businessmen just can't compare with going to the ballpark, suiting up, and winning a game.

When the players report to spring training, it is with great relief. The players greet each other like brothers. Being he-men athletes, they mask the affection with loud banter, lethal insults, and shouts of laughter. With their brothers in baseball they know once again who they are.

John Mayberry and Rico Carty were quite a pair in the spring of 1979. At the time they were the two big hitters on a team of has-beens and not-yets. They stood by the batting cage waiting their turns and started in where they had left off the season before.

"You sure didn't get any better looking over the winter, John," Carty said, the first day of camp, then stood back and watched the outrage.

"I don't know what you're talking about, Rico," Mayberry replied. "At least I didn't get any balder!" Then he grabbed Carty's cap, pulling it off to reveal the hairline, which had snuck a millimetre higher in the off-season.

"Bald! That's not bald," Carty bellowed. "That's a sign of intelligence. You look at all the lawyers and presidents. They all have high foreheads."

The two roared with laughter and players two diamonds away shook their heads with affection. Big John and Rico were at it again, and all was right with the world.

That's a memory of the two I will always carry. Mayberry inside the cage, waiting impatiently for his pitches, hitching up the shoulders of his shirt to give him room to swing freely. Carty watching, his handsome head held high with sideburns like a riverboat gambler, leaning on his bat as if it were a gold-headed cane, taunting Mayberry. Between swings the other man would get his own back, and the players would line up to watch the show.

My final memories of the two are sadder and show another side of spring training, a more poignant side. While Florida is a place where most players begin their career, it is also where some end them, and both Carty and Mayberry were through before they thought they were ready.

The day that Carty was released in March 1980 was stormy. Rain sluiced down the window of his hotel room and a palm tree whipped against it in the wind, punctuating his lament. He sat in an armchair too small for his body, gripping the arms with hands on which rings spelled out his name in diamonds. Gold chains and medallions glittered at his neck, but he looked battered and confused, like a boxer who had defended his title in one too many fights.

It had been sixteen springs since the big Dominican had had to worry about the cuts. For him the annual blood-letting had been something that happened to other people – kids too young or veterans too old – players lacking Major League Stuff. He had felt the twinges of sympathy for them and had been generous with his handshakes and kind words. Now Carty had himself been told to take his final walk, and he was hurt, bewildered, and angry. He blamed Blue Jay president Peter Bavasi. He cited a pulled muscle that had bothered him all spring. He talked about the home runs he had hit in the last two games.

"When I hit that ball over the left-centrefield fence, Johnny Bench said, 'Goddam it, what kind of strength do you have?' He said, 'You're a great hitter.'

"I've been working hard, you ask anybody. Those fans in Toronto are waiting to see me. I told Peter what he did was wrong. His own self knows it was wrong."

The only direction Carty wasn't pointing the finger of blame was toward himself. An honest look in the mirror would have revealed a man who was forty in even the most generous of record books. (Well-meaning scouts in countries where birth certificates are not easily accessible will often dock a few years from a prospect's age. Damaso Garcia, another Dominican, admits to being two years older than the age listed in the book.) Carty had missed a good part of the previous season with an infected hand, the result of a splinter he superstitiously refused to let the Toronto doctor treat. He routinely skipped pregame drills except for batting practice and didn't keep himself in the best of shape. There was more style than substance in Carty's final seasons.

Dave McKay, a former teammate, once described the frustration of playing behind Carty, calling it "backgammon baseball" – one move at a time.

"First they walk Rico," he explained. "The next guy up hits a line drive off the fence, rounds first, looks up, and there's Rico, standing on second." The player would be robbed of a double by Carty's slowness.

He wasn't the player he had once been, but he refused to admit it, and the rather querulous man in the armchair was not the one the fans would remember. That Rico stood in the sunshine with his feet planted firmly in the batter's box, his bat held high and poised like a cobra ready to strike, swaying slightly as the crowd roared his name. When the pitch came, his swing was quick and true. Then for a moment he froze in his final attitude, the bat still dangling from his left hand and watched arrogantly as the ball sailed into the stands. Only then, with a smile, he put his head down and began his home run trot.

Carty still held that image in his internal mirror on the last day of his major league career. "Every ballplayer knows that one day he is going to be released," he said, "but it didn't even come into my mind that it would be like this."

Carty stayed in Dunedin for another week, waiting to clear major league waivers and be free to talk to the other clubs he was sure would be interested. But the calls never came and he went home. In the Dominican Republic he was still a hero, and he still played baseball.

A year and a half later I visited the tacky little stadium that Carty's team called home. It was during the baseball strike, and I was sent to the Dominican to find out how Blue Jays Alfredo Griffin and Damaso Garcia were spending their time. Griffin and I drove from the capital, Santo Domingo, to Garcia's home town, Moca, in the interior of the Republic. The night before Griffin had tried to find Carty, with no success.

The two players held a brief reunion over a couple of beers at Garcia's parents' house, then decided to drive to La Vega, home of Los Indios, to see if they could field some ground balls, take some batting practice, and maybe find Rico.

He didn't show up, but I talked to one of his teammates, a young player who had spent one hopeful season in the low minor leagues with the Blue Jays.

"Oh, Rico doesn't practice," he explained. "He arrives at game time. But he can still hit."

He paused, looking around the dilapidated stadium, with its garish advertisements for Bermudez Rum ("el Ron No. 1 en Calidad") and Presidente Beer ("Cervesa mejore"), thinking of other parks.

"They say he's going back to the big leagues, to the Blue Jays," he said. "Is it true?"

When John Mayberry's turn came, three springs later, he didn't waste any time in self-delusion, which only made his demise that much sadder. After four and a half years with the Blue Jays, Mayberry was traded to the New York Yankees in midseason, 1982, to make room for Willie Upshaw at first base.

It hadn't gone too well for him in New York and when the spring of 1983 came around, he was one of too many trying out for the first-base job on a team with more superstars than it could handle. Owner George Steinbrenner was trying to fit all his free agents onto his roster with a shoehorn and the man they called Big John in Toronto was dying in Fort Lauderdale.

He had done everything that Steinbrenner and Billy Martin, then the manager, had asked him to do. A proud and hard-working man, he had lost the weight they had demanded and reported to camp in better shape than he'd been in years. At thirty-three, he believed that one bad season wasn't enough to finish him off. In return, all the Yankees did was put the handwriting on the wall where he couldn't avoid seeing it.

While Don Baylor, a designated hitter, and Ken Griffey, an outfielder, took turns getting first-base starts in exhibition games, Mayberry sat on the bench as a late-inning replacement. While Baylor and Griffey worked out with regulars Graig Nettles, Willie Randolph, and Andre Robertson, Mayberry did his drills with the scrubbies with the high numbers on their backs. He did it without a word of complaint.

The Captain was just another has-been, forced to scramble for a job he had no chance to get. It was Big Don, not Big John, the fans all hailed. The young players no longer asked his advice. Reporters ignored him. He wasn't a story in the Yankee camp. He was a footnote.

I found him in the batting cage, searching for his ever-elusive stroke against an Iron Mike, a pitching machine immune to reputation, pride, desire, or glares shot like daggers at its mechanical heart. It was beating Mayberry, too, and he left off popping up foul balls gratefully and took a break when a friendly face appeared.

"They got too many first basemans in this camp," he said, realistically if ungrammatically. "I know I'm the best one they've got, but it seems like the job might be decided by the salary the man makes."

Steinbrenner was not going to put one of the millionaires on the bench, but the realization didn't make Mayberry bitter. He asked cheerfully about his friends in Dunedin, Upshaw in particular, the man who had learned enough from him to take his job away. He missed them. As we spoke, a small man in a fedora happened along. It was Tony Pacheco, a scout with the Houston Astros, the team with which Mayberry had started his professional career eighteen years earlier.

Mayberry whooped with happiness as he shook the little man's hand, losing it in his own huge black paw. "Look who's here," he said, the old mischievous smile on his face. "This is my man, my first manager. Oh, man, you worked me so hard. A hundred ground balls every day, all the first year at Covington, a *thousand* ground balls. Next year at Cocoa he's there again and look out, here comes another thousand ground balls. He did it. This man made me the player I am today. This man gave me my career!"

"You still look great, John," Pacheco said warmly. "You're still my favourite."

"Tony Pacheco, good to see you," Mayberry continued. "You did it. You were the man. And I had a good career, didn't I?"

By the start of the season, Mayberry was gone. The Yankees had to buy out the rest of his contract for half a million dollars, but money can't buy back dignity. The John Mayberry who had given so much to the fans and players in Toronto deserved a more graceful exit.

"That's baseball," those inside the sport would say, and unfortunately they would be right.

The Blue Jays didn't forget Mayberry and what he had done for the team during the bad years. Three months into the 1984 season they made him batting instructor for their minor-league system – teaching kids, as he had done so well for most of his major-league career.

For all the spring training triumphs and hopes held high, all the wonderful rookies who win their jobs, it's the falling stars I remember, not the rockets on the rise. Spring is the wrong season for death.

Each spring the same drama comes around again, the eager rookies for whom everything is new and the veterans going through the same old drills. Each puts himself on the line for the six-week trial, but in a way it is the best time in baseball. Spring is a return, six weeks that belong to the players, who can laugh under the palm trees like kids at recess just before it's time for the bell to ring.

Chapter

10

On the Road

It's easy to get spoiled travelling with a major league team. The trip is smooth, all the irritations of ordinary travel made magically to disappear by the men whose job it is to get the group from one place to another.

Take a typical Blue Jay trip. The team is due for a game that night in New York, say. The team and fellow travellers assemble at the airport in the morning, some by bus from the ballpark, some delivered from home by taxi or compliant spouse. Waiting are Ken Carson, the team's trainer and director of travel, who hands out boarding passes, and Jeff Ross, the equipment manager, with a tag for each bag. The men who do these jobs deserve huge salaries and high praise. They get neither.

Even when the team is flying commercial flights rather than charters, there are no lineups, no reservation hassles. Deliver the bag to customs, go to the snack bar for a cup of tea, buy your smokes (reporters) or booze (coaches) or men's cologne (players) at the duty-free shop and stroll to the departure gate.

There is always someone from the airline there to smooth things. They like the business. Each trip involves thirty-five to forty people, but a lot more seats. Under the major league player agreement, each player is guaranteed a first-class seat or its equivalent on each flight. In economy that is "three for two seating," with the middle seat in the row empty for card games.

The press occupies the no-man's land between the players and the regular patrons, who grumble in their cramped quarters behind, complaining about those big guys taking up all the room in front. When they hear the captain welcome the Blue Jays, they warm up a bit and send pens and paper forward for autographs. (In the old days, the grumbling got worse.) On flights with meals, all the players eat first-class food, and on flights on off-days or after a game the drinks are free. Once the flight arrives, the team heads directly through the airport to a waiting bus while Ross waits behind for the luggage.

At the hotel, the room keys are waiting in marked envelopes. The bags are delivered to the room half an hour later. Often, in hotels fighting for major league business, fruit baskets or free drink tokens for the bar downstairs wait in the rooms. (Canny coaches collect the tokens from the non-drinkers and drink free the whole stay.)

This is heaven for anyone used to travelling a lot. For even a short trip, the team travellers have been saved a good hour of lineups, checking in at Toronto, collecting bags at the other end, waiting for a cab at the airport, and registering at the hotel, but some spoiled players can still find something to gripe about. If the bus arrives two minutes late, if a room isn't ready or is in the wrong location (too near the elevator, too far from the elevator), or has the wrong-size bed (queen instead of king), Carson will hear about it. How quickly they forget the beginning of the journey.

It was hard to get much lower on baseball's ladder than Utica, New York, in the summer of 1979. The Utica Blue Jays were in the Class A New York-Penn League, which played a short season from mid-June until the end of August. Technically, Utica wasn't the lowest-level team in the Blue Jay system. The Medicine Hat Jays were in the rookie Pioneer League, one rung below short-season A ball, but the composition of the two teams made their relative importance clear. Medicine Hat was where the team sent the high draft choices like Lloyd Moseby to begin their careers, a training ground for hot prospects. Utica was the dumping ground for the suspects.

Because the Jays had to fill their minor league rosters quickly after expansion, and because American players are all subject to the annual free agent draft for high school and college graduates, the team looked to the south and north in those early years.

They scouted heavily in Latin America and Canada for players who might turn out to have talent and who could be had cheap in the meantime.

They didn't scout them all in ballparks, either. If a youngster looked good in a stickball game on the streets of Santo Domingo or Caracas he was offered a contract for a year, just to see what he could learn. Those players joined the dregs from the draft in Utica in 1979.

The average salary was $500 a month, with a princely $7.50 a day in meal money, with which still-growing adolescents were supposed to feed themselves nutritiously. It was the first salary many of them had ever earned, and too much of it went on video games and down-payments on gold neck chains.

The team had an 8-23 record by the last week in July, and if it wasn't so sad to see the disillusionment and dreams lying broken all over the dugout, it would have been hilarious. The team was truly dreadful.

Chico Esquela was the hero of the English-speaking players. He was the then-popular *Saturday Night Live* comedy character, the Latin American sportscaster whose habitual refrain was "Beisbol's been berry berry goo' to me." The players decided he belonged on their team. "He can't hit, he can't catch, he can't throw, and he can't speak English."

Neither could eleven of the thirteen Latins on the team. The manager, a patient and good-humoured former catcher named John McLaren, spoke little Spanish. He had to rely on the two Latins who had a faint grasp of English to transmit his instructions, often with uncomprehensible results.

"A lot of these kids have never played organized ball before so every morning we have workouts and go over fundamentals: cut-offs, relays, bunt plays," McLaren said with a sigh. "In the afternoon I'll call four guys out early and just work with them. Then they all go out in the game and make the same mistakes over again.

"I don't think we have many real prospects. Alfredo Velasquez has good arm strength. He could become a good defensive catcher, but I don't know about his hitting. Vincent Williams has got the tools, but he gets too excited in game situations and loses the concept of the game. Santiago Tapia is fast, but all he can do is run."

Unfortunately, Tapia was the centrefielder, the linchpin of a Disney World outfield that caused great amusement to the fans in the stands but turned pitchers grey. In one memorable game, the "Blue Hays" took a 3-0 lead into the fourth inning only to lose 29-4. The opposing team scored fifteen runs in the ninth inning. There were ten Utica errors in the game, eight of them on fly balls.

"It's brutal," one of the pitchers told me. "You're in a game with men on base, and they hit a fly ball to right. You look away for a minute and think about the next hitter, then look back and not only has he dropped the ball, he's missed the cut-off man and another run has scored."

The fleet Tapia had stolen seven bases that season, but never when the steal sign was on. When McLaren, who also acted as third-base coach, asked him what the problem was, Tapia explained earnestly that there were so many signs it confused him.

Not surprisingly, this young "prospect" was back in the Dominican Republic by the end of the season. Not one of the Utica class of '79 ever made it to the big leagues.

The conditions in the N.Y.-Penn League matched the level of play. Murnane Field in Utica was typical. The infield was rock-hard and the rightfield fence was only 280 feet from home plate, easy game for lefthanded power hitters. The Blue Jays didn't have any. Other teams did.

At night, the lights gleamed dimly, like a gap-toothed smile, with just enough incandescence to turn night into dusk. As many balls were lost in the shadows as in the lights, but the players never complained about it. With an outfield that lost balls in broad daylight, what would be the point?

The Utica Jays made only four road trips that involved overnight stays that season. Most nights they got back on the bus after a game (sometimes still in uniform because the clubhouse showers didn't work) and headed home. The bus was an old rattletrap. Some seats were sprung; others stuck either upright or semi-prone. There were skirmishes for the good seats. On the trip I took, a unanimous vote stopped the vehicle at the nearest McDonald's where a sweet young upstate New York girl fought hard to keep the regulation smile on her face and the terror out of her eyes as two dozen huge and hungry teen-agers vied for her attention, half of them in English that she couldn't understand.

The team got back to Utica at 1:30 that morning. The players were expected to report for more basic training within hours.

My last view of the Utica Blue Jays was on that old bus as they were heading out on another trip. McLaren sat in the traditional manager's seat, front row, righthand side, the only grownup on the bus. It was hot and humid.

"Will you shut the windows back there, the air conditioning doesn't work with the windows open," he shouted. He waited. The bus driver waited. Nothing happened. McLaren sighed, got up, and looked back in the bus.

"Will someone please tell Pimental, in Spanish, to shut the window," he said, with great weariness.

Kinston, North Carolina, isn't much of a town by anyone's standards. It is small and mean, caught in a time warp in about 1942. The town divides halfway along the main street, with the faces all white in one end of town, all black in the other, and "nigger" is still a common descriptive term. The only bookstore in town sells used books, mostly paperback romances, and the cheery matron behind the cash register and her customer talk about *Princess Daisy* being "kinda dirty" (giggle). In the best hotel in town, fly swatters are the luxury extra, supplied free of charge in every room.

The team is a huge step up from Utica, but the life is still pretty bleak. When I visited there during the major league strike in 1981, I found McLaren again, rewarded for his earlier patience and loyalty with promotion to a team with some real prospects. He even had a coach. (By 1983, he was managing at Double A Knoxville, and I believe he'll manage in the big leagues some day.) While I was there, he learned another lesson about the minor leagues. When he was losing in Utica, the organization left him alone, but in Kinston he won ball games and lost players.

I arrived at the end of June in time to see him say good-bye to two pitchers who had a 21-3 record and eleven saves between them. With them, the team had finished in first place in the first half of the Carolina League season. Without them, things looked less bright. That's the price minor league managers, and minor league fans, have to pay. The better the players do, the faster they move on.

This was also Ray Kuhlman's problem. A retired airline pilot with a lot of romance in his soul, Kuhlman ran the team while his wife Ruth sold tickets and managed the concessions. They also served as surrogate parents for dozens of young players away from home for the first time, and they are remembered by many of them fondly.

It was always a struggle to get people into the tiny, charming ballpark, even with a winning team, but they loved the game enough to fight to make it work. They did all the usual things that make small-town baseball popular. There were scorecard giveaways for chain saws and steak dinners at each game. They invited Little League teams at cut rates. They struggled to keep the dream alive but finally gave up in 1983 and sold the team to another pair of romantics, a Palm Beach lawyer and a sportswriter from Massachusetts, who thought they could make it work. The difference between them and the Kuhlmans was that they had fresher dreams.

The uniforms in Kinston and Knoxville, the next stop up the ladder, in the Double A Southern League, were cast-offs from the big club, faded different shades of blue by sun and wear. Long departed big-leaguers lived on the backs of the kids, their names visible where the letters had been removed, just slightly darker in colour. The players wore different numbers at home and on the road, depending on availability.

The Kinston team was called the Eagles, the name before they joined the Blue Jay organization, which led to some confusion. The hand-me-down uniform shirts had "Eagles" sewn across the chest, the letters different than the numbering or faded names on the back, and on each jersey sat the familiar Blue Jay trying to look as eagleish as it could, which isn't very.

The equipment was old, the conditions and parks were poor, but the mood was full of hope. The players in A and Double A were on their way up, past their first hurdles as professionals. They were finding it a bit tougher at each level, and watched with envy when teammates moved past them, but it was still the real thing. It was a full season of tougher baseball than they had played ever before, and the big time seemed so close they could almost reach up and touch it. They knew others who had made the jump.

Paul Hodgson had done it the year before, called up to Toronto from Knoxville because of an injury. He spent thirty-seven days tasting the good life.

"I miss the air travel most of all, with three seats for two guys," he told me. "Down here if you're late getting to the bus you have to share. Things are really different down here. In Chatanooga, the visiting clubhouse is on the first base side and the dugout is on the third base side. To get there, you have to go in this dirt tunnel that goes under the stadium and around it. You can't get to the dressing room between innings and there's no washroom in the dugout. I guess in Double A you're not supposed to go," he said, wistfully.

Syracuse is one rung from the top for the minor league Blue Jays, and it's where the dreams begin to collide. The players on their way up meet the players on the way down. You can tell the difference in their eyes. The kids' sparkle with energy, high spirits and confidence. The veterans' are wise and wary, ever watchful for a break.

Triple A players are frustrated, especially ones who have been there for a few years. They've been to the major league camp for a few springs; they've spent time in the big leagues in September, when the roster is expanded. They've tasted the life and it's hard for them to be happy down on the farm.

There isn't as much difference between Triple A and major league levels of play as there is between the other steps in the minor leagues, but the move takes longer to make. If the best player in Triple A happens to be a shortstop and the major league club happens to have a good shortstop already, it's tough luck for the minor-leaguer. He can only watch as other, less-talented players move past him because they play a position at which the parent club is weak.

Each spring he's told the same thing: "We're sending you to Syracuse again because you're too good to sit on the bench in the big leagues. We want you to play every day." To the kid who dreams of being in the big leagues, even on the bench, it's not the news he wants to hear. But he goes and plays every day, and waits for the incumbent to get hurt or get traded or get old.

Tony Fernandez spent two more seasons than he needed in Syracuse. In both 1982 and 1983 he was touted as a potential

Rookie of the Year by all the pre-season analysts, but he couldn't crack the roster as long as Alfredo Griffin was the shortstop.

But players like Fernandez will have their day eventually, somewhere. Sadder are those who never will or who already have. Being sent to the minors is terrible for a big league player. It happened to Dave McKay in 1979. He was an average infielder who had parlayed a lot of hard work into almost three years in the majors. He was the Blue Jays' second baseman as the season started, the first time he had a position guaranteed.

But he went into a batting slump in May and the team sent him to Syracuse, promoting in his place Danny Ainge, the twenty-year-old basketball player from Brigham Young University the Jays thought would be the second baseman of the future, a smart-ass kid who had never known failure.

I went to see McKay the next day. He had had nothing to say to anybody about his demotion when it happened, but his wife Lene called me later and asked me to come out. It was a beautiful day. The sun was shining outside. Their five-year-old son Cody ran in and out of the sliding doors to the yard. A radio was tuned to the ballgame as we talked.

"I keep going out and looking at that calendar in the kitchen," McKay said. "I can't believe we've only been playing for a month and a half and I'm being sent down to the minors. If someone had told me I would be sent down to the minors in May this year, I would have said, 'Sure, if I'm run over by a truck or something.' I just can't believe it."

As we talked about their plans, about the difficulties of getting out of their lease in Toronto and finding a place to live in Syracuse, about Cody's disappointment at leaving his friends, play-by-play announcer Tom Cheek suddenly shouted from the radio: "What a beautiful bunt! Rick Bosetti scores and Danny Ainge has his first major league RBI!"

Just like that. McKay grimaced. Several innings later, he heard something wilder. Early Wynn had taken over the play description for a couple of innings, never his strong point.

"It's a hard hit ball that goes between Dave McKay's legs for a hit," he said.

McKay looked at the radio in disbelief before being struck by the ludicrous irony. There was nothing else to do but laugh, and we all did. Except Cody, who looked around at us and asked,

"Why's everybody laughing so hard, Dave?"

I caught up with McKay a month later in Syracuse and saw the bitterness still burning in his eyes. "I'm playing down here," he said. "I'm working hard. It's not bad because we're winning. But I don't have to like it. Don't let anyone tell you I like it."

The Blue Jays had told him that if he improved they would bring him back up later in the season, and he believed them. "Players from other teams keep asking me what I'm doing here," he said. "They know I don't belong here either."

He never made it back up as a Blue Jay, despite Ainge's inability to hit or play second base, and was released at the end of the season.

The story has a happy ending, though. He walked into the Oakland A's spring training camp near his home in Scottsdale, Arizona, for a tryout the next season and hung around for three more major league seasons. He was a hard worker, and when his playing days ended he became a player-coach in their minor league system. By 1984, he was back in the big leagues as the A's bullpen coach.

McKay's story is not an unusual one, and his eventual success is the kind of thing that makes a lot of players hang on in Triple A, long past the time they should have hung up their spikes and gone home to pump gas.

Doug Ault was one of them. He spent two years with the Blue Jays despite only marginal talent, in part because hitting two home runs in their first-ever home game made him an instant hero. By 1979, he wasn't even invited to spring training. Afflicted by a hitch in his swing that resembled St. Vitus dance, he was barely hitting his weight, but he still believed.

"I could get hot," he said. "There might be a scout in the stands."

Ault had one more cup of coffee with the Jays, at the end of 1980, then went to Japan. When he came back, he got a job as a minor league Blue Jay coach, one more thank you for those two home runs.

It would be a lot easier for them all, players and management alike, if there hadn't been countless stories of men who by all appearances were through or lacked big league talent who went on to become stars. Phil Niekro, who will one day be in the Hall of Fame, bounced back and forth between the minors and the majors until he was twenty-eight. At forty-five, he's still winning ball games. And in the minors, there are others who ignore the obvious; they look at Niekro and say: "I could get hot. There might be a scout in the stands."

When you're looking at the big leagues from below, the glamour glitters like someone else's gold, but the life is really just a higher, more expensive level of boredom. The hotels are better, meal money is more ($44 in 1984), but the hours to kill stretch out just as long in Minneapolis or Oakland as they do in Tidewater or Toledo.

The road is home for baseball players and their fellow travellers for half the days between March and October, days that drag by until the games begin and nights that are too short when they're done.

The road gets old, as ballplayers say, pretty quickly. At least it did for me. There was always a moment, just as I woke up, when I didn't know where I was. The absence of husband or cat tangled in the bedclothes told me I wasn't at home, but nothing in the bland luxury around me told me if I was in Cleveland or Kansas City, Baltimore or Seattle. And once I figured out where, there was still a why to answer.

Some cities were a joy. I had friends to lunch with in New York, and Boston was wonderful to walk in. Seattle was one of my favourites, a colourful gem of a city with a terrific waterfront market, McCormick's restaurant for seafood, and Just Michael's for clothes and chat. Once the team moved into the renovated harbourfront in downtown Baltimore, that city joined the top three or four. I could spend hours in the Aquarium.

Minneapolis had a wonderful bookstore right around the corner from the team hotel. But there were few attractions in other places. The worst were Cleveland, Arlington, Oakland, and Anaheim: the first because it sat in the middle of the most depressing downtown core in the league, the latter three because they sat in the middle of nowhere. There seem to be an unusually high percentage of crazy people walking Cleveland's streets and it is the only place outside the Third World where I've seen so many beggars in the streets. It never failed to depress me.

The problem with the other three cities was isolation. The hotels were close to the suburban ballparks, right on highways. Without a car it was next to impossible to get to a bookstore to feed my novel-a-day road habit, and the newsstands weren't much help. In Arlington one year, I could choose among a grand total of eight books, most of them either romances or westerns, neither my favourite flavour of junk.

Most of the ballplayers didn't even have books for consolation – few of them read anything other than the sports section of the daily paper. Their favourite daytime occupations seemed to be lobby-sitting, mall-cruising, and going to the ballpark at 2:00. Video games were popular for some. Roy Lee Jackson was the best I've seen. He could play the same Galaga game for an hour on one quarter. I've even seen the games get a player into trouble. The one time I think I saw off-field activities affect a player on the field, it was Ms. Pacman, not drugs, that did it.

Luis Leal got hooked on the lady in the Anaheim Hyatt lobby. On the day he was scheduled to pitch I made several trips between my room and the front desk during the course of the afternoon: each time Leal was hunched over the game, his hand glued to the lever. That night he gave up six runs, including three home runs, in the three and two-thirds innings he pitched. Pacman hand, I suspect.

An amazing number of players follow the soaps without fail. It was always a bit strange to listen to a bunch of grown men discussing the latest plot twist on *General Hospital* on the team bus heading for the park.

The one player who beat the boredom on the road was Barry Bonnell. Each season he taught himself something new. One year he spent his free time studying advanced flying techniques to upgrade his licence. Another he took up magic and spent hours perfecting card tricks. The season he took up the saxophone was the hardest on his roommate, but it kept him busy.

More players should have followed his lead. More writers should have, too, but it was easier to settle into the torpor, go for a window-shopping walk, buy another mystery, and escape again. All I managed to do was develop a previously unsuspected taste for country music. There was something appropriate to the road in the "here I am agin, sipping misery and gin, sitting with all my friends and talking to myself," melancholy of the country charts, and I could find a good country radio station everywhere in the league, with the snooty exceptions of New York and Boston.

The problem for us all was that we were out of sync with the rest of the world, no matter where we went. Our workdays began as everyone else's ended. It is a problem shared, I suppose, with other road shows. I'm sure actors and musicians have the same sense of dislocation.

As part of the perambulating night shift, I always found myself looking for something to do after work was over, which was usually around midnight. The somewhere available was usually the hotel bar, where the same group would convene almost nightly, mainly writers and coaches. We were out of sync there, too, starting our drinking when the rest of the world was ready to finish, sober when all around us were sloshed. My fondest memories are of the cities that had quiet bars and friendly bartenders.

Ed and Tom were my buddies in Cleveland before the team moved out of the Bond Court Hotel where they work. A trip to Milwaukee wasn't complete without at least one visit to My Office (get it? – "I have to stay late at my office tonight") to roll dice for a round of drinks, and Steve at the Half Shell in Boston was my saviour more than once by putting a Marx Brothers movie on the VCR over the bar and keeping the scotches coming, bless his heart.

The worst were the hotels with popular nightspots, crowded with twenty-year-olds on the make. Oakland was a nightmare, packed every night, filled with disco music and vapid bimbos of both sexes, but it was the only place around.

Players seldom went in the hotel bars. The ones who drank had other watering holes and friends to go with. They did their playing out of sight of the coaches and press. A few, the ones who weren't hiding anything and were interested in nothing more than a couple of drinks, would join us. Jim Clancy and Dale Murray, Ernie Whitt and Buck Martinez, before he quit drinking, were usually there. John Mayberry used to drink with writers, too, and others occasionally dropped in to wind down, but most just disappeared after games.

I made a rule when I began the job that anything said in bars was off-the-record, a rule I don't plan to break now. I saw some misbehaviour over the years, to be sure, but I've misbehaved from time to time myself. I think it goes with the territory. The trips can be long and lonely, and for players companionship is never far away.

I never saw anything dangerous, harmful, or illegal going on, or, for that matter, very surprising. Mostly there was just a lot of talk. My favourite road companions were Larry Millson from the *Globe and Mail* and Bill Lever from the *Sun*, and we closed many a bar with good conversation, not even necessarily about baseball. Bobby Cox eventually took to calling the three of us the Dalton Gang.

On weekends it was easy to get into trouble because day games let us loose early. Ballplayers say that a day game after a night game is the worst of all, but for the writers and other carousers, it's the day game after the day game that will kill you, especially somewhere like Chicago, when they don't even kick you out of the bars at a sensible hour.

On one notable three-day visit I was taken by a local to Rush Street, that amazing avenue where three in the morning is like nine at night anywhere else, lively and fun. Checking out the next morning I ran into Joey McLaughlin, who observed that it was obvious I had tried to beat Chicago. I admitted my guilt, and as the bus pulled out, McLaughlin's voice boomed from the back row: "Final score: Chicago 3, Gordon 0."

The road was the best of the beat and the worst of it, too. I can't understand how some people can stand doing it year after year, but there are people who have spent their entire mature lives on the road, first as players, then as coaches. It's a wonder they're not mad or dead.

Chapter

11

Rooting for
the Home Team

Like the actor who becomes an "overnight success" at forty-five, the Toronto Blue Jays were nobodies until 1983 – names followed in the box scores across North America only by their mums and dads. In their seventh year, the Blue Jays came out of oblivion to spend forty-three days in first place in the American League East, thirty-two of those days consecutively, and became underdog favourites around the league.

Suddenly, the Blue Jays were in fashion, and the sports magazines and big-name baseball writers flocked northward to heap attention upon their heads. My goodness, even Howard Cosell brought his ABC crew to Toronto and pronounced it worthy. Heady stuff indeed, except to a handful of visionaries who weren't surprised at all.

In the calm in the middle of the whirlwind were club vice-presidents Pat Gillick and Paul Beeston, the yin and yang of the organization: Gillick, the quiet one, taking care of the baseball of the business; and the rambunctious Beeston, taking care of the business of baseball. What was happening before them daily followed the optimistic blueprints they had drawn up seven years before. It was happening just as they had dreamed that it would.

When the two first got together with Peter Bavasi, the team's first president, in an empty office on Adelaide Street in downtown Toronto in 1976, all they had was a franchise. They had to find a name for the team, staff a front office, scout for players, and entice people into the cold metal seats of Exhibition Stadium by April 7 of the next year. The three men knew they had a tough job ahead of them. Expansion was a nasty business, and the odds against them producing good baseball in a foreseeable future were almost overwhelming. Kansas City had gone from expansion into first place in just eight years, but the Royals played in a much weaker division than the one the Blue Jays would be contesting. The Jays couldn't expect that kind of success against the Yankees, Orioles, and Tigers, and even eight years was a long time to lose and keep the fans coming in.

They were an unlikely trio, all of them in their thirties, starting from scratch in an old man's game, but they were burdened with none of the impatience of youth. They had learned from watching other teams' development that impatience could be deadly, that jumping for high-priced free agents at the expense of young players could give only momentary rewards. Backed by a trio of supportive owners, Labatt's Breweries, the Canadian Imperial Bank of Commerce, and tycoon R. Howard Webster, they decided to bide their time and build a team from their then non-existent farm system.

It fell to Bavasi to sell the philosophy to the team's new fans. They couldn't have found a better salesman. Bavasi, son of a baseball family (his father was Buzzy Bavasi, the Angel general manager who had spent years in the Dodger organization), was a new breed in the sport. He was as smooth as silk (or slick as an oil patch, depending on your perspective), with a flair for marketing that served the team well. He was also a man who had a lot to prove to baseball (and, one suspects, his father), and wanted to prove it fast.

Bavasi became the front man, with an image of concern for Toronto that charmed the business community. No Yankee carpetbagger, he and his family became landed immigrants and his wife Judy enrolled in a Canadian Studies course. He always dressed impeccably (pointing out that he bought all his clothes in Toronto) and worked hard to maintain the image of a cultured jock who was also a man of the people. He was proud of the fact that he read only hard-cover books. His handshake was soft and clammy, but he answered his own phone.

It was Bavasi who held a name-that-team contest with, it was suspected, one eye cocked toward Labatt's, makers of Blue lager. (Cynics were surprised that the winning name wasn't the Toronto

Blue Bats: translated into French as Les Bats Bleu.) He "sold the sizzle" while Gillick was beating the bushes for the steak.

At first Gillick had to settle for a lot of bologna. It is the nature of expansion that the new teams have nothing but scraps to choose from, players other teams feel no need to protect. They were players either well past their prime or very young and of limited promise, not men around whom a franchise could be built.

Gillick was strictly a baseball man. He had been a pitcher in the Oriole minor leagues for five years before retiring at twenty-six. He went to work in player development for the Houston Astros in that team's first ten years. He left them to become the Yankees' co-ordinator of player development and scouting in 1974, but was glad to jump the Steinbrenner ship when his chance came along. Gillick's looks belie his nature. With his long, thick eyelashes and cross-combed thinning hair, he looks soft, disarmingly gentle. In reality, in business, he is as soft as steel, as other teams and player agents have discovered.

Beeston was the token Canadian of the group, and the youngest, a rollicking cigar-chewer, with accounting in his background but baseball in his heart. He is an attractive, albeit slightly overweight, man with tremendous gusto. Everything rises a few decibels when Beeston is around, and his glasses are, literally, rose-tinted. He is the man who handles all the business – corporate and player contracts, radio and television rights – and he is rapidly gaining a reputation as the only money man in baseball who is willing to pay players more than the baseball people want to.

The first thing Gillick did was reach back into the Yankee organization he had just left and steal Elliott Wahle to run the Blue Jay minor league system. It was the first of many thefts from the Yankees. Because Gillick was determined to resist the temptation of trading potential for instant gratification, the road the Yankees had taken, he was able to take advantage of Steinbrenner's misguided impatience. Gillick's sojourn with the Yankees gave him good knowledge not only of their minor-leaguers but of which buttons to push with the boss.

There were three phases in the development of the Blue Jays, phases that coincided with their three managers. The first was the Roy Hartsfield stage: the Blue Jays simply fielded a team at each level in the organization and hoped people would come to watch anyway. The major-leaguers belonged in Triple A, the Triple A players belonged in Double A, and so on down the line to the lowest level, which was staffed mostly with players who shouldn't be in baseball at all. But there were a few exceptions, prospects that might become players with a bit of patience.

There was a kid down in Utica that first year named Jesse Barfield, for example. In 1978 there was a youngster named Lloyd Moseby playing in Medicine Hat and another called Dave Stieb throwing a ball pretty well in Dunedin. There were also a lot of dogs never destined to make it, but the prospects gave hope to those with an eye on the grand plan.

Novelty brought the patrons out the first season, and baseball-starved fans came from all over southern Ontario and northern New York, especially for series against the Yankees, Red Sox, and Tigers. In the first season, as many fans cheered for the visiting teams as did for the likes of Doug Ault, Steve Bowling, and Pedro Garcia, but 1,701,052 of them paid for tickets. Bavasi had done his job. They were some of the quietest and least sophisticated fans in the league, but they were undeniably there. The Seattle Mariners, created in the same expansion draft, only drew 1,338,511 the first year and slipped well below a million immediately afterwards. The only time the Blue Jays ever dropped under the magic number was in the strike-shortened 1981 season.

Hartsfield wasn't a very good manager, and the players he had to work with weren't very good players. That didn't mean they had no pride, though, and by the 1979 season they were in open revolt against what they saw as an acceptance of losing by their manager and by Bavasi. They complained that the front office cared more about making money than improving the team, and even suggested that the fans should start staying away. It was a bitter, unsettling season; and when it ended, the Hartsfield era ended with it.

The Bobby Mattick stage was on-the-job training, with Mattick as head instructor. The new manager had been the team's director of player development when he was put in uniform and on the field. The first thing he did was dump all the caretaker coaches from Hartsfield's staff and replace them with men who were proven minor league managers and good teachers. Denis Menke came out of the Blue Jay system, where he had managed some of the best young prospects; Jimy Williams came from the Angels organization, where he had managed their Triple A team; and John Felske and Al Widmar came from the Brewers, where Mattick had worked for years.

The baseball college that convened in the spring of 1980 had some impressive students, thanks to Gillick. The baseball man had been busy collecting some new players through trades and raids on other teams' unprotected minor-leaguers.

He already had scored Alfredo Griffin from the Cleveland Indians in exchange for Victor Cruz, a Luis Tiant clone who had delighted the Toronto fans in relief in 1978. Initially enraged by the trade, the fans' boos changed to cheers when Griffin became the 1979 American League Rookie of the Year (with Twins infielder John Castino).

The Yankees helped the team indirectly when they didn't protect Willie Upshaw in 1977; the Blue Jays picked him up for spare change. (Steinbrenner's generosity knew no bounds. He even took Mayberry off Gillick's hands once Upshaw was ready in 1982.)

A lot of the trades didn't work out; a lot were garbage for garbage; and a lot meant giving one more chance to someone else's reject. Because they were always ballyhooed by Bavasi, they inevitably frustrated and disappointed the fans.

Pitching was the problem, and the Jays just couldn't find the solution. Without anything real to offer in exchange, the club had to keep taking flyers on players with problems. They traded for the likes of the Mark Lemongello, Paul Mirabella, and Phil Huffman; and they kept working with their own marginal hurlers, men like Dave Lemanczyk, Jerry Garvin, Butch Edge, and Jesse Jefferson, because they couldn't afford to give up on them. Other pitchers were picked up after they were released from other teams. Don Kirkwood, Dave Freisleben, and Jack Kucek all went through the revolving door, and each new arrival was hailed as the hope of the future.

If Mattick opened camp in 1980 optimistically, the fans were more suspicious. They were tired of hearing about the future. They had just watched two monumental failures in judgement, Danny Ainge and Phil Huffman, embarrass themselves at major league centre stage, and they were running plumb out of patience. If this was the team of the future, they didn't want any part of it.

This was the beginning of the end of expansion.

Starting in the spring of 1980, Mattick and his coaches worked daily and hard with their players. Menke hit thousands of ground balls to Roy Howell to turn him into an adequate third baseman. Jimy Williams worked with Al Woods and Moseby in an outfield that had too often resembled Adventureland in seasons past. Woods finished the season hitting .300, and the team had its best season ever. It was the first time the team hadn't lost more than 100 games, and they even flirted with a winning record in the first half of the season. The grousing in the stands quieted to a murmur.

But the team was playing over its head. The next season was saved only by the mid-season baseball strike. Before it gave them a rest, the Jays had a dismal 16-42 record, daily inventing new ways to lose, and the fans were howling for Mattick's head. But they were 21-27 in the second half and ended the season with their confidence back.

By the end of the 1981 season, Mattick was worn out by losing, and when he was offered the chance to go back to the front office, he decided it would be best to take it. He became the team's executive co-ordinator of baseball relations.

Meanwhile, in Atlanta, events were unfolding precisely according to Gillick's plan. He had known Bobby Cox when he managed in the Yankee organization, and when Cox was fired after four years of managing the Braves, Gillick had the manager he had always wanted, at exactly the right stage for the team. Cox joined the Blue Jays on October 15.

He also brought coaches with him, first base coach John Sullivan, a former catcher, and Cito Gaston, who would serve as the first full-time batting instructor the team ever had. Bobby Doerr had filled the role in the first Blue Jay years, but spent a good part of those seasons either in the minor leagues or with his ailing wife. Gaston arrived not a moment too soon. The team batting average for 1981 was .226.

Williams and Widmar stayed on, but Felske and Menke left, in bitterness and resentment. Menke was offered another job in the minor leagues, which he considered an insult. Felske went on to manage in Triple A for the Phillies.

Just over a month after Cox signed with the club, there was more evidence that the expansion era was over. Peter Bavasi called a press luncheon at which he tearfully resigned because "the thrill of building is gone." Then he opened the bar and buffet and presided over his own wake.

Bavasi's explanations didn't ring true at the time, and the real reason for his resignation was never revealed, but the remaining members of the remarkably stable staff just roll their eyes and groan when the man's name is brought up. He was an unpopular and often irrational and difficult boss. If Bavasi hadn't resigned when he did, the owners would have had to deal with a mutiny by his staff, several of whom were poised to leave. Two years later, when Bavasi was being considered as American League president, it was said that the Blue Jay opposition to the appointment killed any chances he had.

I didn't mind the man. Smarmy and manipulative as he was, he was often kind to me. But I was a member of the all-important press and never worked for him. The one time he tried intimidating me, I hung up on him. He never did it again.

Bavasi also played one unintentional role for which Gillick and the others should be grateful. He so personified the team in those early years that he got all the flak. Bavasi was to blame for everything from bad trades to bad weather. I remember one night in 1978 when the team was losing horribly, as usual. A young man stood up in the stands, turned toward the private boxes, and waved a slice of pizza in the air.

"And one more thing, Bavasi," he shouted in frustration for us all. "This pizza stinks."

When Bavasi left, attention focused more on Gillick and Cox. Luckily for them, the bad days were past.

Once he had had a chance to meet his players and watch them for a couple of weeks in spring training, Cox began to shake things up. The first thing he did was take away John Mayberry's job, a tough move. Mayberry had been one of the team's most popular and productive players since he joined the team in 1978. Just the season before he had signed the biggest contract given to that date, for three years at $800,000 per, and had been named the team's first captain by Mattick. He was also thirty-two years old, coming off a bad 1981 season, and Cox obviously believed the first baseman was through.

Besides, he liked what he saw in Willie Upshaw, the man who had been playing in Mayberry's shadow for five years, and thought he deserved a chance. Upshaw had come to be called Mr. March, a nickname hung on him by my colleague Neil MacCarl because of his habit of hitting well in spring training, only to fold when the season started. Cox understood that Upshaw was a player who didn't do well coming off the bench and he might blossom if he played every day. Mayberry was gone to the Yankees by the first week in May, and Upshaw had the job.

The middle infield was set with Garcia and Griffin, but Cox had a couple more headaches. The Jays had traditionally had problems at third base. Roy Howell had filled the position (more than played it) for most of the first four seasons and Danny Ainge had contemplated a basketball career from the same corner in 1980 and 1981, with the help of several utility players as fill-ins; but there was no one there but Garth Iorg that spring as camp began. There was also no minor-leaguer ready to make the jump.

Cox professed to be unalarmed by the situation, but on the last day of camp, Gillick got Rance Mulliniks, another utility infielder, from the Royals, and Cox announced his plan to platoon the new player with Iorg. Mulliniks, a lefthanded hitter, would play against righthanded opposing pitching and Iorg, a right-hander, against lefthanders.

Mattick had rotated his two catchers, Buck Martinez and Ernie Whitt, in and out of the starting lineup seemingly at random; but Cox decided the two would be most effective in another strict platoon. Whitt started whenever a righthander was going for the other team, and Martinez started against lefthanders.

Cox also decided that Moseby's pathetic batting average (.233) was a mirage and that he would be the centrefielder; and that Barfield was ready to make the jump and could play rightfield, especially against lefthanded pitching. Barry Bonnell, Al Woods, and Hosken Powell were around for backup.

The pitching was no problem with Stieb, Jim Clancy, and Luis Leal at the heart of a starting rotation that was the envy of every other team in the league. Cox hoped that the latest retread, Mark Bomback from the Mets, would flesh it out, but he ended up having to scramble.

The bullpen was an "after you, Alphonse" revolving door of semi-adequacy with no real stopper in sight, but Cox thought he had a team. The catch phrase that spring was "We're going to surprise a lot of people." Including, I suspect, themselves, when they ended up winning 78 games, 11 more than their previous best.

Cox's secret was his consistency. There was very little chance for second-guessing when Cox made out the lineup. The players were delighted. No longer would they have to sidle up to the lineup card on the dugout wall to see if they were in the game. Once the opposing team's pitching rotation was announced, the platooning was automatic.

Cox also kept all his players in every game by automatically switching his platooned players when a reliever who pitched from the other side was brought in. If Iorg had gone three for three and a righthander came in, Cox would call for Mulliniks anyway. This gave him a strong bench because it was rare for a player to go more than a couple of days without getting into a game. The team pinch-hitting average was .271.

Gaston had done his job, raising the overall team average from .226 to .262 in a season. (This was especially pleasing to me because I had been writing for three years that the team needed a full-time hitting coach.)

Cox's faith in platooning was rewarded. Both Whitt and Martinez improved dramatically at the plate, as did the third basemen. Whitt, especially, became a hitter. He raised his batting average 25 points, to .261, but, more importantly, hit 11 home runs. (In 1981 he hit one, on the last day of the season.) Martinez hit 10, double his previous season's high.

The most serious lack in the 1982 season was in designated hitting. Dave Revering and Wayne Nordhagen hadn't amounted to much, and their various replacements didn't do much better. The combination of all the designated hitters came up with only eight home runs, 56 RBIs, and a .236 batting average.

But the first steps toward respectability had been taken, and for the first time the Blue Jays didn't finish dead last. They shared the cellar with the Cleveland Indians.

After the season was over, Gillick did some fine-tuning to improve the designated hitting. He traded for Cliff Johnson from the right and George Orta from the left. The next season the designated hitters produced 34 home runs, 113 RBIs, and a .250 batting average. (Johnson was responsible for 22 of the home runs and 76 of the RBIs. Orta was sent to Kansas City in exchange for Willie Aikens after the season.)

Then, just for old time's sake, Gillick went back to the Yankee well and stuck in his bucket. The best reliever the Jays had in 1982 was Dale Murray, a thirty-one-year-old who had come back from oblivion to save eleven games for the Jays in 1981. The Yankees were interested and the Blue Jays were happy to deal. Murray may have been the best they had that season, but he wasn't overwhelming, and who knew how many years he had left. It was hard to refuse when the Yankees offered speedy Dave Collins and starting pitcher Mike Morgan in return. Morgan was a risk, a young man whose physical talents were hampered by mental wildness, but he was undeniably a prospect.

Collins carried a $650,000 price tag as a result of Steinbrenner's ridiculous overpaying of free agents, but that was no problem either. The Yankees would throw in $400,000 cash as part of the trade. The deal was as good as made when Gillick said that he would be willing to part with a minor league outfielder named Tom Dodd and take a kid named Fred McGriff off the Yankees' hands. Around about the time Willie Upshaw is starting to fade, you can bet the mortgage that McGriff will be ready to take over and that it was he whom Gillick had in mind all along.

In 1983, the mood in spring camp was unlike any year before, one of confidence and high spirits, which wasn't surprising, considering that there was hardly a player on the team who hadn't had his best season in 1982. In Hartsfield's era, spring training had felt like a paranoid ward. In Mattick's time, it had been controlled chaos, with long days of instruction. By Cox's second season, it was smooth, efficient, and optimistic.

New players like Collins, who felt like he had just been paroled after his trade from the Yankees, all commented on the spirit of the spring, and the old guard all talked about how refreshing it was to feel that the team had a real chance. But then spring is always a silly, optimistic time, and when Cox talked about winning ninety games, up a dozen from the previous season, no one took him too seriously. After all, to win that many games, the players would have to repeat extraordinary seasons. That many wins would put the team in the pennant race, and the team was too young, still too new for contention.

Cox patiently pointed to the young players who had yet to come into their own: to Upshaw, whom he thought could get better; to Moseby, whom he knew couldn't get worse (after another bad season in 1982, up .003 points to .236, with only nine home runs); to Barfield, who had spent the winter learning to hit righthanded pitching in Venezuela; to Luis Leal, who had a 9-0 record in the same league; to Jim Gott, who hadn't given up an earned run all spring; and to new players like Johnson, Orta, Collins, and Morgan.

He wasn't completely right, but he came within one game of his prediction. The pitchers, the part of the team no one questioned, let him down. The hitters led the league at .277, their 167 home runs came second only to the Orioles, and the pinch hitters hit .290. They did their job, but the reality of the two-steps-for-ward-one-step-back world of baseball is that nothing can be taken for granted.

But 1983 was special. While the team was learning how to win, it was, for the first time, part of the pattern of the season. Until then they had been in the league, playing the schedule, but out of contention so early that they couldn't get caught up in the pace or understand its demands. They were measuring themselves, as expansion teams must do, against another standard, one they had set for themselves. In 1983, for the first time, they were playing in the same league as their opponents, figuratively as well as literally, and they knew it from the first chilly day of the season in Boston.

They won that day, thumping the Red Sox 7-1, and didn't look back until August. They were caught up in the pattern of baseball, a game bound not by the clock but by the calendar.

Games in April and May tend to be pretty bad baseball, played with frozen fingers, but they have their own special attraction. They are usually intimate affairs with sparse crowds; even good fans would rather sit home by their radios than down the third-base line. At the ballpark, those dedicated or foolhardy enough to brave the cold and damp to stand enthusiastic witness have a special camaraderie.

April and May are the silly season in the statistics pages, which fluctuate more than the Dow Jones average. With limited at-bats and innings pitched, anybody can have a couple of good games and find himself listed in the league's top ten. In April and May teams like the Blue Jays and Texas Rangers can sit proudly atop their divisions for days or even weeks, and Mets fans in Shea Stadium or Cub rooters in the ivy-clad Wrigley Field bleachers can shout "We're number one!" until they are hoarse. It's the season of the underdog, when anything seems possible.

April 1983 was cold and rainy wherever the Blue Jays went and they stumbled through eight wins and ten losses before finding their collective footing, but in May they had the best month in their history (19-9) and suddenly they were noticed. *Sports Illustrated* sent a front-line reporter north for the first time in seven years for anything other than novelty, and attendance started picking up both at home and on the road.

In June, the Jays found themselves in the middle of the rush toward the All-Star break. It is conventional wisdom that the teams on top of their divisions at that symbolic mid-point will be there when the season ends, and even though this has proved so less often than not in the past half-dozen topsy-turvy seasons, there is still some jockeying for symbolic position in late June, a pennant race in miniature.

At the All-Star break in 1983, the Blue Jays were 43-33 and at the top of the American League East. With the Montreal Expos in the same position in the National League East, I went to the All-Star Game in Chicago and conducted a tongue-in-cheek poll of players on both teams about their reaction to an all-Canadian World Series. I made a basic mistake, expecting athletes to react with humour about such an earthshaking possibility.

Dan Quisenberry, the free-spirited Kansas City Royal reliever, thought it would be great for sales of Moosehead Beer, but most of the players took a dimmer view. As well as predictable remarks about snow and cold in October, there was a disturbing undercurrent of real disapproval, a belief that it would be somehow immoral and bad for the sport. It's a ticklish business, nationalism, but I was annoyed at the attitude, all too prevalent among people in baseball. It never occurs to the chauvinistic Americans that there are half a dozen other big league cities as likely to be miserable in October. It snowed in Baltimore on the first day of the 1979 series.

But it's more than the weather they complain of. Everything Canadian is second-rate to many of the players I dealt with, who constantly found reasons to gripe about playing in a foreign country. They didn't like the taxes. They said that Canadians didn't understand baseball the way the Americans do. The fans were ignorant and the sportswriters couldn't get a job with any self-respecting real (*American*) paper. They didn't like to have to stand for two anthems before each game instead of one. They took the customs checks coming in and out of the country as a personal affront. The money looked funny; their wives were bored; and they couldn't wait to high-tail it back to Oklahoma or California when the season was finally over.

Perhaps it is simply in the nature of ballplayers to gripe, but they did great disservice to the Canadian fans who cheered them on, because it was those funny blue and purple bills handed in at the Exhibition Stadium ticket windows that paid their generous salaries, even if they did collect them in U.S. funds.

Oblivious to their unworthiness, Canadians crowded around their television sets to watch the 1983 All-Star Game and cheer for "Toronto's" Dave Stieb, the winning pitcher in the first American League victory since 1971. It was a special game for him. It was the third time he had been named to the team, but the first time the selection was anything more than a token.

Each team in baseball has to have an All-Star representative. Since only the eight starting players are chosen by fan ballot, the All-Star manager (who managed the previous World Series team) makes sure that every team is represented when he picks the rest of his squad. Stieb had been previously chosen because he was the best the Jays had to offer; but in 1983 Harvey Kuenn decided he was the best in the league and honoured him with the starting assignment.

The pitcher had a lot to make up for. His previous appearances had been embarrassing. The first, in 1980, came in his second year in the major leagues, and he didn't look much like an All-Star, giving up two wild pitches, two walks, a hit and a run in the inning he pitched. In his second game, in 1981, his problems weren't on the mound. In the ninth inning, Stieb was called upon to hit.

Since the designated hitter takes the pitcher's place in the batting order in the American League, Stieb hadn't had to heft a bat for anything more than fun for several years, but as a former outfielder he took great pride in his hitting ability. He knew all too well that his teammates would be watching the game on television and remembering his boasts about his batting prowess.

The American League was losing by just one run when Stieb came to the plate, wearing a helmet borrowed from Tom Paciorek and Buddy Bell's glove. He carried one of Rick Burleson's bats. On the mound was Bruce Sutter, one of the toughest relievers in the game. Stieb swung meekly at three consecutive pitches, not even coming close, and went back to the bench with his ears faintly pink. After the game, he groaned as he thought of the ribbing he was going to endure.

"Even if I'd grounded out it wouldn't be so bad," he said. "If I'd just made contact. If I'd even taken a pitch for a ball, I wouldn't be so embarrassed."

He sat with his elbow in a bowl of ice, shaking his head, then remembered he had a question. "Who was that pitcher, anyway?"

In 1983, Stieb was able to erase his bad memories and go back to join a team riding the best high they'd ever known. The eyes of baseball were on the division-leading Blue Jays in July, as people realized that their record was not just an early-season fluke. Even ABC came to town to present the Blue Jays to a prime-time audience for the first time, and made a big to-do about the event. Predictably, some of the media made Howard Cosell the story instead of the Blue Jays, but the team took the spotlight back the night of the game.

Earl Weaver was part of the broadcast crew and he had his own memories of Toronto. Even in their worst years, the Jays were trouble for the Orioles in Toronto. Weaver had suffered one of the most memorable defeats of his illustrious fifteen-year managing career in 1978 when a then-pathetic Toronto team had beaten the Orioles 24-19; Weaver had even used outfielder Larry Harlow and catcher Elrod Hendricks as relief pitchers. He knew how sharp an underdog's bite could be when he came back with ABC, but even he was amazed by the Jays that night.

The star of the 8-2 win over the Royals was Alfredo Griffin. The often underrated shortstop put on a performance in the field that astonished Cosell and delighted the Toronto fans. After one particularly dazzling diving catch of a line drive in mid-air, even Weaver joined the standing ovation.

That was one of the most memorable evenings for the Blue Jays that season. The other one came in early August when they beat the hated Yankees 10-9 and 13-6 in a doubleheader at Exhibition Stadium, packed to the rafters. To beat the Yankees had been sweet for the Blue Jays since they were born, but to thump them twice on the same night was delicious.

Those two nights symbolized the best of that Blue Jay season. The patience of the first six years of expansion had paid off, and the team found itself with a solid core of young, talented ballplayers who had been playing together long enough to work as a team. Cox's platoons were working wonderfully, and players like Lloyd Moseby and Willie Upshaw were undeniable stars coming gloriously into baseball maturity.

Those were the kind of nights that made us all believe it would never end.

Then came the slide.

August is the dog days month in baseball, the time when the season starts to wear the players down. It's hot; they're tired; aches and pains and pulled muscles nag. All they want to do is rest, take it easy for a couple of days, but they can't. They have to play hard because they know what is on the line.

That's how champions show themselves. August is the month when the professional winners take over, teams like the Orioles. When other teams are fading, they are switching into overdrive for the pennant race. When you've been there often enough, you know how much to save for the stretch run.

It was in August of 1983 that the Blue Jays fell. It was the last week of the month when they went to Baltimore and had their hearts broken. The team was almost through playing within the tough eastern division. They had just come from Cleveland and Boston with a 5-3 record and would go on to Baltimore and Detroit for six more games. Then ten at home against the Tigers, Orioles, and Red Sox would send them on to finish the rest of the season against the weaker American League West.

The optimistic believed that all the Jays had to do was finish close to first place in the East, then fatten their record against the likes of the Minnesota Twins, Oakland A's, and Seattle Mariners. The Yankees, Tigers, Orioles, and Brewers would, the reasoning went, kill each other off and, voilà, the pesky Blue Jays would sneak through the middle and win it all.

Heady days indeed. The team was tough, with surprisingly good hitting to go with the pitching that everybody expected. Even the suspect bullpen was giving the illusion of competence. The team had won an amazing nine extra-inning games without an extra-inning loss. It was easy to believe they were touched by destiny's hand. Believers whispered about the 1969 Mets.

It took just a week to burst the bubble. After beating Mike Flanagan (his record against Toronto had been 10-0 in his home park, 15-4 overall), the Jays showed what inexperience meant. They lost seven of their next nine games, two in extra innings, two in the bottom of the ninth. In five of the seven losses, the team blew a lead. The bullpen had broken all their mirrors. It was not at all pretty to see.

The night Oriole reliever Tippy Martinez picked off three base runners in the tenth inning was the absolute bottom. The help-less Toronto fans could do nothing about it. They sat by their radios and television sets listening to and watching the horrible dispatches from the front. The *Sun's* Andy Donato drew a cartoon that summed up the dreadful week: Wife, standing in doorway looking at a broken television screen and a husband imbedded in the wall above it, asks, "Jays lose again?" Broadcaster Tom Cheek complained that his wife Shirley had broken one of their radios during a game. When the week was over, so was the race.

But that's what happens when a team that has never been there before comes up against one that makes contention its permanent address. The only consolation the Jays could grab onto was that they would never be so naive again. That was small comfort going into that particular September.

The last full month of the season is time for watching the scoreboard as much as the games, watching how the rivals are doing all around the league. Even lowly teams can enjoy seeing other teams losing, but there is a sweet excitement in the stands when there's a contender on the field.

The Blue Jays of 1983 were, for the first time, involved in the scoreboard as more than observers; but they were helpless as the Orioles refused to play by the script and streaked away with the championship. They could take their only satisfaction in watching the Milwaukee Brewers, the 1982 league champions, falter and drop behind them into fifth place, and in hoping vainly that they might still finish ahead of the Yankees.

They didn't, but they finished fourth and delighted a whole lot of new fans. The old ones, the ones who had been there since the start, were ecstatic. The biggest surprise, in the end, was how the team had been let down.

The remarkable pitching staff didn't dominate other teams the way they should have. With the exception of Stieb, every earned run average on the team went up from the previous season. If it hadn't been for Doyle Alexander's seven wins at the end of the season, there would have been no joy at all in Hogtown in October.

Oh, yes, Doyle Alexander. The Yankees gave up on him in May and released him, despite the fact that they were bound to him by a contract that lasted through the 1985 season, worth close to two million dollars. Cox had managed Alexander in Atlanta in 1980 and thought he would be worth a look, so the Blue Jays picked him up in June. After losing six games, he won the last seven in a row, and Steinbrenner picked up most of the tab.

The Blue Jay success story is one of wheeling and dealing, high-stakes gambling, and, most of all, patience in the front office and in the stands. But is also a story of boys growing into men, of winning through losing and building success out of the humiliation of failure.

Chapter

12

Closing Day

On October 2, 1983, Ernie Whitt stood on the Exhibition Stadium field and cried. He wasn't alone. In the stands, more than 40,000 people stood and cheered and waved and hugged each other. The season was almost over, and nobody there wanted the magic to end.

It was an extraordinary afternoon, one in which the game being played was irrelevant. The Blue Jays were being brutally beaten by the miserable Minnesota Twins, but it didn't spoil the party for the fans. It became obvious by the second inning that the team wasn't going to give them anything to cheer about on the field, so the fans cheered them anyway, dishing out random standing ovations almost every inning.

Just before the bottom of the eighth, Whitt decided the time had come to give something back and led the players onto the field. Almost casually, they strolled out of the dugout, looking into the stands, a little embarrassed by the fuss.

As the fans began to chant his name, Whitt took off his cap and waved it, then put it back on his head and applauded the fans. Other players followed suit, and for a few moments, the emotion shimmered over the field like a heat mirage. Then the players waved their caps again and went back to work.

This was all for a measly fourth-place team, but one that had never before come so close. It was a celebration of success after six years of failure. It was also well-deserved.

It was a moment of great triumph for the team, and especially for Whitt, who stands as well as anybody for what the Blue Jays accomplished in the first seven years of expansion. Whitt is a big man, his blond hair thinning at a rate he wishes he could ignore, his small, rather closely set eyes a startling sea-blue. He always looks tired and slightly beat up, and usually is. He's a catcher after all. He has a quiet, dry sense of humour, good public relations instincts, and infinite patience. He's a rock.

More than other players, Whitt has grown in his job. Fighting to overcome a reputation that was marginal at best, Whitt, like the Blue Jays, finally won respect through gritty tenacity and fierce pride. He deserved his moment in the spotlight and enjoyed it more than most. Whitt was an original Blue Jay, chosen seventeenth in the expansion draft, pretty close to the bottom of the barrel. The Jays showed their limited expectations for him by immediately trading for two more catchers, Alan Ashby and Rick Cerone.

Whitt was twenty-four at the time and had spent four years in the Red Sox minor league system and eight games in the majors. His chances of beating out Carlton Fisk as the Red Sox catcher were non-existent, so joining the Blue Jays should have been a break. Unfortunately for Whitt, he got stuck behind Ashby and Cerone and spent three bitter years in Triple A, with occasional short trips to Toronto. He came close to quitting the game.

Whitt's career got stalled by one very simple factor: Roy Hartsfield didn't like him, and since Hartsfield was the major league manager, it meant that the catcher had no chance of making it out of Syracuse while Hartsfield was in charge. In 1979 the two had a confrontation in spring training. Hartsfield told him he would never be more than a minor league player because he couldn't hit, couldn't handle pitchers, and couldn't throw out runners at second. Then he handed Whitt yet another ticket to Syracuse.

That was when Whitt almost hung up his mask, but Pat Gillick, the team's vice-president, and Elliott Wahle, then farm director, quietly made it clear to him that Hartsfield was not necessarily the manager of the future. Whitt gritted his teeth and reported to Syracuse, led the league in fielding, and waited his turn.

It came the next season, with Bobby Mattick. So strongly did the new manager disagree with Hartsfield's assessment of Whitt, he told Gillick to go ahead and shop around the incumbent, Rick Cerone. (Alan Ashby was already gone, in one of the worst trades the Jays ever made. They traded him to the Astros for a migraine headache named Mark Lemongello, a crazed pitcher best remembered for beating himself up after games and throwing a heavy crystal ash tray at Bavasi's head when he was sent back to the minors.)

Mattick believed that Whitt could become the major league catcher, although there was no compelling evidence. A .249 Syracuse batting average with seven home runs and 43 runs batted in did not inspire a spontaneous movement to give Whitt the job. Mattick followed a hunch and did it anyway. Cerone went to the Yankees (where else?), along with lefthanded pitcher Tommy Underwood (a chronic whiner they were glad to get rid of) and minor-leaguer Ted Wilborn. The Jays got Chris Chambliss, Damaso Garcia, and Paul Mirabella. (Chambliss was then traded, with Luis Gomez, to the Atlanta Braves for Joey McLaughlin, Barry Bonnell and minor-leaguer Pat Rockett.)

Whitt didn't come through with a Hollywood season, hitting just .237 with little power; but he did begin to mature as a player. What infuriated him was the implication that he was just filling the spot on the roster until the Jays could find a "real" catcher, either in a trade or in the minor leagues.

The following February an arbitrator granted Carlton Fisk free agency when the Red Sox neglected to send him his contract on time, and the Blue Jays chased him avidly. The papers were full of breathless reports on the possibility of the Red Sox star coming to Toronto. In the end, when Fisk decided to change Sox and go to Chicago, Whitt was given a reprieve, but he knew that was all it was. The irony of almost being replaced by Fisk, the man he had once hoped to succeed in Boston, neither escaped nor amused him. His spirits weren't improved when veteran catcher Buck Martinez joined the team in May, and Mattick began to alternate them at whim. Whitt began to sulk, his mind more on his grievances than the game.

Martinez eventually became the key to Whitt's success. He was not only very good at his job, he shared his knowledge with Whitt. He was less impatient than his younger colleague and helped tone down his anger. It would stand them both in good stead in the next Blue Jay era. Together the two became a very good composite catcher, better than most in the league.

Ernie Whitt was not very different when he began his career from any of a number of young men who are now selling real estate and watching the Game of the Week at the corner tavern. Why did he make it? Why was it he who stood on the field with tears in his eyes and chills up his spine on that October afternoon, an unlikely hero? Because he understands the nature of luck, good and bad, and of baseball, and because he has the good sense to take advantage of it. And because he has learned to listen to others' advice.

When Hartsfield told him he was worthless, he tore out of the ballpark with the anger of a man whose pride had been ground into the mud. He was lucky enough to have a wife, Chris, who knew him better than he knew himself and told him the truth. It was she who reminded him how lucky he was to be doing what he wanted most to do, albeit not in the way of his dreams, and that if he turned away from it because of another man's opinion, he would only be hurting himself. At that crucial point, Whitt decided that he would be the one to succeed or fail on his own merit or lack of it.

Two years later, when factors out of Whitt's control made Carlton Fisk decide to go to Chicago instead of Toronto, he realized his vulnerability. But for a decision made by another man on another team in another city, he would have been out of a job. It was another testing point, and Whitt felt put-upon again, especially when Mattick brought Martinez in to threaten his job. Whitt was lucky that Martinez was an intelligent veteran who understood that respect must be earned every day, and he was smart enough to learn the lesson again.

The relationship of Whitt and Martinez, personally and professionally, was a joy to watch. It revived both their careers and helped the young pitching staff immeasurably. The two became the perfect platoon. Instead of being jealous antagonists, they were friends and partners, joining their intelligence and experience in a common cause.

The pitching staff the rest of the league so admires are part of the catchers' cause. Working with pitching coach Al Widmar, they have developed a philosophy of handling the sometimes erratic and usually egotistical young pitchers and they work hard with them to bring out the best in each.

I have learned to have a special respect for catchers, and none more than these two. It is the toughest job on the field, physically and mentally, but it is also the most overlooked. All eyes are on the pitcher, imperial on the mound, or the shortstop, balletic in the field, but no one bothers to watch the catcher, crouched behind the plate. Try it some time, for a whole game. Watch him squat down on his haunches, inches away from the swinging bat, with the umpire leaning heavily over his shoulder. Count the times he catches the ball and throws back to the pitcher, more catches and throws than anyone else on the field. Watch him call all the pitches and go to the mound to calm a pitcher down. Watch him signal the dugout surreptitiously when a pitcher is losing his control or his fastball. Watch how many times he gets hit by foul tips. Watch him jump to his feet, throw off his mask, and chase a wild pitch or back up first base. Watch him absorb the collision of a runner trying to score while catching a bouncing throw from the outfield.

Then watch him come up to bat in the ninth inning with the game on the line. (Oh, and be sure to boo him if he can't run out an infield grounder.) Then ask yourself why catchers aren't the highest-paid players in the sport.

Whitt was not the only symbol of gritty determination that October afternoon. Rance Mulliniks and Garth Iorg were two more men written off by others who rose to flourish in partnership. Iorg was another original expansion draftee, chosen from the Yankee organization four rounds after Whitt. He had his first chance in 1978, when he made the team after spring training, but he was sent down to Syracuse after six weeks and, in his mind, forgotten.

I first got to know him in Venezuela in January of 1980 and was impressed by how hard he worked. While other players saw the Caribbean experience as a bit of a lark, Iorg and Dave McKay, who had just been released by the Blue Jays, took it seriously. I watched the two of them one hot afternoon working in the primitive batting cage at Estadio Barquisimeto and realized how dedicated they were.

This was literally a cage, a box made of chain-link fencing instead of the usual netting, and balls hit ricocheted wildly around, from walls to ceiling to floor. It was like a squash court designed by the Marquis de Sade. When Iorg threw to McKay it was with an odd pitching style, a response to the killer cage. It went: wind up, throw, then duck, glove over the head. Iorg threw pitch after pitch to McKay, and then the two switched places. It was hot, dirty work in the most primitive of conditions, but Iorg didn't shirk it. He even seemed to be able to have fun doing it.

He was very unhappy at the time. He hadn't even been invited to the Blue Jay spring training camp. He felt like they thought he was washed up before he had even had a chance. Even though he was only twenty-five, he believed the organization thought of him as part of the "old team" and that the nineteen games he played in 1978 had been his last chance. He was being written off as a failure because of forty-nine bad at-bats.

Iorg was eventually invited to the big league camp that spring, with good expectations that he would become the team's utility infielder. Instead, he was sent down to Syracuse the day camp wrapped up. He had to retrieve his equipment from the team truck and cancel his family's travel plans.

Through all this, Iorg kept his cheerful perspective. He is a little terrier of a player, as wisecracking as a teen-ager, a clubhouse agitator. He is another of the parade of Mormons the Blue Jays have marched through the organization since it began, but there is nothing sanctimonious about him. It's just that he says "darn it" when he pops up instead of something stronger.

Iorg was back with the Blue Jays six weeks into the 1980 season and he has had a job ever since. Cox's platoon gave him the front-line job he never expected. I suspect that Cox sees in Iorg a lot of the attitude he had when he was a player, eagerness and hustle that can turn a small talent into something bigger.

Iorg and Mulliniks batted .275 in 1983, with Iorg .00016 percentage points lower than Mulliniks. Although the two didn't have the power usually expected from third basemen, they were a perfectly matched pair, and Mulliniks hit thirty-four doubles, one short of the team record, while playing only half the time.

Two other faces define the 1983 season, the faces of two friends who came to symbolize the power and the spirit of the Blue Jays. Willie Upshaw and Lloyd Moseby came onto the field before the last game to accept their trophy as co-winners of the Most Valuable Player award for the season, sharing the award as they had shared so much over years of playing together. Willie Upshaw and Lloyd Moseby were linked in people's minds: Lloyd and Willie, Willie and Lloyd, two fine young men who brought cheers leaping from throats when they approached the plate. The two supplied the excitement of the Blue Jays that season not just because they hit balls out of the park. Cliff Johnson did that, too. Upshaw and Moseby were so loved because they belonged to the Blue Jay family. The fans had watched them struggle, had crossed their fingers and suffered through slumps with them, and when they did everything as well as they did in 1983, the fans all said "We *knew* you could do it! That's our guys!"

For two men who are so close, their personalities are mightily different. Upshaw is quiet and calm, Moseby flamboyant. Moseby *styles* his way through life, making great big splashes as he goes. Upshaw barely leaves a ripple. Moseby wants to get to the Hall of Fame. Upshaw wants to get home before his children have gone to bed.

When I first met Moseby in Venezuela he was twenty, two professional seasons old. He had been chosen second, just behind Bob Horner, in the 1978 draft; and he had hit over .300 in both the Pioneer League and the Florida State League, an All-Star wherever he played. He was big and strong and handsome and alive. His fine-featured face had a slight Oriental cast, and his laughter could fill a room. He talked in staccato bursts about a future without limit. He didn't suffer from excessive humility. On the back of his batting helmet he had written "Sir Lloyd."

In the field, Moseby was unmistakable, a big league grandstander, even in the minor leagues. The hot-dog reputation continued into the major leagues. If a player got mustard on his jersey eating postgame cold cuts, another was likely to ask him if he'd bumped into Lloyd.

Moseby was invited to spring training camp that season, fresh out of Class A, and hit over .300 again, but the team sent him to Syracuse to start the season. They wanted to make sure he could handle higher-level pitching. He kept on hitting down there, and on May 24 he and Iorg reported to Toronto together. Moseby got a bit more ink.

He started off like the clash of cymbals, smashing doubles off the fences against the Yankees in Toronto and New York. He got his first home run in his second game. This was *it*, everyone thought. Here was finally promise of future greatness glorious on the field today.

And then the dream turned inside out. First one pitcher found his weakness, then another, and the word sped through the league. He couldn't hit the fastball around the fists but he couldn't resist trying. He became a mark. His batting average slumped to .229 by the time the first season was over. The next two seasons he hit .233 and .236. He was a pushover at the plate, this great strong young man who looked like a star. He had to learn to handle failure for the first time in his life, and he had to do it on centre stage.

But Moseby never changed. He never stopped approaching the plate with a swagger, eager and confident. He never sulked. He never stopped playing and joking. He never gave up and the Blue Jays never gave up on him.

Upshaw was his friend in those days, quiet Upshaw who was having problems of his own, listening to him and talking quietly, making suggestions to his impetuous friend. Upshaw was a student of the game, one of the few players I encountered who actually kept a book on the pitchers, a small black notebook in which he would make entries after every game describing the type of pitches each pitcher threw him, in what order, and what he had done on each pitch. He also talked to Cito Gaston, the batting instructor, all the time. I remember several times looking for Upshaw after a game in which he had done well and finding him at Gaston's locker, trying to figure out how he could have done better.

Upshaw is shorter than Moseby, though no less strong. He has impossibly broad, sculptured shoulders and arms full of power. His face is impassive, almost brooding, with big hooded eyes, and a smile that is quick and abashed. He seems careful. Upshaw gave some of his calm strength to Moseby when he needed it, and Moseby gave back his confidence in return, and when the season was over the two shared the prize.

Moseby had found himself again and ended the season hitting .315, with 18 home runs, 81 RBIs, 104 runs scored, and 27 stolen bases. Upshaw hit .306 with 99 runs, 27 home runs, and 104 RBIs. Moseby was the first Blue Jay to score more than 100 runs;

Upshaw was the first to drive in more than the century. It was a triumph for them both, and each enjoyed the other's success as well as his own.

On the last day of the season, Jesse Barfield hit his twenty-seventh home run of the season to tie Upshaw, who was the first out of the dugout to shake his hand.

One image of each of them remains from that season. The first is of Upshaw the day he drove in his 100th run. He did it with a single and when he got to first base the crowd was on its feet cheering. Upshaw stood quietly with both feet on the bag, looking impassively at his shoes. Finally, when the cheers refused to die down, he reached up and tipped his batting helmet. As he peered shyly out from under it, embarrassment and pride battled on his face. Embarrassment won.

And Moseby? It's a recurring image that I suspect will keep happening as long as he plays. He's at the plate; he swings; the ball goes high into the air toward the rightfield fence. Moseby pauses halfway to first, with his arms bent upwards and his hands at the level of his shoulders, pushing that ball out of the park. When it goes, he gives a little pump with his fists, claps his hands, and trots around the base path. Afterwards he swears he didn't really *mean* to style, honestly, and he's such a swell guy you want to believe him.

In the fifth inning of that last game in 1983, Bobby Cox sent in rookie Tony Fernandez to run for Alfredo Griffin, the man he was touted to replace, but this was no symbolic passing of the torch. Cox knew that letting Griffin run off the field alone would give the fans a chance to show their appreciation of one of Cox's favourite players. They did, with another prolonged standing ovation.

Griffin had been in a tricky position for several seasons because of Fernandez, who, by all reports, was destined to become a great shortstop, one who could field and throw and hit and run. Griffin, merely a good shortstop, had been playing in a funny sort of shadow, one that was cast forward instead of back, by a player most fans had yet to see. After Fernandez's first Triple A season, in 1981, he was routinely picked as a Rookie-of-the-Year contender by spring pundits. It was assumed that Griffin would be dumped to make room for him, especially after a poor 1981 season.

Cox immediately declared that Griffin was his shortstop until Fernandez took his job away, a refreshing change for players who had watched others lose jobs to rookies. Cox wasn't convinced Griffin was as bad as he looked.

If Griffin could prove nothing else, he could prove he was durable. He played every game that Cox managed. He played with his ankles taped, wrists taped, thumbs taped. He played every game of the 1982 and 1983 seasons, an extraordinary record for a shortstop, and he played each game with joy. Griffin danced in the infield during batting practice, to the beat of the music blaring from the p.a. system. During the game, he never let up.

In the spring of 1983, an interesting thing began to happen. As rumours spread that Griffin was going to be traded to make way for Fernandez, his teammates began to come to his defence and talk about how important he was to the team. They had seen Fernandez play and didn't deny that he had more raw talent than Griffin, but they talked a lot about Griffin's heart.

Leading the plaudits was his compatriot and keystone partner, Damaso Garcia, but this was no ethnic buddy system at work. Black and white and Latin agreed that Griffin was an inspiration to the team with his relentless play, and they wanted him to stay. In fact, it was his teammates who first pointed out that Griffin could be moved to second base, where he played in winter ball, and the immensely talented Garcia traded instead. Some talked about Fernandez's temperament – apparently so similar to Garcia's moodiness – and said that they didn't want two of them on the team even if they could both hit .300.

Moodiness was not one of Griffin's problems. He was one of the most genuinely funny players I ever encountered. Because of his clumsy English the humour most of us saw was purely visual, that of a deadpan clown.

I remember one day when Griffin had played a particularly gruelling game. He had dived hard and landed awkwardly trying to field a hard ground ball, and had tripped rounding second base. When the game was over, Griffin wasn't in the clubhouse to celebrate the win. He waited, then made an entrance from the trainer's room with a giant ice pack strapped to one elbow and another strapped to his knee. Around his neck was a large brace, and his loud groans could be heard even over the hilarity in the room.

He had shown his humour to fans just a few days before the

season ended, the day that Dave Stieb pitched his last game. It had been reported in the papers that if Stieb lasted six innings he would be eligible for a $75,000 bonus for pitching 275 innings in the season. He made it, and the fans, not resenting overpaid ballplayers, leapt to their feet to cheer him. They kept it up for minutes, trying to draw him onto the field, but he had gone into the clubhouse and didn't hear them.

So Griffin calmly got to his feet, walked out of the dugout, and took a bow, doffing his cap and waving to the crowds while the rest of the players rolled around the dugout. That was typical of Griffin, always a joy to be around.

Cox stuck with Griffin through the 1983 season and was rewarded for his loyalty with another good year. But Fernandez was still in the organization, trade rumours constantly flew, and on that last day of the season the fans were saying, "Well done, thank you," and maybe, "Good-bye."

It would be impossible to talk about the success of the Blue Jays without talking about Jim Clancy and Dave Stieb, the team's two winning pitchers. They were the core of the team, especially in the early days when they were the only two pitchers with a real chance to win. It was frustrating for them both to be so much better than the team around them, but they handled it in different ways.

Clancy never seems to change. He is a big, bull-necked, but gentle man, handsome in a diffused way. He and Stieb have similar, rather wolfish, features, but Stieb's are tidier to his head. Clancy's spread out over more ground.

You see their differences on and off the mound. Both throw hard, but Clancy does it without the emotional intensity that leads Stieb to stomp around the mound and glower at umpires, opposing batters, and teammates alike, as if they are all the enemy. The Blue Jays catchers say they wish all the pitchers had Clancy's steady emotional keel.

After a game Stieb carries his intensity into the clubhouse, but Clancy is never a prima donna. He simply goes into the trainer's room for an ice pack, then comes out to meet the press. After a detour to the beer cooler, he will sit at his locker, light up a cigarette, and talk to reporters for as long as they want, whether he won or lost. He is less articulate than Stieb, but every reporter on the beat preferred talking to him.

One story illustrates the difference. When the two signed large multi-year contracts within a week of each other in 1983, a colleague preparing an article on instant sports millionaires called them to find out what they were planning to do with their new wealth. Stieb said he was going to buy a Porsche (he did, with licence plates reading "Stieb 37"); Clancy said that he and his wife were thinking about buying a new dining-room set.

But just maybe the intensity that makes Stieb difficult and unpopular off the field is what has made him the better pitcher. It is also possible that Stieb will yet become as admirable a man as he is an athlete. When, occasionally, he let down the guard, when he felt relaxed, flashes of a nice person came through. Just flashes, mind you. When I saw him kissing his two-year-old son on the plane to Chicago in 1983, just after he had learned he was going to start the All-Star Game, I liked him. For a moment.

But for the most part, Stieb was a chore, a spoiled brat.

Most players hate to lose, but Stieb carries the loathing to extremes. Once in Minnesota, before they put up the ghastly dome, Stieb wandered out of the dugout the day after a loss, looked at the cloudless sky, and growled, "What a rotten day."

"What's the matter?" I asked him. "Do you need a grey day to go with your mood?"

"To go with my mood, the sky would have to be grey, the earth trembling, and the dead people crawling out of their graves," he said.

This hatred of losing, the intense competitiveness, is at the root of his arrogance, and his unpleasantness is linked to his pride, but that shouldn't excuse his behaviour, and Stieb is baseball's answer to John McEnroe.

A Californian with B-movie good looks, he is a loner, not popular with his teammates, as much as they admire his skill. He loathes the press and goes out of his way to make our jobs difficult. After a loss he would ice his arm in the trainer's room for twenty minutes or longer as deadlines ticked down. Then he would brush past us with a glare. A question about the game would get a snarled "no comment" or a flippant "I threw too many strikes."

Stieb was also too ready, like the Orioles' Jim Palmer, to blame his losses on others – the fielder who made an error or the catcher who called for the pitch that was hit out of the park. He had a habit of turning and glaring at the offender, a habit that didn't endear him to the players around him. In the press box we wished his teammates would do the same to him, just once, when he was the one who messed up.

Even after a win, he still carried a chip on his shoulder.

In the beginning of the 1982 season Stieb did badly, while Clancy did well. After Clancy's fifth win, I wrote a story that began with the words, "Dave Stieb? Dave Who?" pointing out that it was the underrated second starter who was the big winner, not the highly touted ace.

At the time, May 20, Stieb had won two games. He never said a word to me about the story, but on June 6, the day he won his fifth game, he broke off a postgame interview as I approached.

"Do you know my name now?" he snapped.

But a team can survive one egotistical pitcher, and in 1983 the Blue Jays were a team in the best sense of that word, an all-for-one, one-for-all conglomerate that was refreshing. With a few exceptions, the players refused to take themselves too seriously or to demand attention for themselves, something other beat writers noticed with surprise. Those of us who covered them were envied by many of our peers, who were fed up with squabbling players and owners, with being treated like insects by men with whom they were forced to share time and space.

And for the writers, too, 1983 was a splendid season. We didn't cheer in the press box, of course, but we had as much fun as the players and fans did along the way.

When the season was over I realized that the 1983 season would always be the best one. The giddiness of winning after the years and years of losing was like the first sip of good champagne. The wine will always taste good, but never like it did the first time.

Chapter

13

Coming of Age

On October 5th, 1985, nine years of Blue Jay history got reduced to a footnote. All the struggling and growing and learning, all the excitement and pain of the early years, all the stumbling and fumbling of expansion became a mere prologue to success.

"It took the Toronto Blue Jays nine years," the record books will now read, "to win their first division championship."

Only the Kansas City Royals had done it more quickly, and they play in a less competitive division.

What the record books won't show, however, is what it felt like. Numbers haven't got hearts. Statistics can't laugh and cry at the same time and turn cartwheels down the street.

Only the ones who lived through it can carry the images of that victory and the sweet memory of jubilation: George Bell falling to his knees with the final out of the division-clinching game; Doyle Alexander waving his hat in the air and, by God, actually smiling as he is carried off the field by his ecstatic teammates; tears and laughter and grown men jumping up and down and hugging each other in the stands.

October 5th was a Saturday of madness in Toronto, a night of dancing in the streets, a flag-waving, horn-honking, back-slapping, yahooing celebration that we never wanted to end. The Blue Jays had beaten the Yankees head-to-head at home in the second-to-last game of the season. A gaggle of no-name upstarts had grabbed the prize from all the big boys: the Tigers, the Orioles, the Red Sox and especially those pinstriped bullies who just wouldn't let them alone. After a long nailbiter of a season, our dreams had finally come true. After nine long years of humiliation, the Blue Jays had found their best revenge.

It shouldn't have been a surprise. If the Jays had played in New York, Los Angeles or Chicago they would have been household names, and their stealthy stalking of the American League East title wouldn't have gone unnoticed. They had, after all, been in first place for part of 1983, finishing fourth, and in second place, where they ended up, for most of 1984. If it hadn't been for the Tigers' phenomenal start to that season (winning thirty-five of their first forty games), they would have been in a dogfight until the end. As it was, Toronto fans got an extra dollop of entertainment in 1985 from watching the Americans trying to figure out just who it was, up there at the top of the heap.

Not that Toronto fans needed more entertainment. Their first championship season gave them a whole photo album full of memories to pore over by the fire all winter long.

* * *

Here's a head and shoulders shot of Jesse Barfield with his trademark smile. Barfield is a joyful man, and it shows in his eyes. He is also a gentle and thoughtful soul, an altogether admirable athlete. In a time when greed and stupidity appear to define too many of our sports "heros", Barfield is a man worthy to be a role model for young kids.

At the start of the 1984 season, Barfield had every reason to believe he was finally ready to play every day. After all, playing only part time in 1983, he had tied Willie Upshaw for the team lead in home runs (27), even though he had just 388 at bats and Upshaw had 579. He had steadily improved at the plate every year since he made the team, and was one of the best defensive outfielders they had. Instead, Bobby Cox platooned him again, playing him against lefthanded pitching only. When a righthander pitched, George Bell moved from left field to right and Dave Collins played left. Neither Bell nor Collins could play the field as well as Barfield, but both hit so well that year Barfield got lost in the shuffle.

Some players would have whined and moaned about it or demanded a trade, but Barfield just kept on doing his best. When Collins got traded in the winter of 1984 Barfield finally got his chance to prove he was an every-day player and came through like a champion in 1985, especially down the stretch.

He was named the team's most valuable player, a difficult choice on a team in which leadership was shared among many. What set him above the others was that he excelled in almost everything he did, on and off the field.

He hit a very respectable .289, with twenty-seven home runs, thirty-four doubles and nine triples. He showed he could run the bases, stealing twenty-two. His major flaw was his strikeout total – 134 – a common failing in sluggers.

Those numbers delighted most fans, but for some of us, they were almost secondary. It was Jesse Barfield in right field that brought us the most pleasure, over and over again.

Barfield patrols his turf with authority. He has an arm that even the fastest runners are learning not to challenge. Despite that, he led the league with twenty-two outfield assists.

It's a joy to watch him when a ball is hit to right, especially when there is a man on third just itching to score. He glances at the runner, reminding himself whether he is fast or slow, then times his approach to the ball perfectly. He hangs back until the last second so that he can charge and catch the ball at full forward speed. Then he uses that momentum to give his arm just that much more power. His aim is unerring and any runner foolish enough to try to make it home is odds-on to be dead at the plate.

No matter how many times he does it, it gives me the same feeling of elation to watch him set up and catch the ball; to watch the runner barrel towards home and to sense that runner's disbelief evolving into respect as he is tagged out. Sometimes a man trying to score from second on a single to right will turn into a cartoon figure as he rounds third and sees the throw on the way: his legs backpedalling like training wheels on a bike as the "Whoa!" balloon flashes on over his head.

And in the stands we settle back in our seats and chuckle in a proprietory way as we ask each other why anybody in his right mind would ever want to run on Jesse's arm.

For those moments alone, Barfield will be a favourite Blue Jay for many years to come.

* * *

Turn the page. Here's George Bell, caught in midair, legs scissored in a flying karate kick aimed at Boston pitcher Bruce Kison. Kison had the audacity to hit the left fielder with a pitch one Sunday afternoon in June of 1985. Bell shouted at him, charged the mound, did his Bruce Lee imitation, issued a swift right-hand combination to catcher Rich Gedman, then retreated to the safety of the Blue Jay dugout and watched while the rest of the players went at it on the field. This tacky display rightly earned him a two-game suspension.

Bell was the MVP runner-up for the second consecutive season. In 1984 it had been Dave Collins who edged him out in the voting by the Toronto chapter of the Baseball Writers of America. In response, Bell refused to talk to the press all season.

No tears were shed in the press box because of this, but it made the writers' jobs more difficult. Bell had had the kind of season worth discussing, but the writers had to find comment elsewhere. His high point came one late August weekend in Chicago when he hit two home runs onto the roof in left field and one into the bleachers in straight away centre field. Comiskey Park is no bandbox, and many power hitters have gone a whole career without ever hitting a ball onto the roof or out in centre field there, let alone three in three days.

Ironically, the weekend could well have been his downfall. He admitted at the end of the season that his approach to hitting changed after that. He began to swing only for the fences, and was next to useless down the stretch. He hit just one home run and drove in eight runs in September and October, when the team really needed him. Even with that slump, though, he finished the season with twenty-eight home runs and led the team with ninety-five RBIs. Without it, he would have won the award he so coveted.

Bell's attitude towards pitchers is understandable, if deplorable. In the minor leagues, he missed most of the 1982 season after having his cheek broken by a pitch. With a background of poverty in the Dominican Republic, Bell takes seriously any threat to his livelihood as a baseball player. But taking runs at opposing pitchers isn't going to make them stop throwing at him. On the contrary. The pitchers who don't know how to get this talented hitter out now understand that if they want to unnerve him, to break his formidable concentration, all they have to do is threaten him with their pitches, and they'll keep on doing it until he learns to control his temper.

When the Blue Jays made the playoffs, Bell broke his silence, but it didn't do him much good. After the fifth game in Kansas City, he blasted the umpires, accusing them of favouring the

Royals because they were an American team. Now he not only has a reputation as a hothead, but as a paranoid hothead. Some fans joked that their biggest regret over the Blue Jays not making it into the World Series was that they never got to see Bell face Joachin Andujar, the temperamental pitcher from the same Dominican home town who loves throwing at hitters.

* * *

The next pair of photos isn't too pleasant to look at, but they show one of the most impressive plays ever, in either league.

The first is of Seattle Mariner outfielder Phil Bradley knocking over catcher Buck Martinez at home plate. It was obvious at the moment of the collision that there was something very wrong with Martinez. His cleats had caught in the unyielding dirt around the Kingdome home plate, and as he fell, his right leg was crushed under him. He hung on to the ball, though, and Bradley was out.

Then the catcher spied Gorman Thomas, who had hit the ball originally, rounding second and heading for third. Despite his injury, Martinez threw to third, but the ball went wildly into left field. George Bell picked it up and threw home, where Martinez, struggling, sat up and caught it. The second photo shows Thomas gingerly trying to tiptoe around Martinez and find home plate while being tagged out. A former teammate of Martinez's, and a good friend, he had the decency not to slide.

The two putouts on the same play with a dislocated ankle and broken leg earned Martinez a place on that night's sportscasts across two countries and a spot on This Week in Baseball. They also put him out of action for the rest of the season, and perhaps ended his career.

It was very hard on him. A thoughtful, dedicated veteran, he had been given a reprieve from oblivion when he was traded to the Blue Jays from the Brewers in 1981. He had teamed up with Ernie Whitt to form a very effective catching platoon, but he had a disappointing season in 1984, when his batting average dropped to just five hits in the first two months of the season. In fact, he barely dodged every ballplayer's worst nightmare, that of going for a whole month without a hit: he was one for May. At one particularly low point, early in June, home fans greeted him with a chant of ".072, .072": his batting average at the time.

He never stopped working with batting coach Cito Gaston, though, watching video tapes of his swing in good times and in bad. In June they finally found his problem and he began to turn around. It was his home run that won one of the most dramatic games of the year, a double shutout against the Detroit Tigers that lasted twelve innings on June 6th. He hit .313 for the month, to bring his average up to .162 by July 9th, when he was injured.

Once he was mobile, on crutches, Martinez rejoined the team. He did daily exercises to hasten his recovery, insisting until the last that he would be able to play again before the season was over.

It wasn't hard to understand his attitude. At thirty-seven, aware that his career was in its last stages even if he hadn't been injured, Martinez didn't want to miss being part of the team's long-awaited success.

In fact, he didn't miss it. Even on crutches, he was part of the team. His advice was invaluable to the younger players around him, involved in their first pennant race. Martinez had been through it before, with the 1976 Kansas City Royals as a backup catcher.

Martinez was also a part of the team in the eyes of the fans. He popped up from time to time as colour commentator on both radio and television, and was in the dugout for every game. Early arrivals at the ballpark could see him leaning against the batting cage, his crutches beside him, watching his teammates take their cuts. It was a poignant sight.

The Jays tried to replace Martinez, first with Gary Allenson, a journeyman who had been playing in Syracuse, then with Jeff Hearron, a rookie from the Double A team at Knoxville, and finally with National League veteran Steve Nicosia, who they signed after he had been released by the Expos. None of them could fill the role, so more and more of the catching load fell to Ernie Whitt, who suffered, finally. As part of a platoon, Whitt had become a good catcher over the years, but taking almost full-time responsibility for the second half of the season hurt him. By the time the playoffs came around, he was too exhausted to provide the spark he had in the first half of the season.

During the winter, as the Jays shopped around baseball for a replacement, Martinez still vowed he could come back, and if sheer determination was the only necessity, he would.

* * *

Here's Bobby Cox, the manager, hands tucked into the waist-band of his pants, walking to the mound with his strange rolling gait, boos raining down on his head because he has waited just one batter too long. If the Jays had lost the division by one game instead of winning it by two, Cox would have been the goat of the year instead of manager of the year. It would be hard to find a winning manager anywhere whose every move was more suspiciously examined by the increasingly sophisticated and demanding fans. The race was so close all season that every loss was dissected. The second-guessers were particularly tough on the way he handled his pitchers.

He trusted them too much, it seemed. Especially Alexander and Dave Stieb. It happened over and over again that season. Stieb or Alexander would begin to struggle in the late innings of a close game, giving up hits or walks. Cox would go to the mound to consult with the pitcher, pat him on the bum, then head back to the dugout. Inevitably, it seemed, the next hitter would hit a home run to tie the game or go ahead by a run, and the manager would trudge back out, scowling and signalling the bullpen.

Cox left after the season was over, lured back to Atlanta, where he had previously managed, to become general manager. He said he was making the move to be near his family.

Scoffers questioned Cox's motivation, suggesting that it had to be greed that led him to leave the Jays, or a lust for front-office power, but I believe that Cox made the move for just the reason he stated. As much of a baseball man as Cox was, his family played a very important role in his life. Perhaps because it was his second marriage it mattered more. This was refreshing in a world in which too often family comes in a distant third after the player's own well being and that of his team.

In the time I travelled with the Blue Jays, I was struck by Cox's devotion to his wife and kids. Every time the team had an off day, Cox would fly to Atlanta to spend it with them, even if it meant a great deal of inconvenience. He encouraged his players to show equal devotion to their wives and children.

Anyone who knows him has to wish him well, but the idea of Cox out of uniform is a strange one, and he will miss sorely being on the field. He was always one of the first at the park, and liked nothing better than sitting in the dugout with his coaches, hours before game time, swapping stories and keeping an eye on his players. Hanging out in board rooms in a suit and tie won't be the same.

If the move turns out to be difficult for Cox, it was a real break for the Blue Jays. The Cox era had ended with the division win. It was time for a change, but firing him was out of the question. How could you can the man who brought the team from last place to first in four years?

But if he had stayed, the team would have stagnated, and the pressure to get rid of Cox would have grown. Aside from his questionable ability to read his pitchers, Cox was open to criticism for his rigidity. As a field general, he had become too predictable, and didn't use all the weapons in his arsenal.

Baserunning was one weak area. In 1985, the Jays had the best overall team speed in the league, but Cox never really took advantage of it. He could have taken a leaf from Whitey Herzog's book. Herzog, manager of the St. Louis Cardinals, won the National League championship by keeping his opponents off guard with double steals, squeeze plays, hitting and running. The Cardinals drove opposing pitchers crazy because they never knew what to expect.

Cox seldom caught anyone off guard. He bunted so seldom that opposing infielders simply laid back and waited for the double play grounder whenever there was a man on first.

He was so inflexible with his platoons that he could be out-managed. If a righthander was brought in to replace a lefthander, Cox would pinch-hit for his righthanded hitters, then be left with an empty bench later in the game when a lefthanded reliever was called upon.

Cox's replacement, Jimy Williams, has never managed in the major leagues, but was successful in the minors. He has long been touted by baseball people as one of the best managerial prospects around. It was only a matter of time before he got his chance somewhere (he was a prime candidate for the job in Oakland in 1985) and it works out for the best all around that he got it in Toronto.

Williams is liked and respected by the players on the team, and knows all their strengths and weaknesses well. If a manager had been brought in from outside, he would have had to spend his first season learning what he had to work with. Williams has been with the Blue Jays since the 1980 season, and has known most of his players since they were rookies.

The fans have yet to see what Williams' style might be, but at the very least, he will bring the feeling of a fresh start. Bill Caudill, for one, could use that.

Caudill's was the most baffling story of the 1985 season. Obtained from the Oakland A's for two very popular Jays, Alfredo Griffin and Dave Collins, after the 1984 season, Caudill arrived with more hoopla than any player in the team's history. It was justified, too. Here was a proven reliever, a stopper, for a team that had been hurting for years because their bullpen couldn't do the job. Although Caudill had had a strange on-and-off career, he had saved twenty-six games for the Mariners in 1982 and 83, and thirty-six for the A's in 1984.

He had only one year left before he could become a free agent, so the Jays spent a good part of the winter negotiating a multi-year contract. The rumours surrounding the process filled the papers with rumours and crowded hockey off the front sports pages until February 20th, when Caudill signed a five-year, $8 million contract.

He was the toast of the town in spring training, the centre of attention from the press and fans. Every small clubhouse prank, every one-liner from Caudill's lips, was breathlessly sped north-ward, and everyone began to see signs of spring.

Caudill didn't come through as expected as the season began. He won three games in April, but it isn't a reliever's job to win games. He got his first save on April 18th, but by the twenty-seventh was being booed by the home fans for giving up a lead in the ninth inning and losing to the Royals. When Jim Acker began to pitch well, Cox anointed him as the stopper, ignoring Caudill.

Caudill never recovered, and only he will ever know for sure why. Perhaps the expectations put too much pressure on him. Some said it was because he had changed his delivery and wasn't throwing as well as he had. Others suggested that he was simply being misused. Or maybe it was one of his infamous off-years.

As all relievers tend to do, Caudill said when he joined the Jays that he preferred to be used often. Cox chose to ignore that particular piece of advice. Perhaps he resented having a player tell him how to do his job. Cox was capable of that kind of bull-headedness, certainly, and as a former position player, didn't seem to have much sympathy for pitchers' fragile psyches.

There is a strong argument to be made that that early season experience messed up Caudill so completely that he never recovered. He finished the season with fourteen saves and a 2.99 E.R.A, but he never became the kind of overwhelming stopper that Jays had thought they signed.

And yet, if you had to choose an image of Caudill, it would be of him bounding out of the dugout to congratulate the pitcher after a win. It was Caudill, with Acker, who carried Alexander off the field on October 5th. His positive attitude even softened the fans' hard hearts, and by the end of the season, he was greeted with cheers whenever he came in from the pen.

By the end of the season, though, the fans had a new stopper to cheer. Tom Henke, who the Jays had plucked off the Texas Ranger unprotected list in compensation for losing Cliff Johnson as a free agent in 1984, was a man who had never before proven himself in the big leagues. Always successful in the minors, the twenty-seven-year-old had bombed out in his three short trips to the majors with the Rangers. He did well in spring training, but was sent to Syracuse to start the season.

The Jays brought him up on July 28th, when Jim Clancy went on the disabled list with tendonitis. He had eighteen saves in Syracuse, an earned run average of 0.87 and a better than ninety-mile-an-hour fastball. He took over as the Jays' fireman.

A lanky, laconic, bespectacled blond from small-town Missouri, Henke quickly became a fan favourite. There was a Clark Kent feeling about him, this inconspicuous guy with the superhuman powers. He wasn't given to emotional displays or theatrics on the mound.

By the end of the season, he had saved thirteen games in thirty innings pitched and had an earned run average of 2.03. He struck out forty-two and walked only eight.

He also became the first Blue Jay to have a song recorded in his honour, "The Ballad of Tom Henke", a country talking-blues with a chorus that went something like this:

Terminator, Terminator.
You can bring him in now but he's even better later.
Terminator, Terminator.
Well he blows it by 'em, never throws a tater.

Yes, it got pretty silly around Toronto near the end.

* * *

Here's Dave Stieb's page, with an unusual snapshot. I chose it optimistically, as a possible portent of change.

It was taken during the first inning of the first game of the play-offs. Tony Fernandez had just made a lovely play at short, and before Stieb threw the next pitch he stepped off the mound, called to Fernandez to get his attention, then made a pistol of his forefinger and gestured his approval. Fernandez managed not to faint in surprise.

This is not to say that Stieb in 1985 abandoned his usual tricks, glaring at fielders for balls they ''should have'' had or glowering at the catcher for the pitch he called that got hit out of the park. This is not to suggest for a moment that he stopped treating writers like scum or fans like nuisances. He did all of that, and more, but by the end of the season, there were indications that he was starting to mature.

This came about, I suspect, as the direct result of a column written by Wayne Parrish in the *Star* which took Stieb to task for his selfish attitude, for putting his own statistics ahead of the success of the team, and for showing up his teammates both on the field and in the clubhouse. Parrish bluntly suggested that Stieb should get his act together and stop blaming his disappointing won-lost statistics on anybody but himself. In all, it was the toughest piece ever written about Stieb, but one which reflected the feelings of a lot of people who deal with him regularly. Because Parrish was a columnist, not a beat writer, he didn't have to worry about having an ongoing relationship with the pitcher.

It got to Stieb. After the column was published, he took aside at least one beat writer to ask if people really saw him in that way. After his next start he made a point of sitting for forty minutes in the clubhouse discussing his game, and his personality, with the press, trying to explain his intensely competitive nature.

On the field, gestures like the one he made to Fernandez showed that, on the surface at least, his attitude was changing. And if finishing the season with a mediocre 14-13 record and losing the final game of the playoffs didn't humble him, nothing ever will.

If there is indeed a new Dave Stieb emerging, it's about time. He has a lot of ground to make up, all around the league.

Red Sox first baseman Bill Buckner was speaking for a lot of people after a game late in the season when he said that all teams like to beat Stieb "because everybody hates him."

* * *

Tony Fernandez is frozen in memory four feet off the ground. His glove is stretched as high as he can reach and, incredibly, there is a line-drive captured inside it. The play is one I remember vividly from the 1985 campaign, but it was just one of many stunning, acrobatic plays the young shortstop made in his first full season on the job. He had been ready to play regularly for at least two years. He had, in fact, been picked as a rookie-of-the-year candidate for several springs running. But the Jays had a shortstop, Alfredo Griffin, so Fernandez had to wait his turn, playing only occasionally in 1984.

Liberated from this backup role by Griffin's trade to Oakland, Fernandez showed signs of becoming the sensational player pundits had been predicting for years. Teamed with Damaso Garcia at second, he quickly grew into his job and made people forget about the popular Griffin.

His play wasn't entirely brilliant, of course, and he made some outrageous blunders that were as memorable as the sensational moments. One of the funniest, although not at the time, came in New York, in the hysterically hyped September series in the House that Ruth Built.

It was in the first game of the series, and the Jays had a comfy 4-1 lead going into the seventh inning with Stieb on mound. With one out, Fernandez fielded what looked like a routine double play grounder. All he needed to do was tag second, throw to first and the inning would be over. Instead, he tossed the ball to second. Garcia, who had seen the play unfolding and assumed that Fernandez could handle it himself, turned his back just as the throw was being made, the ball hit him between the shoulderblades, and everybody was safe. Given the gift of two extra outs, the Yankees went on to score six runs in the inning, aided by another Fernandez error and Ron Hassey's home run.

But the man is still young, still learning, and is already better than a lot of shortstops in baseball. His attitude that night showed more poise than most twenty-three-year-olds can muster. After he had calmed down (when the reporters came into the clubhouse, Fernandez at first ducked them by pretending not to speak English), he said, "One thing I know for sure. It's not the end of the world. The world will begin again tomorrow morning."

Fernandez looks earnest, poised for play, all legs and arms and disproportionately large head. He is gawky in repose, but to see him go into the hole or turn a double play is to watch grace incarnate. He has great range and sure hands and his characteristic flip throw is usually right on the money.

What surprised and delighted many of us in 1985 was his power. A switch hitter, he only hit two home runs, but he had solid line-drive punch. He was tied for second place in doubles on the team (he and Willie Upshaw each hit thirty-one; Barfield hit thirty-four) and led it with ten triples. He ended the season batting .289.

Fernandez is the kind of player you can build a team around. He's terrific in the field, dangerous at the plate, and has speed that hasn't yet been exploited. The Blue Jays, either through brilliant design or extraordinary luck, have been able to find and develop a number of young players who combine several skills, especially through their Dominican connection.

Epy Guerrero is the scout who combs the Republic for prospects. The ones he finds, in the sandlots, on the streets, or in organized leagues, spend time at his training complex, a primitive baseball school near Santo Domingo, for more training. The best of those make it into the Blue Jays minor league system.

If the Blue Jays have indeed become Canada's team, Guerrero deserves an Order of Canada for putting so many of the pieces together.

And if the Blue Jays are Canada's team, they are also the Dominican Republic's. Reporters who travelled there during the pennant stretch, in hot pursuit of yet one more story to satisfy the voracious appetite of the city's sports editors, found Blue Jay fever as epidemic as it was in Toronto. It seems that half the cab drivers were wearing Blue Jay caps or T-shirts, that half the pickup teams were called the "Azujelos", and that Fernandez, Bell and Garcia were local heros bigger than Reggie Jackson or Dave Winfield.

Other teams have Dominican players, but the Jays were the only ones who had three starting players, another (Manny Lee) on the bench and several more in the minor leagues.

Manny Lee's yearbook picture shows him sitting on a stool in front of the dugout bench watching, always watching. If the weather was even remotely chilly, he would be wearing a toque and jacket, with his hands in big mitts.

Lee wasn't one of Guerrero's prizes. The young infielder had been signed by the Houston Astros. The Jays took him out of the unprotected player draft at the 1984 winter meetings. He and Lou Thornton, a New York Mets farmhand, weren't protected by their respective parent clubs because they were so inexperienced that the Mets and Astros thought no other club would take the chance on drafting them. A minor leaguer obtained in this draft had to be kept on the major league roster for a full season or offered back to the original club at half the $25,000 purchase price.

For this reason, not many clubs take players from this draft, especially contending teams, but the Jays have done it for years. Immediately after expansion they did it because they were hungry for players. Later, they did it because it worked: Willy Upshaw, Jim Acker and George Bell came in through this back door and were key players by 1985. Kelly Gruber, a Triple A prospect who was a backup player in September, was also drafted this way.

It was a risk, but the Blue Jays won with it. Not only did they carry Thornton and Lee on the major league roster for the year, each of them helped to win several games in a very close season.

Ironically, the system hurts the players involved more than the teams who draft them. Lee and Thornton would have been better off playing every day in the minor leagues instead of watching from the bench in the bigs. Exciting as 1985 was for them, their careers would have been better served by playing.

But it was the Players' Association that insisted upon the provision that forces the team to carry the players on the major league playing roster.

*   *   *

Poor Lloyd Moseby. The most indelibly etched memory of his 1985 season, in the minds of the fans and in his nightmares of the long winter nights, is of the play he booted.

By October 4th, everybody was ready for the Blue Jays to stop messing around and clinch the pennant. They had needed but one win to do it for almost a week, but had lost three straight in Detroit while the Yankees were winning elsewhere.

That Friday night, home again in Toronto with the Yankees in town, they knew that they had to win one of the three to win the division. In the stands and in the dugout, everyone wanted that win quickly. The suspense was starting to wear us all down.

The house was packed to watch Jimmy Key, the unflappable young lefthander who had won all our hearts that season, starting against Ed Whitson, whose season-long woes had most recently included a barroom brawl with his manager, Billy Martin. A foregone conclusion, right?

The championship looked even more certain when Whitson was replaced on the mound by the equally mediocre Rod Scurry and Tom Henke started the eighth with a 3-2 lead.

In the ninth, with two out and the crowds in the stands cheering and chanting, on their feet with delirium, Henke, "who never gives up a tater", gave one up to Butch Wynegar, a man whose bat is not his ticket to the Hall of Fame.

Score tied. The next two men got on base. Hearts stopped, ulcers flared, as Don Mattingly, who would later be named league MVP, came to the plate.

He swung and hit a harmless fly ball to right centre field. Moseby took a bead on it, calmly settled under it, then, unbelievably, dropped it. The lead runner scored, and the Yankees took a lead they kept until the end.

He dropped it. How could he drop it? How many times had we seen him make that play? A thousand, no, a million times at least, he had caught that ball, but that crucial night he dropped it.

I have never felt as sorry for a player as I did for Moseby that night. This wonderfully flamboyant man who normally played with such deftness had failed with more hopes pinned upon him than ever before, or probably ever again, in his career, and he would never be able to forget it.

Later, when the championship was neatly tucked away and the error was nothing more than a footnote, the reason for it became obvious. There was one crucial difference between the way Moseby approached every other fly ball and the way he approached that one: the one he dropped was the only one in living memory he had tried to catch with two hands. Abandoning his usual stylish approach to fielding, Moseby had played by the book and gone for the safety play. Fielding the way every Little Leaguer is drilled to, Moseby had simply blown it. That'll teach him!

* * *

Cliff Johnson is there in the album, standing at the plate, idly swinging his bat and jawing with the umpires. He came back to the Blue Jays in August, from the Texas Rangers in a trade, swallowing the bitter words he had spoken when the Jays had let him slip away to free agency the year before. He became the righthanded counterpart to Al Oliver, both as designated hitter and as self-styled baseball guru to the younger chaps on the team.

The two were hailed as saviours by some who believed that these two great veterans were just what the team needed to pace themselves down the stretch. That was a grave overstatement, according to those most familiar with them.

The morning after Oliver joined the team in July my brother Charley, an Expos fan, called me from Ottawa to commiserate on the Jays' losing their shot at the pennant. He remembered too well the years Oliver had played in Montreal. All talk, no clutch play, was the rap. But, like Johnson, he could be counted upon to issue sanctimoniously humble homilies after every game. (Of the, "I don't care about my own personal statistics, as long as I can help the team," variety.)

When Johnson came back, while some fans were popping champagne corks, a veteran beat writer was sighing to me over the phone: "Oh, they'll just locker Cliff and Oliver at one end of the clubhouse and issue earplugs to the other players."

While the two were never as good as their own opinions of themselves, there is no denying that they helped the team down the stretch. Oliver had the game-winning hit in two of the playoff games, and Johnson won his share, too, even if he did it with nothing more than an inning-extending walk or poochy single that blooped in for an RBI. He seemed to have left the home-run bat he had been hired for in his locker in Texas.

The man he replaced was Jeff Burroughs, an enigmatic slugger who had never quite lived up to his potential. He had played in the majors for thirteen years when Cox, who remembered him from his last .300 season in Atlanta, plucked him from the Oakland bench after the 1984 season. It was probably his last chance in baseball, and although he didn't come through, he played when he was called upon with stoic dignity. His popularity with the team was obvious.

It seems odd that the Blue Jays, with all their drafting and trading acumen have only had one year, 1983, when they solved their designated hitter problem satisfactorily. While there seems to be a surplus of players around who can still hit, if not play a position, the Jays have yet to find one or two that can do the job with the authority of Don Baylor or Hal McRae.

In 1985 they had, in Johnston, Oliver, Burroughs, rookie Cecil Fielder, and early departures Len Matuszek and Willie Aikens, six nominal first basemen who might as well have left their gloves in the trunk of the car, but who, collectively, didn't provide the consistent threat at the plate a designated hitter must. Given their narrow failure in the American League playoffs, that lack was a serious one.

* * *

No baseball album would be complete without pictures of the fans: big-eyed children with oversized gloves and senior citizens nodding in the sunshine; drunken louts stumbling up the aisles and staid businessmen in three-piece suits; teenage girls in breast-hugging T-shirts and solitary eccentrics with scorebook and pencil. There were so many of them that season: more than 2,000,000 tickets were sold, another team record.

It was odd for the old fans to find baseball suddenly so fashionable. Where once we had gathered in small but appreciative numbers we now found mobs of strangers. It changed the game, for better and for worse. It was a lot livelier at the ballpark, but the quality of the experience was diminished. And didn't we all get tired of the newly minted baseball fans with their "expert" opinions on everything about the team.

It's churlish to complain, though. Those fans wouldn't have appeared if it hadn't been for the success of the team, after all. Would we rather be members of an elite group watching ineptitude on the field? Some days, when the park was crowded with rowdy louts who knew nothing about baseball, I wasn't sure, but the winning sure was fun.

My season was similar to that of other fans, and it took us all by surprise. It was the year I crossed the line into total, irredeemable fandom. It was the year I lived and died with "my" Blue Jays and cut the last ties with the objectivity of the press box. My spirits rose and fell with the fortunes of the team, I attended, watched or listened to virtually every game they played. I stumbled through the mornings after night games on the west coast had lasted until the early hours of the morning. I cheered myself hoarse during the pennant stretch and grieved for a week after the playoffs were over. By the end of the season, I had forgotten that baseball was only a game.

It was a tough season for new and old Blue Jay fans alike. Although the Jays were in sole control of first place from the 20th of May onwards, they were never far enough ahead to let us relax. There was always another team closing in, and there were enough close games to keep us gnawing our knuckles from beginning to end. In the 161-game season (one game was lost to the mid-season strike), there were 48 one-run games played by the Jays (they won 27 and lost 21) and 32 games decided by two runs (17-15). Every time the team lost a close one, we feared they had blown the whole season. We could never savour winning because we feared losing so much.

Roger Angell described it for all of us in his end of season wrap-up in the *New Yorker* when he said that the Blue Jays fans' season had been like walking down a long dark alley waiting for a jaguar to jump out and bite us on the bum. It would have been far easier, he suggested, if we had been chasing the leader all season long. We didn't know how to behave in first place.

As the season began and the Jays were picked to be contenders in their division, the two questions most raised were whether they could do it with two rookies on the bench and whether they could handle the pressure. The first was valid, the second a stupid cliché. It was the kind of question asked by those reporters who believe in other intangibles, like the ever-popular *momentum*, in sport. Or desire.

At the time, I thought the real question was whether the fans could stand the heat, and as the season unfolded, it became obvious that we couldn't.

We were fine, at first. We sailed through the start of the season, laughing in the spring sunshine and smelling the flowers. When the team moved into sole control of first place on May 20, we gloated a bit. When the team was in first place at the All-Star break, we had even become smug. That was the easy part. We'd done that before, in 1983. But as July turned to August, clutch time, we began to stumble and look back over our shoulders in panic. By September, hysteria had set in. The question we asked wasn't whether the Blue Jays would choke, but how and when they would do it.

Early in the month, I called Angell for advice. Surely a die-hard Red Sox and Mets fan of such perspicacity would have valuable advice for all of us in the throes of our first real pennant race.

"It's like a terrible illness," he said, "but you do finally get better, one way or another."

That was small consolation in the third week of September, the week the Blue Jays went to New York for what had become the most important four-game series in the team's history. They were only two-and-a-half games up, and we knew in our palpitating hearts that this was where they could crumble. The Toronto newspapers, which had been losing all sense of proportion for weeks, went nuts. The *Star* alone sent eight writers and photographers to cover the series. CTV and THE SPORTS NETWORK scrambled to get the games on the air.

A lot of fans went, too. My husband Paul and I hopped in the car after work on Thursday, having declared Friday a religious holiday. We listened to the first game on the car radio, with the signal fading in and out on the hilly highways through the Adirondacks. We heard the Yankee fans booing our anthem, we heard the Jays take the lead into the seventh. We laughed and honked the horn into the inky darkness of the deserted country road, then lost the signal entirely. When we arrived at the inn near Cooperstown where we had arranged to stay for the night, we found out about Fernandez's errors and Hassey's home run and sat stunned at the bar with our hosts listening to the last inning by candlelight – the electric lights interfered with the radio reception. The gloom of the room matched our mood.

When we got to New York, the papers were all talking about a Yankees-Mets World Series. It was a bit premature. The next three days were crazy and wonderful, with emotional highs colliding like bumper cars at a county fair. There's nothing like beating the Yankees in their own hallowed park, and all the shenanigans surrounding the series made the three subsequent wins even more splendid.

On the subway platform after the Friday night win, a crazy lady came up and began to rant at us. ''B'ue Jays stink,'' she spat. ''Yankees gonna kill'em.''

A couple nearby turned to watch, smiling at us.

''We're from Canada too,'' the woman said. ''You're not going to believe this, but we were at an Expos-Mets game at Shea Stadium and she sat behind us and said the same things about the Expos.''

The crazy lady ranted on at me (I attract them, somehow) as we chatted. Then three young men behind us unzipped their jackets to show the Blue Jay T-shirts they were wearing underneath, and nodded conspiratorially. Finally, a young Oriental man sidled up and pulled a Blue Jay button out of his pocket to show us.

''I'm from Toronto, too,'' he whispered, and we all grinned like canaries as the crazy lady ranted on.

On Saturday night, the Jays won again, but the game was upstaged by the anthem, butchered by the new infamous Mary O'Dowd. A saloon singer brought in to help celebrate Irish-American day, she not only forgot the words, but the tune. The booing that night was from the Canadians. After the game, George Steinbrenner unloaded one of his habitual tirades, and we felt even more smug.

Sunday's win, which saw Yankee fans booing their own players, was gravy. As it ended, one fan, who had begun the game by heckling us, paused in his rather drunken exit to turn and salute us. ''Hey, Blue Jay lady,'' he shouted. ''God bless ya!''

The weekend broke the Yankees' spirit and they began to lose while the Blue Jays, sailing along at .500 against the Red Sox and Brewers, watched their lead increase to seven games. At home we began to feel robbed, since with just one Blue Jay win or Yankee loss necessary to clinch, we were sure they would win it on the road in Detroit.

Silly us. After the season of anguish they had put us through, the Jays were going to end it easily? Forget it. It all came down to that final series against the Yankees at home.

I've already described the first game of that series, and won't put you through the agony again. We watched it on television at home, since we had given our seats away for that night in the beginning of the season. When the game ended we didn't speak a word to each other. There was nothing to do but go to bed and pull the covers over our heads. It was too painful to contemplate.

In the morning as I woke up the images of the game flooded back before I had even opened my eyes. I went downstairs, where Paul had made breakfast, sat down at the table and burst into tears.

"Pain and caring is what it's all about," Angell had said a few weeks before. "The big thing about suffering is that it's what really makes you a fan. You're not really a fan until you've gone through it."

If that was true, I came of age as a fan that morning, and so did hundreds of other people I have since talked to about it. The agony we all felt, the frustration and the fear of coming so close and losing it, surprised us all. Maybe baseball was only a game for everybody else, everywhere else, but it was more than that for us that morning.

A good part of what we were feeling was anticipatory humiliation. After weeks of uncharacteristic braggadocio, of thumbing our noses at Yankee fans and taking altogether un-Canadian glee in beating those bastards at their own game, we were sure we were going to have to eat our words. I for one couldn't stand the thought.

That morning I sat and imagined the Yankees streaming out of their dugout jumping and embracing and high-fiving all over Exhibition Stadium while their boorish fans waved index fingers in the air: Number One. I could see Billy Martin smiling as he was hailed as the genius who had engineered it all. I could see the American writers limbering their fingers to write reassuring stories about how, after all, the better team had won and there wouldn't be any fear of post-season play being snowed out, or of dog sleds bringing relievers into the game. I wanted to throw up.

Less than twelve hours later, I was crying and laughing and hugging my friends in joyous disbelief as we assured one another that we hadn't doubted it for a minute.

That evening we ignored the raucous celebrations that stopped traffic on Yonge Street in the heart of town and went to the place we had gone after so many games over the years, the Underground Railroad, where we knew we would find friends.

The Underground, as its regulars call it, is a restaurant that specializes in southern-style cooking, soul food, and is a home away from home for many baseball players, especially blacks, Blue Jays and visitors alike. The owners, Anne and John Henry Jackson, have served as surrogate parents to many a homesick rookie over the years, and the two care as fiercely as any natural parents about their young friends. It's a pleasant place to drop in after a game for post mortems.

That night was a night for quiet remembering over several bottles of champagne. The rowdies were all on Yonge Street. In the bar of the Underground we weren't shouting, just smiling wearily, glad it was all over.

I found myself thinking a lot about the old Blue Jays, the ones who were long gone. Many of them were out of baseball entirely by then, but they too were a part of that happy evening, because they were a part of the history of the team. Even if they had done nothing more than fill spaces on the roster until the stars of 1985 were ready to take over, they too were Blue Jays and I hoped that wherever they were that night, they were smiling too.

So I raised my glass in a private toast to John Mayberry and Tim Johnson; Dave MacKay and Alvis Woods; Otto Velez, Rico Carty and Luis Gomez. I drank to Dave Lemanczyk and Phil Huffman; Butch Edge and Jerry Garvin; to all those players who were here when the times were tough. Maybe some of them had made those times tougher, but never mind. Maybe the revellers on Yonge Street had never heard of them, but it was important that those of us who remembered them, especially remembered them that night.

Ten nights later, we were back at the Underground after the seventh game of the playoff series. The Blue Jays had finally folded, had finally run out of the magic and had lost three straight to the Royals. We were cold and exhausted and sad, but we couldn't go home yet. We had to be with friends and share what comfort we could. It was a season worthy of prolonging, just for a few more hours.

Al Woods was there that night, too. He and his wife Denise had flown to Toronto for their third wedding anniversary, just two weeks after ours, and we had arranged to meet them for a drink.

There was no champagne that night. We talked quietly about everything but the series. Woods talked about how he was sure he would make it back to the major leagues soon, with the Twins. Anna and John's son Cosby came back from Willie Upshaw's apartment, where he had been baby sitting, looking close to tears. The pianist played "The Party's Over." We went home.

* * *

After the season ended, there was some brave, "wait 'til next year" kind of talk, but it couldn't hide the hurt. On New Year Day, CBC radio replayed an item first broadcast in Octob splicing high- and low-lights from the season into a recording of Barbara Streisand singing "The Way We Were." It was corny hell, but as I listened to the play-by-play description of the Ji Sundberg triple that put the last game out of reach, and to Rance Mullinik's postgame remarks about how good the team was, and how badly they felt, I wanted to cry all over again.

Angell was probably right. Toronto baseball fans would never be the same. We thought we knew what it was to lose before but, as he said, "Losing when you never had a chance to win isn't the same as losing when you should have won."

The analogy has been used often enough in this sort of situation to deserve consignment to the trash can of clichés, but, dammit, the season *was* like falling in love for the first time. The elation was just as exhilerating and the heartbreak was just as cruel. And, as in love, when it happens next, the quality is bound to be better, but the intensity will never be so strong again.

More's the pity.